VISITORS

A New Look at UFOs

by Kelly Bell

Fontaine House Publishing

First Edition

ISBN:

17 18 19 20 21 22 23 24 25 / 9 8 7 6 5 4 3 2 1

Fontaine Creative Enterprises

Longview, TX

Dedication

DEDICATED TO MY FRIEND and mentor Phillip E. Mahfood, whom our Heavenly Father sent to provide me with the support and guidance that made these pages possible. He went Home before they were published, so by now he has learned the truth.

Introduction

IN KELLY BELL'S *VISITORS: A New Look at UFOs,* readers will find a handy overview of the field of ufology with insights and a historical perspective from many different angles. There is an intriguing look at the broad spectrum of sightings, a re-visit to the story of Roswell, and a nice primer on the appearances of anomalous objects in paintings and descriptions from antiquity. A welcome addition to any library, but especially for those new to the research into UFOs. *Visitors: A New Look at UFOs* is an all-in-one handbook for quick reference and insightful observation.

— Dr. Bill Birnes, Ph.D, host of the television program *UFO Hunters.*

Inscription

THE GLOWING DOT MOVED slowly from south to north at what seemed to be very high altitude. It repeatedly changed colors, from blue to green to yellow to red. Upon reaching the absolute zenith, it halted, turned white and slowly faded from sight.

Foreword

RICKY HUDSON IS NOT certain of the exact date, but it was just before Christmas 1988, at about 9:00 p.m. He was driving south on Highway 155 approaching Tyler, Texas when he saw a bright red light in the sky ahead. At first he assumed it was an airplane, but it seemed to be coming directly at him, so he pulled over and got out for a better look.

It was not descending toward him as he had first thought, but following a northerly, horizontal course. The device flew so low he could easily have heard its engines had it been a conventional aircraft, but it was totally silent. It also seemed to be moving much too slowly to have been a plane (much less a meteor,) and it had no blinking, airplane-style running lights.

Hudson later described it as circular and about the size of a typical delivery truck. It "looked like it was on fire," and "was bright enough to be seen miles away."

He estimates he watched the object for about five minutes, during which it passed directly overhead. It was still visible and following its northward heading when he got back in his car and left.

The night was clear, so it was impossible to tell if the peculiar aircraft was above or below a cloud line. Hudson is certain it was no balloon.

Highly visible, silver-colored upper atmosphere scientific research balloons are not uncommon in the skies over this area because of the proximity of the National Scientific Balloon facility in nearby Palestine, Texas. This NASA contractor's periodic launchings of large, bright balloons ordinarily precipitate a flurry of UFO reports. However, when telephoned by this author, the center reported it had sent no balloons aloft since the previous September.

Another Tyler-bound motorist had an even more memorable meeting with an aerial something. It was the spring of 1981, and she was driving east on Interstate Highway 20. She had just left Mesquite, Texas. It was late afternoon, and she was headed away from the setting sun when a bright light startled her. At first she thought it was the sun reflecting off an airplane's wings, but the light suddenly became markedly brighter. It was so intense that despite the bright sunshine outside it markedly lit up her car's interior.

The strength of the beam made it difficult to discern the outline of the object from which it was emanating, but the witness is nevertheless certain the device changed shape. She could not tell how far away it was, but it maintained its distance.

"I could tell it wasn't a helicopter," she said later. It traveled too slowly to have been an airplane, and too fast for a balloon. It followed her for about 70 miles, the whole time illuminating the inside of her car with its mesmerizing light. When she exited onto Highway 69 the object continued to follow Interstate 20. She admitted she was relieved at its departure.

"It made me feel funny. Frightened."

In the spring of 1975 high school senior Woody Johnston was driving south on Highway 155 outside Tyler, Texas one night when he noticed a brilliant light approaching his car from the rear. Its intensity lit the highway like it was midday.

Looking back, Johnston could see only the well-illuminated roadway, and realized the source of the light was directly above him. Peering out his window he saw a round object "like a ball that was lit up." It was pacing the car and directing a beam of light onto it. At first he thought it was a helicopter, but then realized it was silent.

Accelerating so that it was slightly ahead of the automobile, it maintained this position for about half a mile at 55 miles per hour until it abruptly shot ahead and was lost from sight "in at most a second."

The significance here is that this is the first time these three events have been reported via any medium other than casual word-of-mouth. The three witnesses are personal acquaintances of the author, who made no effort to solicit the reports. I overheard them accidentally, in passing.

This emphasizes the magnitude of the saucer mystery. It has become an everyday occurrence that one does not have to dig for to find. Perhaps we have come to regard it as commonplace and to be taken for granted, and are therefore not as aware of it as we should be.

The phrase "Unidentified Flying Object" has metamorphosed from an obscure technical term into what we now must be reminded is still one of the greatest riddles of the modern world. The intent here is point out a new direction that could be taken in the study of UFOs. This book is meant to inform those who already believe in the existence of flying saucers—not to convince skeptics.

Unfathomable devices from points beyond our present ken may have been bisecting our skies for a very long time. What they are, where they come from, what their occupants want, and if they even exist must (for now at least) remain tantalizing, unanswered questions. Yet, perhaps, not for much longer.

By dividing the science of ufology into separate and distinct sub-categories researchers may learn there is no single, overall answer to the entire discipline, much in the way cancer is caused by multiple factors that are wholly distinct and independent from each other. We need to overhaul our methods of researching flying saucers by assigning each case history to the files of the potential cause that appears most appropriate for it. Only then are we likely to start learning the answers…one after another.

--The author

Some Significant Sightings

Part 1

1 The Camel Killer

IT TOOK A FEW days for news to leak out about the cryptic flying machine that crashed in a remote area of southern Somalia on March 26, 2007. It was no April Fool's story that came out five days later of the sparkling contraption embedded in a crater 24 miles north of the community Buulo Burde Town.

A local resident, Ilyas Ali, watched the UFO pass overhead seconds before it crashed. "In the evening of last Wednesday a large device flew over our heads, and moments later we heard a large sound, 'BAM!'"

Ali also described how the object glittered brightly in daylight, and at night it flashed lights and spoke in a strange language the natives could not understand as it managed to stay in operating condition despite having crashed with such violence that it killed a camel grazing nearby.

After the initial reports from this isolated region nothing further was heard about the camel-killing crash. [1]

2 English Channel Colossi

A BRITISH AIRLINER PASSED near a couple of gargantuan UFOs hovering over the English Channel on April 26, 2007. The flabbergasted aircrew estimated the flying machines as being *a mile across*!

Aurigny Airlines pilot Captain Ray Bowyer saw the first colossus hovering at 2000 feet ten miles west of the channel island of Alderny.

"It was a very sharp, thin yellow object with a green area. It was 2000 feet up and stationary. I thought it was about 10 miles away, although I later realized it was about 40 miles from us," he said. "At first I thought it was the size of a [Boeing] 737, but it must have been much bigger because of how far away it was. It could have been as much as a mile wide."

As Bowyer continued his approach into the airport at Guernsey he noticed an identical object farther west.

"It was exactly the same, but looked smaller because it was farther away. It was closer to Guernsey. I can't explain it," he said. "At first I thought it might have been a reflection from a vinery in Guernsey, but that would have disappeared quickly. This was clearly visible for about nine minutes."

The passenger jet's flight path took it closer to the second unknown, and the intrigued Bowyer considered going nearer for a close look.

"I was in two minds about going towards it to have a closer look, but decided against it because of the size of it," he said. "I had to think of the safety of the passengers first. I'm certainly not saying it was something of another world. All I'm saying is that I have never seen anything like it before in all my years of flying."

Trained to make meticulous observations, airline pilots make excellent eyewitnesses, and Bowyer turned out not to be the only one to note this pair of giants. The duty officer at Guernsey Airport, Paul Kelly, listened to both Bowyer's report and one from another pilot who saw the second UFO from the opposite direction. Their descriptions matched.

"The description was very similar to Captain Bowyer's, and they described it as being in exactly the same place, but they were looking at it from opposite sides," Kelly said. "Both pilots placed it at exactly the same altitude."

Neither craft appeared on the airport's radar, but this is to be expected because this kind of radar filters out stationary objects. [2]

3 Where Did the Time Go?

A YOUNG COUPLE FROM Allentown, Pennsylvania preferred to not be identified when they related a baffling UFO experience. They maintained a summer cottage in the Pocono Mountains. On a Saturday morning in July 1966 they climbed into their car and set off on the 30-minute drive to their lofty little retreat.

The first inkling that something was amiss was how the normally bustling Pennsylvania Turnpike was eerily devoid of traffic. Suddenly a large round object loomed ahead of them and appeared about to land on the highway. However, when the husband pulled the car onto the shoulder of the road and stopped, the craft stayed slightly aloft and slowly came closer. The couple later described it as being a shiny metallic color with big black spots spanning its circumference. It flew low over them, and then quickly departed. The husband restarted the car and they resumed their trip, but the real surprise was still ahead. When they arrived at their cottage they looked at their watches. They had left home at 9:30 a.m. It was now 1:30 p.m. The 30-minute trip they had made numerous times had taken four hours that day.

They had experienced the same thing as countless saucer witnesses. When dealing with UFO incidents, missing time is a recurring factor. [3]

4 Get Out of the Way!

NEAR MISSES BETWEEN UNIDENTIFIED flying objects and commercial airliners became almost commonplace in the 1950s, and in one ghastly case in May 1953 an English-built Comet jetliner was destroyed over the plains of India. Crash investigators concluded the plane had struck "...some heavy solid object while in flight." [4]

A similar incident occurred on the evening of April 1, 1959 over the mountains outside Tacoma, Washington when a military C-118 carrying four men went down under very strange circumstances. The first indication something was wrong was an emergency transmission received at 7:44 p.m. The pilot radioed, "We've hit something, or something has hit us!" A few seconds later, "Mayday! Mayday!" Then more silence. Suddenly came the last transmission, "This is it! This is it!" Nothing more. The huge plane slammed into a mountainside. There were no survivors. [5]

Investigators discovered the tail section near Mount Rainier, above which it apparently had been knocked loose from the rest of the aircraft, the wreckage of which was found miles away. The pilot had been correct. The C-118 had had a midair collision. Tailless and out of control it had crashed a few miles from the site of the original message.

Ground witnesses told representatives of the Aerial Phenomena Research Organization (APRO) that two yellowish-orange objects closely followed the stricken transport. They trailed it until the instant it crashed, and then zipped out of sight.

An earlier collision was documented on the night of July 22, 1956. The airplane was a twin-engine C-13-D Convair troop transport piloted by Air Force Major Mervin Stenvers. The impact occurred at 16,000 feet. The plane plunged to 7000 feet before Stenvers was able to regain control. He startled ground controllers by yelling into his microphone, "Struck! We've been struck by a flying saucer!" Air traffic controllers cleared him for an emergency landing at Bakersfield, California. [6]

Nobody could understand how Stenvers landed the crippled machine. Government representatives told reporters the plane's tail was thoroughly smashed by something that hit it from "…above. We don't know yet what it was." Decades later the military still cannot explain what caused the damage. [7]

Not all transportation sightings have come from airplanes or automobiles. October 3, 1958 was the date of the most intriguing UFO *railroad* sighting ever reported. Before sunrise, Monon Railway's train #91 was southbound on a 90-mile jaunt from Monon, Indiana to Indianapolis. The crew consisted of three men in the locomotive, and two in the caboose. They maintained contact via a low-wattage FM radio. FM radio was also the only communication between the train and the dispatcher located in Lafayette, Indiana. At 3:20 a.m. fireman Cecil Bridge was first to notice the formation of odd lights low in the sky ahead.

"They were moving in a sort of V formation. By that I mean there was not actually a light at the front and center of the formation, just the two wings of two lights each, angled off at about 45 degrees from each other." [8]

Bridge was an Air Force veteran with more than 450 hours of logged flight time as a heavy bomber crewman. He was no novice when it came to identifying aircraft, and he later said he was, "…dead certain these were not planes!" He went on to say, "They were moving at about 40 or 50 miles an hour when they crossed the tracks about half a mile ahead of us. Just four big soft white lights."

Because of the length of the train (about half a mile) the men in the caboose could not see the objects, but a radio report filled them in on what the men in the locomotive were seeing. The lights abruptly shot out of sight to the east, "…barely above the treetops," said Bridge. A minute later they were back over the tracks ahead of the train, but this time they were high enough that the men in the caboose could see them.

Conductor Ed Robinson climbed into the caboose cupola for a better view. He described what he witnessed: "I saw four gobs of light about half a mile ahead of the caboose—the full length of the train. Then I realized they were coming toward us. Sosby (the other man in the caboose) was in the cupola, and he saw them too. They were going north, and we were going south. They were pretty low; not more than a couple of hundred feet above the cars, and they passed over the full length of the train, but going in the opposite direction. I would not say they were going over 50 miles an hour at the most, but that is only an estimate. I just know they were not moving very fast. It took too long for them to run the length of the train."

The train drowned out any sound the craft may have made, but nothing obstructed Robinson's and Sosby's view as the glowing things passed overhead. According to Robinson, "They were four big, disk-shaped things maybe 40 feet in diameter. They glowed like white fluorescent things, sort of fuzzy-looking around the rims."

They allowed the train to pass under them, and then gathered in a cluster over the tracks, waiting until the caboose was about a mile and a half away. At this point they accelerated eastward in single file, their luminosity increasing with their speed.

The men lost sight of the disks, but in a couple of minutes they reappeared, still behind the train, but now overtaking it rapidly. Both Robinson and Sosby were struck by the strange formation the devices now assumed. The two outer disks were vertical while the inner ones were slanted at opposing 45-degree angles, so that they resembled a giant, flying letter M.

Robinson turned a powerful five-cell flashlight on the objects. They jerked to the right as if to escape the light beam. When they reassembled over the tracks he turned the light on them again. Again they scattered.

"I had the feeling they didn't like being in the light all that much," Robinson said later.

The UFOs continued to trail the train (at a greater distance) until it reached the outer limits of the township of Kirklin, about 35 miles north of Indianapolis. Then, according to Robinson, "They zipped off to the northeast and we never saw them again."

5 Meltdown

NOT ALL UFOS HAVE displayed the same degree of shyness. The one that appeared over the eastern seaboard on the night of April 18, 1962 made no effort to conceal its presence, and apparently was in dire distress. First reported over Oneida, New York it was moving slowly on an easterly heading (for the moment.) Ground observers described it as being at extremely high altitude, higher than any known Earth machines were capable of flying at that time except for the rocket-powered X-15. Yet this device maintained its lofty position far longer than an X-15 could. It trailed red flames. Witnesses sighted it over Kansas, Utah, Montana, New Mexico, Wyoming, Arizona and as far west as California, indicating it was following a meandering course.

The North American Air Defense Command (NORAD) scrambled jet fighters to intercept the intruder, but it was far above their altitude ceiling. It is possible these planes produced the rumbling sounds reported by residents of Nephi, Utah as the UFO passed directly overhead, although nobody on the ground reported seeing any jets. The bizarre interstate air drama ended abruptly when the object suddenly exploded over Nevada, about 70 miles northwest of Las Vegas. The streets of Reno were lit midday bright by the detonation, which was seen as far away as California and mistaken by most witnesses as an atomic test.

There had been no nuclear test. The Atomic Energy Commission denied conducting any blasts in North America that night. Considering the power of the explosion it is sobering to consider the implications had it occurred at a lower altitude.

An interesting sideline to this story was brought to light when United Press International announced that a huge flying machine had landed next to an electrical power station in Eureka, Utah that same night. An Air Force spokesman said the "impact" of the UFO's landing temporarily disabled the plant. Whether these incidents involved the same or separate craft is uncertain, but it is undeniable that some kind of doomed vessel made its last flight that spring evening, and its crew, although apparently unable to achieve escape velocity from Earth's gravity, managed to maintain a high enough altitude to protect those on the ground from the impending detonation.

6 Captain Mantell's Last Flight

ONE OF THE FIRST tragic UFO episodes occurred January 7, 1948. A shiny metallic saucer whizzed over the town of Madison, Indiana. The area lies on the Indiana-Kentucky border, and when repeated calls from Lexington, Fort Knox and Elizabethtown alerted the military at nearby Godman Field, three incoming F-51 Mustang fighters were ordered to investigate.

By this time (3:00 p.m.) the contraption was directly over Godman. After observing it through binoculars, Colonel F.G. Hix described it as a shimmering disk about 150 feet across. Fifteen minutes later one of the pilots, Captain Thomas Mantell, was close enough to the ascending UFO to get a clear look. It had changed shape.

"I've sighted the thing," radioed Mantell. "It looks metallic, and of tremendous size. It's rotating rapidly and surrounded by reddish streamers. It looks like an ice cream cone topped with red, intermittently flashing at the top." Mantell's transmission continued.

"It's still above me, making my speed or better. I'm going to 20,000 feet, and if I'm no closer I'll abandon chase."

According to the United States government's official press release these were the young captain's last words. Later, however, one of the staff in the Godman control tower told a representative from the British Flying Saucer Bureau that Mantell had sent another message just before his plane was destroyed. The transmission was simply, "My God! There are men on it!" [9] The next thing ground control heard was a deafening blast of static, and then silence.

The next day Mantell's body was found among the scattered wreckage of his plane. The press was not permitted access to the crash site. The official explanation for the wreck was of the genre that would become familiar to saucer investigators. It explained that Mantell had flown too high and passed out from lack of oxygen in his non-pressurized cockpit. With an unconscious man at its controls the unguided Mustang had spun to Earth. The report stated that the object this highly trained aviator had fatally chased was the planet Venus. A later explanation was that a cirrus cloud that deceived Mantell. When this did not fly either, the government more credibly concluded the captain had encountered an "unknown object of uncertain origin."

The plane's wreckage was strewn over an entire field, as if it had disintegrated in the air rather than crashing into the ground, as it would have had the unconscious pilot theory been true. There was no impact crater, and the mangled fuselage was peppered with what investigators called "tiny perforations, and to be almost porous or rough." This could indicate the plane had been caught in a powerful blast of intensely hot, abrasive thrust.

7 Mayday!

ANOTHER CASE IN WHICH a terrestrial aircraft ran afoul of a saucer took place south of the Rio Grande in June 1949. A four-engine bomber was en route to its base in Texas when the routine flight became otherwise. While over the Yucatan Peninsula the pilot and co-pilot noticed a star-like point of light hovering motionless ahead of them. They first assumed it was a weather balloon, but as they neared it the thing took on a most unballoonlike disk shape. At this point the captain alerted his crew to the object's presence and proximity. It was immobile at 8000 feet and surrounded by white vapor.

As the bomber came within a mile of the UFO it commenced wobbling on its vertical axis as a spinning top does as it loses momentum. Without warning it charged the bomber.

"What's he doing?," cried the co-pilot. "He's coming right at us!"

The disk shot past the plane, barely missing the port wingtip. In an attempt to escape, the pilot dove to 3000 feet, but could not shake off the saucer. It turned and charged again.

Trying to describe the incident to ground control, the pilot yelled into his microphone, "He won't go away! That damn S.O.B. is going to wind up crashing into our wing unless…" This was all the captain had time to transmit. His engines cut out and the B-17 was tumbling helplessly downward. The crew bailed out, and as they floated to Earth they watched their aircraft crash and burn. Their attacker hovered long enough to observe the results of its attack, then zipped out of sight.

One of the toughest bombers in the history of martial aviation was destroyed without a shot having been fired by the assailant. Chalk this one up to technological superiority.

8 Just Taking a Quick Look

THE STEAMSHIP *LLANDOVERY CASTLE* was one day out of Mombassa on the East African coast. As it steamed toward Cape Town on the evening of July 1, 1947 its passengers and crew enjoyed the calm winter weather while passing through the Strait of Madagascar.

At about 11:00 p.m. the lookout and some passengers saw a bright light approaching rapidly from behind the ship. Dropping to about 50 feet the dazzling object flashed a blinding searchlight onto the steamer and matched its speed. The beam was abruptly extinguished, and the shipboard witnesses got a good look at the object. They later agreed it was a gigantic metallic cylinder, cigar-shaped, with no windshields, windows or portholes. Its size was staggering. The onlookers estimated it was at least three, possibly, four, times the length of the *Llandovery Castle,* making it about 1000 feet long with a diameter of roughly 200 feet.

After about a minute of quietly pacing the steamship the colossal flying machine slowly, soundlessly ascended to about 1000 feet. Orange jets of thrust erupted from the aft, and the aircraft swiftly rose until it was lost from sight. [11]

9 Recharge

MANY UFOS SEEM ATTRACTED to electric power plants. These visits have rather startling (but generally harmless) effects on the installations. A power plant in Uberlandia, Minais Gerias, Brazil had such an adventure August 17, 1959. It all started when four automatic keys at the main facility unexpectedly turned themselves off, terminating the power flow to all substations. Technicians were unable to pinpoint the problem, and the situation became even more confusing when one of these substations called in a UFO report. The manager telephoned to report that all his keys had suddenly kicked into the open position as a glowing UFO passed overhead at low altitude. The chief engineer did not believe the manager, and hung up on him.

Moments later, however, the chief changed his opinion when he had the same thing happen to him. Again the UFO passed over at treetop level, and followed the power lines into the jungle. At this point the power returned to normal at the main station. Investigation revealed no damage or evident reason for the outage. It was almost as if the passing UFO had absorbed a few hundred thousand kilowatts.

10 All Shook Up

IT IS NOT UNUSUAL for UFOs to be first spotted over water, and then head inland. During the small hours of March 27, 1968 two Mexican vessels in the Gulf of Mexico, the *Alfo Mex II* and the warship *Guanajuato,* spotted a blazing object which roared over them, leaving the previously calm sea churning in its wake.

Moments later it passed over the coastal city of Vera Cruz. An unearthly rumbling awakened locals to a terrifying scene. Resident Angelita de Villalobos Arana would recall, "It was as bright as day, and the terrible noise kept on. I felt cool, then cold, and the light kept getting brighter and brighter!"

The terrified peasants testified that they had seen "…two or three objects in the center of a bright ball of fire." They reported feeling the ground shake, and the darkness banished by a blinding light. They agreed the fireball looked as if it would crash into the Earth, but it regained altitude and charged out of sight.

The official government report read like most. It was a mixture of explaining what the UFO was *not,* and an admission that the powers-that-be did not know what it *was.* According to Ernesto Dominquez, head of the Mexican Department of Meteorology, the official report read in part:

"This probably was not a meteorite. We cannot say for sure what it was. We do know that it did not fall to Earth, or collide with the Earth. Its trajectory was curved. Imagine a jet or spaceship suddenly going out of control and plunging directly toward Earth. Then, as if control was suddenly regained, the object or objects suddenly veered away from the Earth only moments before collision point, and went out over the Gulf of Mexico. But I think it did not fall into the sea. It could have gone upward."

A meteorite would hardly do such a thing. [12]

11 Taking the Plunge

NOT ALL UNIDENTIFIED FLYING objects are actually flying. Ground sightings are well documented, and at least one encounter with an unidentified *floating* object is on record.

The steamship *Fort Salisbury* was churning along uneventfully just off West Africa slightly after 3:00 on the morning of October 28, 1902. Suddenly the lookout sounded the alarm, warning the pilot to take evasive action to avoid colliding with something in the water dead ahead. Second Officer A.H. Raymer came on deck and had the searchlight turned on to illuminate a giant metallic mass floating in the sea.

It was huge, and as *Fort Salisbury* pulled alongside what her crew assumed was a disabled ship clanking noises and what sounded like excited voices were plainly audible from inside the craft. Two reddish-orange lights glowed at one end, and greenish-blue ones at the opposite end (since they were identical it was impossible to tell which was fore and which was aft.) The strange object was about 600 feet long, with a diameter of approximately 100 feet.

Raymer shouted to his sailors to prepare to assist the vessel. Whatever it was, it clearly was sinking. He ordered his signal officer to open communications with the craft and to begin rescue operation maneuvers, but the sinking vessel did not respond. With very little fanfare the unidentified object slipped under the waves and out of sight.

After more than a century the *Fort Salisbury* encounter remains one of the most intriguing of all unexplained sightings. [13]

12 Convoy

THE EXTREME DIVERSITY OF our visitors is continually demonstrated. On the night of February 9, 1913 a procession of glowing objects bisected the sky over Canada and beyond.

First reported passing over a rural area of southeastern Saskatchewan, the convoy displayed little in common with the generally solitary, silent and swerving saucers that later came to typify UFOs. Two farmers spotted a line of four bright lights, followed by a second group of three abreast with two more bringing up the rear. Slowly and deliberately this parade crossed the heavens heading in a southeasterly direction. Loud rumbling sounds similar to those produced by latter-day jets marked their passage.

Providentially, a noted astronomer witnessed the procession. Professor C.A. Chant of the University of Toronto gave the event a fully detailed description. In describing these "meteorites" he said, "There suddenly appeared...a fiery red body seen to be followed by a long tail. In the streaming of the tail...it resembled a rocket, but unlike a rocket the body showed no indication of dropping to the Earth. On the contrary, it moved forward in a perfectly horizontal path...without the least apparent sinking to the Earth. It moved on to the southeast, where it simply disappeared in the distance."

Chant also recorded the other, following objects until they were al lost from sight, describing the entire episode as lasting "perhaps 3.3 minutes."

After they left Canadian skies and flew over the Atlantic Ocean, shipboard reports recorded their passage over New York City, Bermuda and as far south as Cape Sao

Roque, Brazil, still bound southeast. They were not reported after this point. Although these peculiar night fliers became known as "Chant's Meteorites," there is virtually no possibility they were some kind of natural occurrence. Their airspeed was far too slow for meteorites, which never fly in orderly formations anyway.

Earth technology was too primitive in 1913 for the objects to have been terrestrial. It may be noteworthy that each formation of UFOs appeared only *after* the preceding one had disappeared over the horizon. Should a squadron of spacecraft be hovering outside the atmosphere preparatory to entering, it stands to reason that one detachment will not enter until its predecessor achieves secure passage, indicating it is safe for the next to proceed.

This fantastic episode had a sequel the following day. *The Toronto Star* reported the widely witnessed flight of three groups of dark objects over the city in broad daylight. "They passed from west to east, at great altitude, in three groups. They then returned from the west, in more scattered formations, seven or eight in all."

The world in 1913 was not ready for the possibility of visitors from outer space (or elsewhere.) We had neither the technology to detect them, or the sophistication to understand the full implications of such a statement. The entire event passed away with virtually no speculation as to what it may have been. [14]

13 The Dixie Cloud Sailors

THE YEARS IMMEDIATELY BEFORE and after the dawn of the 20th Century produced numerous spectacular instances of unexplained aerial machines. 1897 was vintage for sightings of airborne conveyances whose descriptions do not match those of more contemporary UFOs.

April 9 was the beginning of a weeklong spectacle over the American Midwest. A single huge object patrolled the heavens day and night from St. Louis to Denver. Generally moving at relatively slow speed and at great altitude it was viewed by millions. Telescopes revealed it to be cigar-shaped with broad, short wings. At night it flashed red, white and green lights. On April 16 it abruptly disappeared, but the drama was not ended. The same (or similar) UFO cruised over the hamlet of Sistersville, West Virginia during the predawn of April 19. At low altitude this time, an enormous machine at least 200 feet long wandered the sky while shining blinding searchlights over the area, and sported the same blinking red and green lights. Shaken townspeople could discern a loud humming. After several minutes the thing extinguished its lights and flew off eastward at high speed, never to reappear.

The southeastern states were favored by mysterious airships at this time. In January 1910, an elongated UFO visited Chattanooga. It was a gleaming metallic white, about 100 feet long, wingless and reported by many as emitting a loud chugging. After meandering slowly over the city for almost an hour, it suddenly zipped away, appearing over Huntsville, Alabama (75 miles away) a few minutes later.

This tantalizing, beautiful craft returned to Chattanooga the next day. Watched by multitudes, it flew low over Missionary Ridge, slowly rose into the drizzling clouds and never returned.

Probably the best chronicled of the 1897 airship reports came from two lawmen, Deputy Sheriff John McLemore and Constable John J. Sumpter, Jr. of Garland County, Arkansas. Their two signed affidavits chronicling this encounter, and the following first-person account was printed in the May 13 issue of the Helena, Arkansas *Weekly World*:

While riding northwest from this city on the night of May 6, 1897 we noticed a brilliant light high in the heavens. Suddenly it disappeared, and we said nothing about it as we were looking for parties and did not want to make any noise. After riding four or five miles around through the hills we again saw the light, which now appeared to be much nearer the Earth. We stopped our horses and watched it coming down, until all at once it disappeared behind another hill. We rode on until about half a mile further, when our horses refused to go further. About at 100 yards distant we saw two persons moving around with lights. Drawing our Winchesters, for we were now thoroughly aroused to the importance of the situation, we demanded, "Who is that, and what are you doing?"

A man with a long dark beard came forth with a lantern in his hand, and on being informed on who we were, proceeded to tell us that he and the others, a young man and a woman, were traveling through the country in an airship. We could see the outlines of the vessel, which was cigar-shaped and about 60 feet long, and looking just like the cuts that have appeared in the papers recently. It was dark and raining, and the young man was filling a big sack with water about 30 yards away, and the woman was particular to keep back in the dark. She was holding an umbrella over her head. The man with the whiskers invited us to take a ride, saying that he could take us to where it was not raining. We told him we preferred to get wet.

Asking the man why the brilliant light was turned on and off so much, he replied that the light was so powerful that it consumed a great deal of his votive power. He said he would like to stop off in Hot Springs for a few days and take the hot baths, but his time was limited and he could not. He said they were going to wind up in Nashville, Tennessee after thoroughly seeing the country. Being in a hurry, we left and upon our return about 40 minutes later, nothing was to be seen. We did not hear or see the airship when it departed.

(signed) John J. Sumpter, Jr.

John McLemore

Subscribed and sworn to me on the eighth day of May 1897.

C.G. Bush, J.P. [15]

The 1897-1910 airships were never identified, and their mission(s) remain equally obscure. Some ideas have been advanced, and certain situations have come to light since those early sightings. They will be addressed in later chapters.

14 A French Connection

FRANCE WAS STILL IN revolutionary turmoil in 1790. Chaotic social conditions contributed to the ensuing obscurity of an enthralling UFO sighting witnessed by two mayors, a police inspector, a doctor and several other officials. Inspector Liabeauf conducted a meticulous investigation. His report, in part, was as follows:

At 5:00 a.m. on June 12 several farmers caught sight of an enormous globe which seemed surrounded by flames. At first they thought perhaps it was a balloon that had caught fire, but the great velocity and whistling sound that came from that body intrigued them. The globe slowed down, made some oscillations and precipitated itself towards the top of a hill, unearthing plants along the way! The heat which emanated from it was so intense that soon the grass and small trees started burning. The peasants succeeded in controlling the fire, which threatened to spread to the whole area. This sphere, which could have been large enough to contain a carriage, had not suffered from the flight. It excited so much curiosity that people came from all parts to see it. Then all of a sudden a kind of door opened and, this is the interesting thing, a person like us came out of it, but this person was dressed in a strange way, wearing a tight-fitting suit, and, seeing the crowd, said some words that were not understood and fled into the wood. Instinctively, the peasants stepped back in fear, and this saved them because soon after that the sphere exploded, in silence, throwing burning pieces everywhere, and these pieces burned until they were reduced to powder.

Searches were initiated to find the mysterious man, but he seemed to have dissolved. [16]

If this landed UFO stayed on the ground long enough for people to "come from all parts to see it," it must have been under observation for quite awhile, as well as viewed by a considerable number of eyewitnesses. This virtually precludes the possibility the encounter was some sort of elaborate, seemingly pointless, and incredibly advanced (for its time) hoax.

The "mysterious man" who "seemed to have dissolved" adds yet another dimension of confusing fascination to this incident occurring outside the farming village of Alencon.

15 The Phantom Flying Corps

BEGINNING IN 1933 THE skies over Scandinavia were routinely frequented by formations of mysterious airplanes the local press dubbed "Ghostfliers."

In December the Swedish Air Force attempted to intercept a flock of these machines that appeared in weather so atrocious that two Swedish planes crashed, and others were unable to get airborne. The Ghostfliers, however, seemed totally unaffected by the storms, and blithely flew at low altitude over the mountainous region until contact was lost.

The planes were described as huge, six-engine craft devoid of any insignia. Shortly before the outbreak of World War II they ceased to appear. [17]

16 A Postwar Puzzle

IN 1946 THE SKIES over the Baltic Sea came alive with a bewildering assortment of phantom flying machines. In May, people in northern Sweden began reporting objects that looked like flaming rockets or missiles shooting through the upper atmosphere.

They came to be called "ghost rockets" and "spook bombs." It was generally assumed it was the Soviets experimenting with V-2 missiles and other advanced weaponry recently captured from the Germans. Moscow repeatedly denied responsibility, and for once Joseph Stalin may have been telling the truth. Many of the spook bombs bore little resemblance in appearance or behavior to V-2s or any other flying armaments in service at that time.

Descriptions accumulated of cigar-shaped, football-shaped and round missiles. Some witnesses saw things that reminded them of fireballs or whirling pinwheels. One observer watched a flying something he described as resembling a "headless seagull."

Some ghost rockets zipped across the sky at incredible velocity, while others crept along. There were intricate maneuvers, rolls, dives, climbs and direction reverses. Hardly the sort of performances to be expected from a V-2, designed to fly in a simple rainbow arc.

The modern flying saucer era had not quite arrived, and to a world dazzled by the technological leaps spawned by the just-ended war the ghost rockets seemed just another magical gadget in its testing stage. However, military establishments on both sides of the Atlantic were in a position to know better. Investigations were launched, with the U.S. sending General Jimmy Doolittle to aid in the inquiry.

Meanwhile, Denmark, Sweden and Norway, fearful of Soviet aggression, imposed a news blackout on the sightings to head off potential widespread panic should plans for an imminent Russian invasion be uncovered. The fact-finding teams unearthed no latent military threat from the East. They determined that most of the spook bombs were, in reality, nothing more than misidentifications of conventional aircraft (particularly of the newly developed jet fighters.) But not all of them.

The Swedish Defense Ministry catalogued more than 200 sightings of objects that could not have been airplanes or any other "phenomena of nature or products of the imagination." This sort of official exasperation would soon become commonplace. The halcyon days of flying saucers were just around the corner. [18]

17 Dogfight

IN A FATEFUL 1954 encounter the two-man crew of a jet interceptor lost their plane to a saucer's heat ray. Radio operators at Griffiss Air Force Base in upstate New York detected an unidentified aircraft approaching at noon on July 1.

No planes were supposed to be in the area, so the base command scrambled an F-94 Starfire interceptor to head off the intruder. In the rear seat of the plane the radar operator quickly found the unknown on his screen and unerringly directed the pilot to it, establishing visual contact in about two minutes.

By this time the craft was motionless several thousand feet above the jet. It was a large, silvery disk, and made no effort to evade the rapidly closing warplane. The radar man attempted to contact the UFO via his radio. As he did so the jet's engine suddenly cut out, and a searing blast of heat engulfed both men. The pilot desperately checked his instruments, but could find nothing to account for the heat or mechanical failure. Realizing they were running out of time, he shouted for his comrade to abandon ship. Both managed to eject, getting a brief look at the huge silver saucer.

Their stricken fighter tumbled into Walesville, New York and killed four people, two of them children. The dazed airmen told a crowd of civilians what had happened, but Air Force officers soon arrived and silenced the fliers. The military did release to the press a description of the saucer. When it was sighted again later that same day over other sectors of New York State no more jets were sent to investigate. [19]

18 Countdown

THE WORLD NEVER KNEW how close it came to World War III after the early warning station at Thule, Greenland noticed a flight of unidentified aircraft heading toward North America from the direction of Soviet Russia on the morning of October 5, 1960.

The Strategic Air Command (SAC) sprang into action, sending formations of nuclear bomb-laden B-52 bombers aloft worldwide. While the military worked feverishly to establish the intruders' identity and calculate their probable destination, the American bombers circled, awaiting confirming orders to head for selected targets deep within the USSR.

Then, in the midst of all this panicky international activity, the blips abruptly vanished from the Thule radar screens. After a thorough, fruitless search, SAC recalled the bombers and Armageddon was placed on hold. The incident received little publicity. Several months later this brush with global nuclear war was mentioned briefly in newspapers on both sides of the Atlantic.

Whatever the objects were, they evidently were not Russian warplanes because their dematerializing act was beyond the technological ability of any terrestrial craft, but it was incredibly well timed. Had these UFOs maintained their course a little longer our planet might well have been reduced to a radioactive barren by a mistakenly launched nuclear war. [20]

19 How Much is Enough?

OVER A NINE-MONTH PERIOD beginning in August 1957 a series of incidents took place in which UFOs closely approached humans in the air and on the ground. They incapacitated planes or facilities, but departed before the situations became critical. Most of the encounters were in South America.

At 9:00 p.m. on August 14 a Varif Airlines C-47 cargo plane lifted off from Porto Alegre, Brazil en route for Rio de Janeiro. The seasoned fliers were Jorge Araujo and co-pilot Edgar Soares. They leveled off at 5700 feet and 160 miles per hour. Because they were above the cloud layer they had excellent visibility.

Soon a bright object appeared to the left of the C-47, slightly behind and below it. It passed the plane, then at extreme speed cut in front of it from left to right. The device was plate-shaped with a dome on top. As it passed in front of the plane, the C-47's engines sputtered and almost died, its lights dimmed and radio communications almost faded out. After a few seconds the saucer dropped into a cloudbank, and the airplane's electrical and mechanical systems recovered.[21]

On the night of November 3 a Varig C-46 piloted by Captain Jean de Beyssac departed Porto Allegre for Sao Paulo. After cruising at 7700 feet for several hours de Beyssac, at 1:30 a.m. on the fourth, spied a glowing red craft pacing them below and to the left. The pilots assumed it was another plane, but it suddenly shot toward them, closing to very tight quarters, and then withdrew. The crewmen noticed a smell of something burning. An equipment check revealed the aerial direction finder was burned out, as was the radio transmitter. The generator for the starboard engine was also affected, disabling the engine.

The stunned pilots managed to coax the crippled transport back to Porto Allegre, where they wrote out and signed a full report. Afterward, de Beyssac confessed, "I went home and got drunk." [22]

That same night a heat-spewing UFO assaulted a Brazilian Army base at Itaipu. A glowing orange sphere descended to hover over the darkened encampment. A quizzical sentry stepped into the open for a better look, and was joined moments later by a second soldier. The strange aircraft gradually lost altitude until the two sentries became alarmed and attempted to set off the camp's warning system, but the installation's power grid abruptly went dead and a blistering surge of heat blasted the hapless guards. By the time emergency power was turned on moments later the UFO was gone, leaving two severely burned soldiers who required prolonged hospitalization. [23]

The next event occurred three days later, on November 6, but it was thousands of miles to the north, in Merom, Indiana. The family of Rene Gilham were taking their evening meal when a neighborhood child interrupted them, begging them to come view the odd star hovering overhead. The Gilham children ran outside with their friend, and were back inside moments later, pleading with their parents to come see for themselves.

What they saw outside shocked them. The neighbors who had already come outside were standing transfixed by the silent disk hanging motionless 200 to 300 feet above them. It looked to be no more than 40 feet across, and when it commenced playing blinding blue beams over the area, the ground observers figured it prudent to withdraw—except for Rene Gilham, who laughingly told his wife, "Take the kids and go on inside. I want to see this thing."

See it indeed. For about 10 minutes he stood under the object, with the blue rays repeatedly flashed on him. Next the disk "…made a sizzling like a high-speed motor, and away it went."

Two days later Gilham noticed his face was itching and swelling. The next day the top of his head was swollen and red, and he consulted a physician, Dr. Joseph

Dukes, who had him hospitalized for what looked like burns inflicted by an electric welding torch, something Gilham had not been around for three weeks. In fact, he could not recall being in close proximity with anything that could have burned him, except presumably the blue light-flashing flying saucer.

While recovering in the hospital, Gilham was visited by two Air Force officers who did not identify themselves. They suggested he would be wise to not discuss what had happened to him with anyone else. Too late. Gilham had already spoken about it to his doctors, friends and the press. He recovered from his injuries, but the rash of UFO-related burnings was not over. [24]

On May 5, 1958 Carlos Rodriquez was flying a single-engine airplane over San Carlos, Uruguay near the Curbelo Naval Base when a glowing disk approached to within 700 yards, halted and commenced a regular rocking motion. Rodriquez then felt a stifling heat far in excess of what could have been caused by the afternoon sun. He opened the plane's windows, took off his jacket, and even opened the door, seeking relief from the sudden, oppressive temperature.

Nothing helped, but the heat wave ceased a few seconds later when the saucer zipped away seaward, its path marked by a thin vapor trail. [25]

This sequence of events seemed to indicate a series of tests aimed at men and their machines, possibly to determine how much heat and electrical interference was required to disable them. Although motives are undeterminable, this may have indicated latent hostility, or the saucerians may merely have wanted to learn how well they could defend themselves if attacked by us. Judging from these reports, fairly well.

20 A Midsummer Night's Dream

THE EIGHT BLIPS THAT appeared on the Civilian Aviation Authority's traffic control center in Washington D.C. at 12:40 a.m. on July 20, 1952 were moving abnormally slowly. They progressed at 100 to 130 miles per hour across the sky near Maryland's Andrews Air Force Base, 15 miles southwest of the capital. When they changed altitude they rose or dropped vertically like helicopters.

The air control center at the national airport was also monitoring the objects, and the staff were stunned when one suddenly ascended to the upper stratosphere and whizzed along for eight miles at 7200 miles per hour. The formation then broke up and these spherical UFOs dropped low over the city, flagrantly violating the strictly proscribed airspace over the White House, Capital Building and Pentagon.

Ground observers noted that there was one glowing ball markedly larger than all the others, all of which generally followed it, but at somewhat greater altitude. The UFOs were a variety of colors. Two jet interceptors out of the airfield outside New Castle, Delaware arrived to investigate the peculiar aerial goings-on over the governmental nucleus, but upon their arrival they found nothing but a serenely empty sky, the UFOs having disappeared moments earlier. When the fighters departed, however, the lighted globes reappeared, "dancing in the air like young deer," as one onlooker described them.

When senior air traffic controller Harry G. Barnes radioed the jets to return the UFOs vanished a second time, even before the pilots could reverse direction. This gave Barnes the impression his coded military transmissions were being monitored and deciphered.

Scores of prancing lights continued their heavenly gyrations throughout that night, effortlessly evading hurtling warplanes and disappearing at dawn.

Six days later, on July 26, Washington again was titillatingly buzzed when, at 9:08 p.m., twelve luminous white orbs cruised in from the northeast at the sluggish speed of 40 miles per hour. Once again, the New Castle jets played a frustrating game of cat-and-mouse with quarry that dissolved into nothingness at the approach of a conventional aircraft.

At 3:00 on the morning of the 27th a transport plane approached the vicinity in which the UFOs had been cavorting. The devices responded by shooting straight up until their altitude was too great for radar to track.

These persistent Washington overflights ceased after the night of August 5, when a formation of cryptic craft bobbed and weaved over the federal buildings, entertaining a large crowd. They again evaded fighters by ascending above their altitude ceiling.

After a lone UFO traveling 4000 miles per hour streaked in a perfectly straight line over the length of South Carolina on the morning of August 20, the summer of intrigue ended. The 1952 flying saucer wave (also called a "flap") concluded, and the newspapers, after contributing a little space to "explanations," went back to covering the development of the hydrogen bomb. [26]

21 Russian Roulette

IN THE SUMMER OF 1961, near Moscow, construction was underway on new missile emplacements when an enormous UFO appeared overhead, surrounded by smaller disks. The startled battery commander had his men fire a rocket salvo at the huge craft, but the missiles exploded far short of their target. A second volley suffered the same result, and a third was aborted when the battery's electrical systems went dead. [27]

22 Arizona Cover-Up

SHORTLY BEFORE 10:00 ON the night of July 2, 1947 residents of Roswell, New Mexico made numerous reports of a large UFO streaking through their city's stormy skies. Later that night, northwest of Roswell, rancher Mac Brazel noted an enormous, reverberating explosion that drowned out the thunderclaps. The next morning Brazel found his property littered with fragments of what looked like foil. Although thin and pliable the material was extremely tough. He also found a small disk that he turned over to the intelligence officer at Roswell Army Air Field.

The military later announced the wreckage was debris of a crashed meteorological forecasting device, and permitted reporters to photograph the fragments from a distance. After the newsmen later complained their photos were taken from too far away to show detail, the military held a second news conference. However the journalists claimed the material at this second exhibition was not the same as the first, but had been switched.

UFO investigators spent the next 40 years accusing the Air Force of conducting a cover-up. Then, in 1987, old government papers turned up which purportedly revealed an unidentified flying machine had indeed crashed, and its wreckage and the bodies of four occupants had been recovered and kept hidden from the public. Later evidence and statements from individuals in the Roswell case (some testimonials were made on deathbeds) resurrected the affair, exhuming a maze of governmental intrigue and deceit.

Army Major Jesse A. Marcel was base intelligence officer at Roswell at the time of the crash. Thirty-one years later he came forward with a tale that staggered international ufodom. Marcel claimed to have been one of the officers who hurried to Brazel's spread immediately after hearing of the explosion and crash. The soldiers found a 500-foot-long furrow gouged in the hard ground, and a 3500x300-foot area littered with graying metallic debris. Despite its shattered condition, the wreckage seemed unbreakable. The soldiers could not bend, break or cut it, and some of it was embossed with purple hieroglyphics. There was also material resembling aluminum foil. It too was incredibly tough, and when crumpled would unfold with no trace of wrinkling.

Ordered by their commanding officer, Brigadier-General Roger Ramey, "not to say anything to anybody," the men loaded the wreckage onto trucks and hauled it back to the base.

Meanwhile, base commander Colonel William Blanchard had not been informed of the gag order, and placed the Army in an awkward position by telling the press a flying saucer had crashed and its wreckage recovered. Ramey attempted to quash this release by contradicting it with the weather balloon story.

By 1991, investigators, pointed in the right direction by Marcel's account, began to close in on the truth. Kevin D. Randle, a former Air Force intelligence officer, and Donald R. Schmidt, Director of Special Operations for the Center for UFO Studies (CUFOS,) published their laboriously gathered findings in a book titled *UFO Crash at Roswell*. It turned out there had been a second crash site two and one-half miles southwest of the first. Although this find yielded considerably less bulk than the first (from which three C-54 transport planes were filled with material,) it was by far the more interesting. Here the military investigators found what appeared to be a crumpled escape pod containing the lifeless bodies of four nonhuman crewmen.

An archeological party and a surveyor lucked into the otherworldly tableau before anyone else. When the soldiers arrived they immediately cordoned off the area and threateningly swore the civilians to silence on the matter, but threats did not prevail. The surveyor, Grady L. Barnett, told a friend, L.W. Maltais, what he had seen that morning. After Barnett's death, Maltais gave his statement to investigators.

Barnett had seen a "pretty good-sized" grayish, metallic conveyance at the top of a ridge. The object was split open, and four crumpled bodies lay on the ground. Their one-piece suits had no zippers, buttons or snaps. With their pear-shaped heads and spindly limbs the four-foot-tall beings looked to Barnett to be "from another planet."

In 1989 a terminally ill woman in Florida revealed she had been one of the archeological students who happened upon the crash site. Her recollections closely paralleled Barnett's, and more reports began to surface. A year later another archeologist described driving over a ridge and encountering the destroyed capsule. He had examined one of the bodies, and described it as having an oversized head and eyes, a tiny mouth and no nose. The grim military detachment arrived before he could further examine the scene.

One of the soldiers, Sergeant Melvin E. Brown, was on his deathbed years later when he told his daughter Beverly how he had collected corpses of creatures with leathery, yellowish-orange flesh that was beaded.

Schmidt and Randle also tracked down a Roswell mortician, Glenn Dennis. His curiosity piqued after receiving numerous calls from the base, requesting information on embalming techniques, Dennis had driven out to the military hospital. As he strolled down a corridor an agitated nurse suddenly appeared and loudly informed him, "My God! You're going to get yourself killed!" At that point two military policemen dashed up and escorted the befuddled Dennis out of the building. The following day he spoke to the same nurse. She disobeyed orders by telling him three nonhuman carcasses had arrived at the hospital. Apart from the large eyes and heads, they had thumbless, four-fingered hands. After examination the three bodies were frozen, sealed in mortuary bags and shipped (she thought) to Wright-Patterson Air Force Base outside Dayton, Ohio.

The resolute investigators sniffed out another witness who told them the crate containing the corpses was loaded into a B-29 commanded by a Lieutenant Joe Shackleford, and flown east to a stopover in Fort Worth, Texas. The reasonably certain route of the cadavers ended in Fort Worth. Randle and Schmidt could find no trails leading out of Texas, but they kept digging.

There was an illuminating report from a woman who, in the summer of 1947, had been in Dayton visiting a friend whose husband was a guard at the air base. He came home while his wife's visitor was still there. He was greatly excited by the arrival that afternoon of four nonhuman bodies. While checking the refrigeration connections in the cold storage room where the shipment was temporarily being kept the guard had actually lifted the lid of a large case and seen a thoroughly unfamiliar type of corpse.

There were others who corroborated this report. One individual who refused to give his name claimed to have attended a cloak-and-dagger conference at Wright-Patterson and to have been shown a dead ufonaut deep frozen in an underground vault.

Another deathbed report came from a woman named Norma Gardner. She told UFO researcher Len Stringfield, "Uncle Sam can't do anything to me once I'm in my grave." She followed up this indisputable truth with a description of her 1940s job as a security-cleared secretary at Wright-Patterson. She claimed to have logged pathology reports from autopsies of dead aliens.

Information kept pouring in daily. The Randle-Schmidt team hit the jackpot when they interviewed the Roswell base pathologist who had examined the cadavers, Dr. Jesse Johnson. He was one of several witnesses who described the beings as ranging from three and one-half to four and one-half feet tall, weighing about 40 pounds, with huge almond-shaped eyes that had no irises or lids, and only vestigial ears, noses and mouths. The arms reached almost to the knees, and the thumbless hands had long fingers with what seemed to be suction pads on their tips. Their legs were short and atrophied. The pink, leathery flesh, when viewed under high magnification, was found to have a meshed structure. Their circulatory system contained a watery, lymph-like fluid, and there were no evident reproductive organs or digestive systems.

The most crucial testimony, however, came from Brigadier-General Arthur E. Exon. At the time of the 1947 Roswell crash, Exon had been a lieutenant-colonel stationed at Wright-Patterson. From July of 1989 to July of 1990, Randle and Schmidt interviewed him four times, and the general confirmed everything the intrepid pair had uncovered. After arriving at the base the debris had been taken to the material evaluation laboratories. According to Exon it underwent:

"Everything from chemical analysis, stress testing, compression tests, flexing. The boys who tested it said it was very unusual. They knew they had something new on their hands. A few of them thought the material might be Russian-made, but the overall consensus was that the pieces were from space. [28]

When asked about the bodies, Exon relied that "the strongest information was that they were brought into Wright-Pat." Three of them, anyway. The general believed one corpse was sent to a Denver "mortuary outfit."

He also shot down the weather balloon cover story:

"General Ramey and the people out at Roswell decided to change the story while they got their act together and got the information into the Pentagon and the President." [29]

It was an astounding revelation, and in conclusion Exon stated flatly his belief that "Roswell was the recovery of a craft from space."

This witness' credentials as a top-ranking Air Force officer with an exemplary record of 135 combat flights during the Second World War made his statements as weighty and credible as any possibly could be. They irrefutably documented the Roswell incident as being precisely what it long had been whispered as being—the fatal crash of a UFO. Furthermore, they finally confirmed the existence of the long-suspected cover-up program. [30]

23 Down on the Farm

AT CHERRY CREEK, NEW York, about 50 miles south of Niagara Falls, the Butcher family had a large, football-shaped UFO visit their farm twice on the evening of August 19, 1965. At 8:30 p.m. 16-year-old Harold Butcher was milking cows in the barn when static suddenly flooded his AM radio. A bull tethered to a pole outside vented a screech Harold later said he had "never heard from an animal before." Although tied through a ring in his nose, the panic-stricken animal was bending the pole in his frenzy to distance himself from the silvery object hovering at treetop level about 450 feet from the barn.

Demonic presences have a history of producing terror in animals. In the Cherry Creek case we encounter a theistically significant instance of a *saucer* having this effect.

Trailing reddish and yellow vapors the machine flew horizontally to a large maple tree and descended next to it. The craft was about 50 feet long and 20 feet thick in its middle. It was totally silent except for a distinct beeping.

When Harold ran outside for a better look, the "football" shot skyward, emitting a sonic boom. The boy ran to the farmhouse, where his mother was wondering what was causing the interference with her radio. He shouted for his family to come outside for a look. His 14-year-old brother Robert ran out just as the UFO disappeared into the clouds.

Mrs. Butcher called the state police at Fredonia, but the device returned before they could arrive. Another teenager, family friend Kathleen Brougham, ran inside screaming, "It's here again!" She hurried back out, closely followed by Harold,

Robert and the oldest Butcher child, William, Jr. In the gathering twilight the four adolescents watched the glowing green aircraft cruise southeasterly over a pasture, leaving a luminous yellow vapor trail.

Later, with the state police, the witnesses investigated the spot by the maple tree where the object had landed. At first they found nothing but a pungent odor, but the next day Harold found a purple fluid that "smelled like 3 in 1 oil." Over the following days milk production dropped sharply.[31]

24 Saucers Invade New England

AT APPROXIMATELY 2:00 A.M. on September 3, 1965, 18-year-old Norman Muscarello was walking on Route 150 between Amesbury, Massachusetts, where he had been visiting a friend, and his home in Exeter, New Hampshire. He was passing through Kensington when a large UFO abruptly descended from the sky above an open field and slowly approached him. The shocked teenager thought it would land and crush him, so he dove onto the shoulder of the highway, but the object veered off to hover unsteadily over a nearby house. Muscarello darted for the house and pounded on the door, screaming hysterically. He got no response. At this point a car passed by, headed for Exeter. Norman flagged it down and caught a ride to the Exeter police station, where Officer Scratch Toland listened in bewilderment to the terrified young man's story.

"Look," sobbed Muscarello, "I know you don't believe me, but you've got to send someone back out there with me!"

Toland got on the radio and summoned Cruiser #21. Momentarily, patrolman Eugene Bertrand arrived with a strange tale of his own. He had come across a car parked on a bypass of Route 101. A lone, frightened woman was at the wheel. She told the police officer that a giant, soundless aircraft had been following her very closely. It sported bright, pulsating red lights, and when she approached an overpass the craft shot skyward and was lost from sight within seconds.

Toland turned slowly to the boy and asked, "This sound like the thing you saw?"

"Sounds exactly like it!," Muscarello replied.

At 3:00 a.m. Bertrand and Muscarello arrived back at the site of the encounter. It was a warm, moonless night, and the two walked into the open field. Abruptly the horses in a nearby corral became agitated, whinnying loudly and kicking at their enclosing fence while dogs commenced a fearful howling.

Muscarello shouted, "I see it! I see it!"

A brightly illuminated circular craft was rising from behind a tree line. As it fluttered toward the men it lit up the area within at least a 100-yard radius with a glaring red light.

Retreating with Norman to the cruiser, Bertrand radioed, "My God! I see the damn thing myself!"

From inside the car they watched the device hover over the field, swaying like a rocking chair. The intensity of the flashing red lights made it difficult to discern an outline or shape. It remained totally noiseless, but the terrified animals continued their din.

Next, Patrolman David Hunt, who had been monitoring the radio transmissions, arrived in his cruiser. Both policemen walked to the edge of the field to watch as the thing moved haltingly off to the east. Meanwhile, at the police station, Toland had just heard from a night telephone operator who had received a call from a hysterical man in a phone booth. He had shouted that a flying saucer was coming straight at him, but the connection was broken before she could get his name or patch him through to Toland. He never called back. [32]

The eventful late summer of 1965 was the kickoff of an unprecedented wave of UFO sightings that swept the Northeast for months, and seemed to concentrate on Exeter. Locals quickly learned what areas their celestial guests favored, and began congregating nightly in hopes of making sightings. They were seldom disappointed.

These UFOs had a predilection for cruising over high-voltage power lines, and the spectators who sat up nights for the air shows stuck close to the wires. The onlookers also noted how inclement weather seemed to discourage the craft from appearing.

Jittery officers at nearby Pease Air Force Base actually ordered their pilots to shoot down the objects. One airman told a journalist he simply ignored this directive because the UFOs he had encountered were far too maneuverable to hit. Besides, he felt it might be imprudent to antagonize them, whoever they were.

In one notable sighting, Joseph Jalbert in Fremont, Massachusetts watched a red, cigarlike machine hover over nearby power lines for several minutes. Suddenly it disgorged a small, reddish-orange disk that drifted down to within several feet of the wires. A silver tube emerged from the little disk and came to rest on the lines. After about a minute, the tube was retracted and the small disk zipped back to the waiting UFO, which then cruised along the lines until Jalbert lost sight of it.

It ran in the family. Joseph's mother had a virtually identical sighting near Manchester, Massachusetts. [33]

On the evening of November 9, at the height of the flap, virtually all of New England and parts of Canada suddenly lost power. An area five times the size of Switzerland and 36,000,000 people were abruptly consigned to darkness by what became known as the Great Northeast Blackout. The Exeter vicinity was strangely unaffected. Several local power companies *totally detached and independent from the main system* simultaneously failed. [34]

Even more incredible was the absence of detectable damage. Utility repair crews searched frantically and vainly for something to fix. When service finally was restored it was with the same equipment that had mysteriously ceased to function a few hours earlier.

Chairman of the Rochester Gas and Electric Corporation, Robert Ginna, stated in exasperation, "Suddenly we didn't have it. We don't know what happened to the 200,000 kilowatts. It just wasn't there." [35]

There were some interesting sidelines to the outage. At 5:15 p.m. on November 9, private pilot Wheldon Ross was approaching Hancock Field outside Syracuse when he saw a giant, blindingly bright red ball hovering over power lines under him. It looked to be about 100 feet in diameter, and was over the intersection of two 345,000-volt power lines of the New York Power Authority and the New York Central Railway's tracks running between Hancock Field and Lake Oneida. A student pilot flying with Ross corroborated his account, and three other persons also reported the sighting. Seconds later the lights went out.

The blackout was the precursor of a series of others that struck internationally. On November 16, large areas of England lost power. On the 26th parts of St. Paul, Minnesota went dark amid numerous reports of UFOs. December 2 saw a sprawling area of the Southwest blanketed by a power failure that extended deep into Mexico. Finally, on December 26, parts of Argentina, including the entire city of Buenos Aires, lost power. That same day inhabitants of south-central Finland were shivering as their electricity deserted them in the dead of winter. [36]

The Great Northeast Blackout has eluded a conventional diagnosis to this day, and the ubiquitous flying saucers and spheres hung around New England well into 1966. Some say they *never* completely departed.

25 The Case of the Michigan Swamp Gas

IN A SEQUEL TO the Exeter experience, beginning in March 1966, fleets of flying saucers descended on the area around Ann Arbor, Michigan. On the evening of March 14, citizens in several counties watched glowing craft cavort overhead, combining impossible speed with incredible maneuverability. On the 17th they returned for another nocturnal air show. On the following night at least one of them touched down.

It was about 7:30 in the town of Dexter, 12 miles from Ann Arbor, and something was disturbing Frank Mannor's dogs. When the 47-year-old stepped outside to investigate he saw a most peculiar "meteor."

"It stopped and settled to the ground, then rose again. It was about half a mile away. I called my wife and my kids out, and we watched it for 15 minutes."

Mannor and his son Ronnie decided to have a closer look, and approached to within about 500 yards of the object.

"It was sort of shaped like a pyramid, with a blue-green light on the right-hand side, and on the left a white light. I didn't see no antenna or porthole. The body was like a yellowish coral rock, and looked like it had holes in it. Sort of like you took a piece of cardboard box and split it open. You couldn't see it too good because it was surrounded with heat waves like you see in the desert. The white light turned to blood-red as we got close to it, and Ron said, 'Look at that horrible thing!'" [37]

At the sound of the young man's voice the device vanished.

While her men were investigating, Mannor's wife Leona called local police on her party line. Neighbors were eavesdropping as she told the lawmen, "We've got an object out here like they call a flying saucer. It's got lights on it down by the swamp."

By the time the time police arrived, the road was blocked by carloads of eager UFO watchers. The contraptions came back the next day as out-of-this-world air shows entertained hundreds of eyewitnesses in the Ann Arbor vicinity. Some of the craft were at very low altitude.

In one of the most famous UFO sightings in history, 87 coeds at Hillside College watched a football-shaped object with multi-colored lights cavort through a swamp for more than four hours on the evening of March 21. At one point it suddenly charged the dormitory from which the girls were watching, but halted as abruptly as it had started. [38]

Alerted by the media's uncharacteristically thorough coverage of the situation, the Air Force sent its civilian UFO investigator, Dr. J. Allen Hynek, to look into the Michigan swamp frenzy.

After he arrived in Ann Arbor, Hynek tried to commence fact-finding and analysis, but his efforts were stifled by swarms of reporters, television crews and out-of-town sightseers. On his first night there he went on a wild ride in a police cruiser with officers eagerly chasing what they had convinced themselves was a UFO. It turned out to be the star Arcturus.

While trying desperately to dig some relevant information from the circuslike turmoil, Hynek received a message from the Air Force ordering him to hold a press conference on March 25 and explain what was happening. All the harried professor had to go on was a phone call he had received from a botanist at the University of Michigan. The man had pointed out that methane gas produced by rotting vegetation, especially in swamps, occasionally ignites spontaneously, producing silent, flickering columns of flame. Known as will-o'-the-wisp and foxfire, this naturally occurring phenomenon struck Hynek as a valid possibility for explaining the *nocturnal swamp sightings*. It was all he had to offer the throng of journalists clamoring for a single, all-encompassing explanation for *all the sightings*.

Going to great lengths to qualify his swamp gas theory as a *possibility* for *some* of the sightings did Hynek no good. He later recounted how he watched in dismay as a reporter skimmed through the statement, "found the phrase 'swamp gas,' underlined it and dashed for a telephone."[39]

The following day news reports and headlines announced the Air Force's official UFO consultant's "explanation" that swamp gas was the cause of many (if not all) saucers--not just those in Michigan, but everywhere. Predictably, this misrepresentation of Hynek's statement caused widespread resentment among witnesses and other interested parties. It was taken as an official announcement they could not tell the difference between burning methane gas, and saucer-, pyramid- or football-shaped flying machines.

Public dissatisfaction over how the case was being officially handled was such that Congress thought it prudent to take action. Under the prodding of Michigan State Representative and House Minority Leader Gerald Ford, the first-ever congressional hearing on UFOs convened as a closed session of the House Committee on Armed Services on April 5, 1966.

Ford wanted a far-reaching investigation, with UFO witnesses and high-ranking members of the government's executive branch testifying. Instead, Committee Chairman L. Mendel Rivers of South Carolina called only three witnesses: Air Force Secretary Harold Brown, director of the Air Force's UFO investigation agency, Project Blue Book, Major Hector Quintanilla, and Hynek.

Qunitanilla said little during the session, but Brown testified that of the 10,147 UFOs investigated by the Air Force since 1947, all but 646 had been explained as misidentifications of "bright stars, planets, comets and meteors." Of the remaining 646, Brown stated that there was inadequate information available to properly classify them. He concluded with, "The past 18 years of investigating UFOs have not yet identified any threat to our national security, or that the unidentified objects represent developments or principles beyond present-day scientific knowledge, or any evidence of extraterrestrial vehicles."

Upon hearing this Rivers evidently decided the subject was no longer important enough to be kept congressionally concealed, and admitted the mob of reporters waiting outside the chambers. He then had Brown repeat his testimony. He next called Dr. Hynek.

Eighteen years of trying to clarify the flying saucer enigma had changed his attitude. When he had first begun studying the subject, Hynek was a hard-core skeptic, regarding UFOs as an "utterly ridiculous" fad that would quickly pass, but years of persistent, convincing reports and the subject's stubborn eluding of any concrete diagnosis had forced him to open his mind to other possibilities. It was time, he declared, for an efficient, objective investigation into the "UFO problem."

Hynek went on to castigate the Air Force for investigating all saucer sightings under the assumption they were generated by error, hallucination or fraud. He pointed out that this close-minded attitude had stifled scientific advancement throughout history. "As a scientist," he told the committee, "I must be mindful of the lessons of the past. All too often it has happened that matters of great value to science were overlooked because the new phenomenon simply did not fit the accepted scientific outlook of the time."

After an hour and 20 minutes the congressional inquiry was over. The hearing, as far as Hynek was concerned, was entirely too limited in its scope, and never did have a legitimate interest in getting to the bottom of the UFO problem. The brevity of the hearing was more damaging than he could imagine at the time. Three years later, partially because of funding cuts, and partially because it was obvious the government had a very limited interest in the study of UFOs, Project Blue Book, the "unofficial" 19-year UFO tracking and recording program maintained by the U.S. Air Force, was terminated. The government of the United States had made its decision. Unidentified Flying Objects were not worth the time or money to study.
40

26 Are You Following Me?

IT WAS STILL DARK on the morning of April 17, 1966. Sheriff Deputies Dale Spaur and Wilbur Neff were investigating a car wreck outside Ravenna, Ohio when they received a dispatch to watch for an unidentified aircraft reported headed their way at low altitude from the west. Resuming their patrol, the two stopped to check out an abandoned car, then Spaur saw the shining disk hovering about 1000 feet above some nearby trees. The device had a protuberance on top resembling a shark's fin, and seemed to increase in size as they watched. It brilliantly illuminated the predawn countryside.

"I had never seen anything this bright before in my life," Spaur later declared. The lawmen ran back to their squad car, where Spaur grabbed the radio's microphone and excitedly described the contraption to the dispatcher.

"It's about 50 feet across, and I can just make out a dome or something on the top, but that's very dark. The bottom is real bright. It's putting out a beam of light that makes a big spot underneath. It's like it's sitting on the beam. It was overhead a minute ago, and it was as bright as day here. Our headlights didn't make nearly as much light as it did, and this is no helicopter or anything like that. It's perfectly still, and it just makes a humming noise!" [41]

Headquarters dispatched a unit with photographic equipment and ordered Neff and Spaur to keep the UFO in sight. It took off southeast over Route 14, with the deputies following below at about 90 miles per hour. Because of their speed and the dispatcher's erroneous belief they were on Route 14A, the camera car never found them.

East Palestine, Ohio police officer Wayne Huston had been monitoring the radio transmissions, and when he saw the object hurtle overhead he joined the chase. Huston later commented on how the saucer made no discernible attempt to evade its pursuers. "It's a funny thing, but when the object got too far ahead of us it appeared to stop and wait." The low altitude and flight path directly over the highway also seemed to indicate that whoever was piloting the craft wanted to be followed.

When the bizarre chase entered Pennsylvania, Huston notified the state police, who called the greater Pittsburgh Airport to ask if they were tracking the aircraft. The air traffic controllers responded they saw nothing unusual on their radar screens.

The chase had now covered 85 miles, and Spaur was running out of gas. He pulled into a filling station in Conway where they were joined by police officer Frank Panzanella. Now that it was no longer being chased, the UFO halted and began to ascend. Then a call came through from the airport. The controllers were now tracking the object, and as the four officers watched, an airliner (United Airlines flight 454) passed under it. The device then shot upward until it was lost from sight in the brightening sky.

Because of the recent sightings in Michigan, public fascination with flying saucers was at a high point. When Spaur and Neff got back to Ravenna, they found reporters awaiting them. Spaur described the chase in detail, which was awkward for the Air Force because his description was not at all compatible with the official explanation, which was that the three police officers had been pursuing the planet Venus across Ohio and Pennsylvania.

When this statement was released, the military was scathingly criticized from high and low. Ohio Congressman William Stanton railed, "The Air Force failed in its responsibility. Once people entrusted with the public welfare no longer think the people can handle the truth, then the people, in turn, will no longer trust the government."

The Air Force refused to alter its woefully inadequate explanation, however. They declared the peace officers had merely been chasing a planet, inferring that all three men had mistaken an object in outer space for something as close as the tops of trees.

This announcement's reflection on his veracity and common sense devastated Dale Spaur. Haunted by the stigma, he quit his job and marriage and drifted into obscurity and poverty. When a reporter tracked him down living in a seedy motel the ex-deputy moaned, "If I could change all that I have done in my life, I would change just one thing, and that would be the night we chased that damned saucer!" [42]

27 A Dark and Searing Night

SOUTH TEXAS WAS COLD and dreary just after Christmas 1980, especially late at night. Fifty-one-year-old Betty Cash and 57-year-old Vickie Landrum were motoring on a lonely road outside Houston, and this typically private setting hosted a very nontypical UFO encounter. It started when Landrum's seven-year-old grandson, Colby, noticed a blazing light hurtling over the pine forest that lined the highway. Cash stopped the car as the craft, flames spewing from its underside, paused over the roadway.

From about 65 yards the UFO resembled two cones, placed end-to-end, standing vertically. Landrum later referred to it as a "diamond of fire." Despite what should have been a very frightening experience, neither woman wanted to leave the scene. Instead, livid with curiosity, they got out of their car for a better look. Emitting a beeping sound the machine began to radiate searing heat, forcing the women to return to their car. Cash had to wrap her coat around her hand before she could grasp the metal door handle.

The mystery deepened yet further moments later when the craft began to gain altitude. About 20 military-type helicopters appeared and seemed to try and surround the strange object, but it sped away closely pursued by the noisy, metallic swarm. Within hours both women and Colby developed dysentery, nausea and sunburnlike blisters on their exposed flesh. Cash became so ill she had to be hospitalized for two weeks for treatment of these symptoms so uneasily reminiscent of radiation poisoning.

Other local witnesses later reported the burning object and its sizable helicopter escort (which appeared strangely immune to the blast of heat that so affected the ground onlookers, who were much farther away.) The observers identified from photos the copters as CH-47 Chinooks. The area military bases, however, unanimously denied sending aloft any such aircraft during the time frame in which the eyewitnesses made their sighting. In fact, the whole affair reached such proportions that the federal government felt it prudent to announce it was in no way responsible, and did not have an explanation for the bizarre case of the searing UFO and its helicopter retinue cruising over the Rio Grande Valley. [43]

28 Back in the USSR

On October 9, 1989 the official Soviet news agency TASS released a report of a landed UFO and occupants in a park in the city of Voronezh, about 300 miles south of Moscow. The account stated, "…a large shining ball or disk was seen hovering over the park. It then landed, a hatch opened and three creatures similar to humans, and a small robot came out."

These beings were described as standing at least 10 feet tall and having abnormally small heads. After a stroll around the park, the visitors re-boarded their saucer and flew away. Those witnesses who would talk about what they had seen said they had been overwhelmed with fear, and this fear stayed with them several days.

Scientists who examined the landing site allegedly found two chunks of hard material, presumably left by the UFO. One authority, Dr. Genrikh Silanov, described the nuggets as resembling "sandstone of a deep red color. However, mineralogical analysis has shown that the substance found in the park cannot be found on Earth."

Onlookers also reported a peculiar "banana-shaped object passing overhead."

TASS, noted for its staid, no-nonsense approach to news reporting, made a point of upholding the veracity of all the witnesses.

29 Saucer in the Monastery

LATE ON THE NIGHT of May 29, 2015 monks in the Buddist monastery called Baita Temple in Anhui Province, China were awakened by an intensely bright UFO that flew into the temple's main hall during a violent thunderstorm and set off security alarms. Video surveillance camera footage shows an apple-shaped hovering object that changed into a disc-shape before assuming the outline of a sitting Budda. After seven minutes of silently hovering and changing shape the device commenced a rapid spinning before suddenly zipping from the temple and out of sight into the stormy heavens. Like the rest of his monks, Father Shi Xingkong was totally bewildered by the eerie visitation.

"When I heard the alarm I got up to turn it off before going outside to check, and didn't see anything unusual," he said. "It was only when I looked at the monitor that I could see the UFO."

He added that this was the first time he ever had seen an unidentified flying object.

Chen Songzheng, a temple staff member, added, "Had the UFO not entered the temple hall it would not have set off the infrared alarms and we would not have known it was there."

30 Destruction in the Desert

EVENING PRAYERS WERE JUST concluding on October 27, 2016 in the Saudi Arabian town of Riyadh when residents were startled by a tremendous explosion from the desert east of town. With Houthi rebels waging a rebellion against the Yemeni government just across the border such occurrences were not rare, but when word leaked out about the strange nature of this engagement the Saudi government sealed off the area and released no information.

Almost two months later word leaked out to the West. Onlookers said it was definitely not a meteor because it glowed blue-green and shot out flashes of green light. One eyewitness who identified himself only as Khalid said he was "baffled and have never seen anything like it." The aircraft flew southward over the Yemeni desert while making numerous minor direction changes until a Houthi rebel soldier shot a shoulder-fired 9K-32 anti-aircraft rocket at it, scoring a direct hit and downing the craft. A Saudi helicopter crewman took a photo showing the crashed UFO with what looked like someone standing next to it. Residents as far away as Kuwait claimed to have heard the crash, and those in the immediate vicinity felt the ground shake upon the object's impact.

31 Ground Zero

DURING THE WANING YEARS of Holy Russia an event occurred in Siberia that would not be studied for what it apparently was until years later.

On the morning of June 30, 1908 seismographs around the word recorded a titanic explosion near the Yenesei River in the Tunguska province. People 40 miles from the detonation were knocked off their feet by the shock wave from a blast as mysterious as it was powerful. The remoteness of the site plus a world war accompanied by bloody political upheavals delayed investigation of what became known as the Tunguska Meteorite. Not until the 1920s would the chaos in the newly created USSR simmer down to the point that the government could concentrate on exploring the enigmatic occurrence.

An expedition arriving in 1927 found a charred, lifeless area that only could have been created by incredible heat. Also, trees were flattened for a vast distance around the presumed center of the explosion. However, the absence of an impact crater puzzled investigators. Clearly, whatever the object was it never reached the ground. One noted scientist, Dr. Alexander Kazentsev, who was part of the excursion would not see another such scene for 20 years, and then it was at the site of a nuclear bombing.

Kazentsev was a member of the scientific team later sent to postwar Hiroshima to study the effects of the atomic bomb that immolated that city. He was shaken to realize the devastation he saw in what was left of the hapless Japanese metropolis looked familiar. It was unmistakably the same kind of ruin he had viewed so many years earlier from the banks of the Yenesei River. After making his report on these recollections, he received orders from Moscow to return to the Tunguska region with a data-collecting group. Their Geiger counters went wild when checking radiation levels. The team tracked down a few eyewitnesses to the blast, and these people described an enormous, roiling fireball that rose high into the heavens before flattening into a strange, mushroom-shaped cloud. They reported many of their friends and relatives began dying shortly afterward of an unknown illness.

On an earlier expedition locals had told an ethnographer named I.S. Suslov that the explosion "…brought with it a disease for the reindeer; specifically scabs that never appeared before the fire came."

Kazentsev and his companions painstakingly picked through huge quantities of soil from the blast zone. They recovered a few metal particles they were not able to identify, but which were definitely not like any known meteoric material. The researchers exhumed some of the victims of the mysterious sickness and sent them to Moscow for autopsy. They were found to have died from radiation poisoning.

After sifting through all this evidence the scientists concluded that some enormous, nuclear-powered device had exploded 1.2 miles above the Siberian countryside. Kazentsev believed it was a spaceship, and said:

"Whether we approve or disapprove, we must admit the thing which was long known as the Tunguska Meteorite was in reality some very large artificial construction weighing in excess of 50,000 tons, which was being directed to a landing when its atomic engines exploded. In the catastrophe along the Yenesei River in 1908 we lost a guest from the universe."

Kazentsev was not alone in his evaluation. In 1921, 38-year-old Leonid Kulik was assigned to the first of several expeditions to investigate the Tunguska explosion. He began by visiting communities in the region, interviewing witnesses and searching out and meticulously studying old newspaper accounts. In the town of Irkutsh, about 400 miles north of the blast zone, Kulik found a newspaper article that took him totally by surprise. The piece was based on eyewitness reports taken down immediately after the event, when it was still fresh in the memories of those interviewed. The reporter quoted people who had watched

"…a pipe-shaped body shining with a bluish-white light too bright for the naked eye, moving horizontally for about 10 minutes."

This object came sharply about and commenced a rapid descent, but was still at extreme altitude when it exploded with indescribable force. The distant observers watched as "…a huge cloud formed, all the buildings shook and a forked tongue of flame broke through the cloud."

From the beginning Kulik had assumed he was investigating the fall of a large meteorite, but the data he had so far uncovered were thoroughly dissimilar to those of any meteorite impact he had ever heard of or encountered. How could a meteorite be pipe-shaped, shine with a bluish-white light or travel horizontally for a full 10 minutes, indicating it was moving impossibly slowly for a meteor, and how could it make a 180-degree turn in midair? As Kulik penetrated deeper into the Siberian wilderness these maddening questions ate at him constantly, and the mystery would thicken.

Reaching a point about 40 miles from where the "meteorite" was thought to have hit, Kulik questioned a peasant who described a wave of heat so intense, "My shirt was almost burned from my back!" This was followed by "…an explosion that threw me several feet from the porch."

Finally reaching the area directly beneath (as it turned out) where the explosion had taken place, Kulik surveyed the eerie, frighteningly large (800 square miles) region. Charred, flattened trees pointed outward from a central spot where burnt, lifeless trees still stood. Like Kazentsev, Kulik was nonplussed by the lack of a crater. He closely examined the standing trees, took notes and departed more bewildered than when he had arrived.

Although Kulik, Kazentsev, Suslov and others were stunned, awed and stumped by what they found in Tunguska their findings made for some intriguing conclusions and theories. Kulik spent the rest of his life trying to prove the blast was a meteoric event. He led almost annual expeditions into the bleak Siberian Taiga, but could never make the facts he uncovered fit his theory, despite each junket being better equipped than its predecessor. The scores of relatively small, flat-bottomed depressions he found in the winter-frozen swamp in the center of the blast zone (which he called the "Great Cauldron") turned out not to be impact craters. Rather they were formations caused by the explosion's incredible heat suddenly melting the permafrost underlying the surface.

This wave of searing heat was another problem for the meteorite explanation. No other recorded meteorite fall had been accompanied by immolation, but the 1908 event charred an area scores of miles in diameter, and did so in the twinkling of an eye. To a scientist of the 1920s a meteorite was the sole imaginable explanation, and it is not surprising Kulik was so pertinacious about the only answer conceivable at that time. In exasperation he formulated a theory that the mysterious burning was caused by a "giant bubble of superheated atmosphere" pushed ahead of a swarm of meteors. Because of the old problem of no impact craters this idea found little support among his contemporaries, and when Leonid Kulik died in a Nazi POW camp in 1942 the case of the Great Siberian Explosion remained wide open.

With the advent of the nuclear age a very exotic possibility presented itself. Subsequent to the blast, trees sprouting in the Great Cauldron exhibited drastically accelerated growth rates, towering 55 to 72 feet high when measured in 1958. Normal would have been about 30 feet. Radioactivity-boosted growth seemed the only feasible explanation.

Later suggestions that the explosion was caused by the collision of Earth with a fragment of antimatter or a black hole (an ancient star that has collapsed in on itself to a state of density so extreme that its gravitational attraction sucks in even light) were hamstrung by the same old snag of no impact crater. Furthermore the eyewitness descriptions did not lend credence to a black hole or antimatter impact. Kazentsev's theory about the explosive flying object having been artificial was resurrected.

Every factor that did not fit into other hypotheses tended to support the notion that it had been a spaceship that blew up over Russia. In 1959 and 1960 another researcher, Dr. A.V. Zolotov, led expeditions and came up with another facet of the event that favored the spacecraft notion.

The oddly elliptical shape of the devastated area had puzzled investigators for decades. Zolotov suggested the strange pattern was the result of the explosive (a nuclear reactor?) having been encased in an elongated container. Yet another interested scientist, aerodynamics professor Felix Zigel, agreed:

"The directivity of the explosion was due to the inhomogeneity of the container, which consisted of at least two parts: a substance capable of nuclear explosion, and a nonexplosive shell."

In 1961, after examining data derived from scrutiny of standing burnt trees, Zigel further stated: "The Tunguska body described in the atmosphere a tremendous arc of about 375 miles in azimuth. No natural object can do this."

He also reported, "It turns out the Tunguska explosion's temperature was several tens of millions of degrees…a chemical explosion is excluded without a doubt."

In 1962 Soviet airplane designer A.Y. Manotskov and rocket specialist Boris Liapunov made public their findings that the object had been traveling through the atmosphere at 1500 to 2000 miles per hour. This was far too slowly for a meteor, and they found that in its trajectory and velocity it behaved like a supersonic aircraft.

Based on so many facts the nagging suspicion was compelling. It appeared that a nuclear-powered spaceship had developed a severe problem with its power plant, and was attempting to land in the desolate, sparsely populated wilds of Siberia, but ran out of time. Meltdown occurred while the vessel was still over a mile high, and the ship and crew disintegrated in a radioactive supernova.

The site of the blast may be another clue. Could the doomed crew have selected such an isolated spot not only to avoid detection, but also to spare mankind one of the worst disasters in its history? If the object had exploded over a city like Shanghai, literally millions would have died.

There are still plenty of opinions on precisely what happened that morning in Siberia, but more research would appear to be in order. A definite, factual answer could be revolutionary. [44]

Up Close and Personal

Part 2

TYPES OF UFO CONTACTS are almost as varied as the physical appearances of the saucerians themselves. Some seem to be mere chance encounters. Others may be geared to obtaining data through conversations and medical examinations. Some would seem to convey messages, often warnings, especially concerning this world's predilection for nuclear weapons.

1 No Nukes

Two young casino employees, Carlos Peccinetti and Carlos Jose Villegas, had just left work in Mendoza, Argentina at 3:30 a.m. on September 1, 1968 when their car abruptly stalled. When they got out to check under the hood they noticed a huge circular craft hovering nearby. Three overall-clad beings emerged. It was then that Peccinetti and Villegas realized they were completely unable to move. A voice with an unidentifiable accent spoke to them telepathically, saying, "We have just made three journeys around the sun, studying customs and languages of the inhabitants of the system. Mathematics is the universal language."

A round screen materialized next to the ship, and the image of a lush waterfall appeared. The screen next showed a mushroom cloud, followed by a repeat of the waterfall scene, but without water this time. After delivering this simple message the creatures re-boarded their craft and zipped off into the night. The two young Argentines were again able to move and their car started readily. Muscular paralysis and demobilization of motorized vehicles are typical of reported UFO encounters. [1]

2 Step Into My Parlor

ON NOVEMBER 23, 1953 a UFO was detected by radar at Kimross Air Force Base in Michigan. Flight Lieutenant R. Wilson, flying an F-89 jet fighter, pursued the object for 160 miles, until radar operations at Kimross saw the two blips on their screens suddenly merge. At this point radio communications with Wilson abruptly ended.

Wilson was never heard from again, and no wreckage or any other trace of the pilot or his plane was found during the ensuing massive search. [2]

3 Meanwhile, Back at the Ranch

RANCHER PAT MCGUIRE AND his large family had good reason to fear the UFOs that began frequenting their spread outside Laramie, Wyoming in the mid-1970s. At first the craft made it their practice to steal and mutilate cattle. Later they ceased molesting the livestock, but persisted in making such frequent overflights of the property that the McGuires not only lost their apprehension of them, but even came to take the strange devices for granted.

Then one night McGuire was taken aboard one of the UFOs by strangers about six feet tall, bald, with thin lips and oversized eyes. As is often the case the witness came away from the meeting with only fragmentary memories of it, but Dr. Leo Sprinkle, a parapsychologist from the University of Wyoming, was able to hypnotize McGuire and bring out some highly unusual (and profitable) information.

His hosts had told the rancher that if he drilled a well on a specific high plateau he would find a large water deposit. Geologists advised against the venture because the land indicated by the ufonauts was 7000 feet above sea level, and a most unlikely place to strike water. Undaunted, McGuire purchased the land commenced drilling, encountering a massive subterranean stream at 350 feet.

With 8000 gallons of fresh water per minute gushing from this bountiful well McGuire was able to transform 5000 acres of dry sagebrush into green, well-irrigated grazing range. In 1980, after making extensive studies of the case, Sprinkle reported:

"I believe the craft appearing over his farm could be goodwill ambassadors of an alien civilization. I believe people like Pat McGuire are being chosen to spread the word that they are among us, and I believe we will see full-scale contact over the next decade or so." [3]

4 Take a Message

AFTER TAKING A SERIES of excellent photos of a UFO maneuvering wildly over Salvadore, Brazil, Helio Aguiar passed out. When he regained consciousness he was clutching a note written in his own handwriting. It read, "Atomic experiments for warlike purposes shall be definitely stopped. The equilibrium of the universe is threatened. We will remain vigilant and ready to interfere." [4]

5 May I Ask You a Question?

ONE OF THE CONTACTS seeming to indicate mere curiosity is the enigmatic rendezvous reported by a man named Dewitt Baldwin near Eden, New York on March 1, 1967. While hunting, Baldwin heard a strange noise and saw a round, golden-hued craft land. He later recounted the meeting:

"While I was watching it, a door opened—like a sliding elevator door—and a man walked out and down the incline of the machine. He was dressed in a sort of black, tight-fitting suit and had on some sort of helmet and goggles. He asked me what I was doing. He wasn't white and he wasn't a Negro. He spoke very plainly with no accent. I told him I was hunting. He asked me if I was born there, and I said no, that I was born in Georgia. He took my gun, looked at it and handed it back to me. He told me he would be back, walked up to the saucer, got in and seconds later zipped out of sight."

Baldwin later found a crack in the muzzle of his shotgun where the being had handled it. [5]

6 The Flatwoods Monster

AT DUSK ONE EVENING in September of 1952, Flatwoods, West Virginia was the setting for a frightening encounter with a sky-borne creature that came to be called the Flatwoods Monster. It began when a group of five youngsters saw a wobbling, glowing disk flutter unsteadily over some nearby trees where it settled onto a wooded hilltop. Two boys, Eddie May, 13, and his 12-year-old brother Fred ran home and told their mother they had seen a flying saucer land on one of the foothills bordering town. The skeptical Mrs. May was quickly converted when she stepped outside for a look. A large, pulsating red light was clearly visible on the promontory's summit. Mrs. May sent her boys running to fetch a neighbor, Gene Lemmon, who was a member of the National Guard.

Lemmon grabbed a flashlight and accompanied the boys back to the May home, where they were joined by three other youngsters—14-year-old Neil Nunly and two 10-year-olds. Lemmon and Nunly were slightly ahead of the others and first to notice a slight mist and disagreeable smell that grew stronger the higher they went. Lemmon and Nunly reached an old gateway from where the shimmering red object was in plain view. The witnesses later likened the craft's appearance to a faintly glowing mass of red coals. It was about 25 feet in diameter, and six feet thick.

The group's attention was so riveted on the device that if not for the dog that had accompanied them they might not have noticed what was in the bushes about 25 feet to their right. The dog growled and backed away, and Lemmon shone his flashlight among the brush to see what the animal had detected. The light illuminated a colossal being about 10 feet tall, wearing a helmet and clad in dark bluish-green or greenish-gray reflective garb. The face was round and dark red with greenish-orange eyes that reflected the flashlight beam the way a cat's would. The undergrowth obscured the lower body, but when the thing moved, the observers agreed it seemed to slide its feet rather than walk in a conventional manner. At this point the pungent odor became overpowering.

Mrs. May screamed, Lemmon dropped his flashlight and the panicked party raced back down the hill. Upon reaching what they considered a safe distance they phoned the sheriff. Lemmon later led an armed group back to the hilltop, but the UFO and its terrifying occupant were gone. Only the stench remained, along with unmistakable skid marks where the giant had stood. [6]

7 Roadblock

AT 2:00 A.M. ON November 28, 1954, truck drivers Jose Ponce and Gustavo Gonzales left Caracas, Venezuela for a short drive to Patare. According to a sworn statement they later made to police they were less than halfway to their destination when they rounded a sharp bend and almost collided with a luminous, hemisphere-shaped machine hovering several feet above the road. Ponce and Gonzales got out of their truck for a closer look, and a small, manlike being came running at them out of the darkness.

Gonzales, intending to have this "man" arrested for obstructing the thoroughfare, grabbed him only to be hurled about 15 feet. Ponce lit out for a police station a block away and saw two more diminutive humanoids sprinting for the UFO. They carried uprooted plants, were dressed in light brown loincloths, and covered with short, bristly hair.

Stunned, Gonzales pulled his knife and stabbed his assailant in the shoulder, but the blade glanced off ineffectually. Gonzales felt something strike him at this point, but managed to escape. Both men made it to the police station. They were given sedatives and allowed to rest before making their statements.

Surprisingly, a doctor the police called to examine the pair of traumatized witnesses later stepped forward to corroborate their story, having seen the otherworldly incident while returning from an emergency call. He decided to confirm the men's story providing his identity was not revealed. [7]

8 Not Quite Kidnapped

ON DECEMBER 20, 1958 two young Swedes were returning from a dance near Halsingborg when they stopped their car to investigate a huge luminous sphere in the woods lining the highway. As they drew near they were able to discern a disk-shaped craft resting on the ground. The ship was supported on metal legs about a yard high. As the men gazed in amazement four beings about four feet tall abruptly attacked them.

One of the Swedes broke loose, reached the car and leaned on its horn in an attempt to attract help. The other human, 25-year-old Hans Gustavsson, was unable to break free, but did manage to grab a metal highway sign that he clutched with desperate strength as the saucerians tried to pull him toward their ship. After several minutes the peculiar struggle ended when the creatures suddenly bolted for their conveyance and flew away.

Gustavsson later remarked, "The one thing I can never forget about this terrible experience is the sickening smell of those creatures. It haunts me!" [8]

9 Prophecy

ONE FREEZING NIGHT IN upstate New York, Rita Mallory, a lovely young mother of two, was headed home on Route 34, bound for Ithaca. Her five-year-old son Dana was sleeping in the back seat at about 7:00 when she noticed a red glow lighting up the car's interior. Since she was speeding she first thought it was a police car chasing her, but when she looked in her rear view mirror she saw nothing but the red light "covering everything." Rounding a bend in the highway she spotted a red, brightly glowing object to her left, hovering over a telephone pole. It was December 12, 1967—a date that remains fresh in her memory.

"It must have been 50 to 60 feet in diameter, with a domelike thing on top. I was terrified!"

A beam of light shot from the aircraft and took total control of the car. Mallory's eyes were burning, she had trouble swallowing, and despite her mounting panic she was unable to scream. These symptoms may have been side effects of her hysteria, exacerbated by her concern for Dana.

The car halted and began to slide sideways off the highway and into an alfalfa field. Its headlights and dash lights faded out, leaving the red and green flashes from her aerial hijacker as the only illumination.

At this point the witness began hearing what sounded like the low buzz of a swarm of bees, hardly expected in such frigid, snowy weather. The hum abruptly stopped and was replaced by a chorus of disembodied voices speaking broken English. She believed the voices were definitely audible, not some kind of mental transmission. She was able to glean enough words from the babble to discern a prediction of the impending death of a man in a nearby city. Although Mallory was not acquainted with the man, she did know his sister. The deceased-to-be would be killed in a traffic accident while driving a tractor-trailer.

After a few minutes her car began to slide back onto the roadway, the steering wheel moving of its own volition. The engine spontaneously restarted, the lights came back on and the automobile set off down the highway under control of the UFO, now flying above it. When Mallory noticed other cars coming toward her the flying saucer vanished, leaving her in control of her vehicle.

She went directly home. The shaken young woman had trouble sleeping. When she finally did drop off she quickly awoke screaming. A low humming was coming from outside her window. It was a television antenna vibrating in the wind.

The next day Mallory learned to her horror that nothing from the previous night had been hallucination after all (as she had fervently hoped.) The man mentioned by the otherworldly chorus was killed while driving a tractor-trailer in the specified city.

Here we see a precognitive event associated with a UFO. The ability to see into the future is another criterion the saucers share with demonic forces. [9]

10 The Case of the Dying Crew

SOUTH AMERICA HAS BEEN the site of innumerable UFO adventures. One of the most unique was reported from Bahia Blanca, Argentina. On May 7, 1955 the Caracas, Venezuela daily newspaper *El Universal* published the account a prominent engineer gave of his experience from across the border in Argentina. He had spotted a saucer-shaped object sitting in a field beside a highway. There was a blinking light atop a central dome, and a door was open on one side. The engineer squeezed through the door and was shocked to find three tiny men in a circular control room.

They wore tight-fitting brown overalls. One was seated at a control panel, and the others were lying on curved lounges. He guessed them to be about four feet tall with dark brown flesh and yellow eyes. All three were dead.

The witness dashed off to get some friends to witness the tableau, but by the time they returned the craft was hovering high overhead. They photographed the departing UFO and collected some hot gray powder from the landing site. When the Argentine government later asked for this powder the engineer handed it over and never saw it again. [10]

11 Working on the Railroad

QUAROBLES, FRANCE WAS THE site of a brief encounter reported by a metal worker named Marius Dewilde. At 10:30 p.m. on September 10, 1954 Dewilde's dog began barking wildly. Marius reached for his flashlight and stepped outside for a look. Living on the Franco-Belgian border, he assumed smugglers were at work on the nearby railroad tracks, but when he switched on his light he was stunned to see two child-sized individuals in silvery jumpsuits with transparent helmets completely encasing their heads.

The befuddled Frenchman could think of little else but to slam a nearby gate to prevent the creatures from escaping. At this point a blinding beam of light from something on the railroad tracks struck and paralyzed him. Several seconds later the light went out and Dewilde arose to find himself alone on the deserted stretch of track.

Later investigation indicated an extremely heavy object had rested on the track's wooden cross ties. Gravel in the roadbed had been subjected to such intense heat that it had crumbled into powder. [11]

12 Float as Well as Fly

On July 2, 1950 a mining engineer and his wife were picnicking at Steep Rock Lake in Ontario. They were on the shore of a secluded spot called Sawmill Bay. Their car was parked under some trees and out of sight. They were brewing tea over a small fire when the air seemed "to begin vibrating." The quizzical engineer climbed a huge boulder overlooking the bay and saw a shiny disk on the lake's surface several hundred yards away. His wife joined him and they watched the craft and its occupants for what they later estimated was a full ten minutes. Several hatches opened and 8 or 9 humanoids emerged. All wore bright blue skullcaps, except one who wore a red one and remained in the top hatch the entire time. Moving with robotlike motions the beings shoved a green hose into the water, and after several minutes climbed back into their ship. The saucer then rose vertically while changing colors from a collage of rosy and blue hues to white. It was out of sight within 20 seconds. [12]

13 Father Gill's Encounter

IT WAS A QUARTER to seven on the evening of June 26, 1959 in Papua New Guinea, and Anglican missionary William Gill had just finished the evening meal with his congregation. As he stepped out of the dining hall he was bolted to the spot by the sight of an aerial "sparkling object which to me was peculiar because it sparkled and because it was very, very bright, and it was above Venus, and so that caused me to watch it for awhile. Then I saw it descend toward us."

A mission teacher named Stephen Moi gauged the size of the aircraft by holding his arm outstretched toward it and observing that his clenched fist covered "about half of the object."

As a crowd of entranced parishioners gathered, in Gill's words:

"Men came out of the object and appeared on top of it, on what seemed to be a deck on top of the huge disk. There were four men in all, occasionally two, then one, then three, then four...They seemed to be illuminated in two ways: By reflected light, as men working high up on a building at night caught by the glare of an oxyacetylene torch, and by this curious halo which outlined them, following every contour of their bodies."

At about 8:30 two smaller saucers appeared. One hovered over the ocean, the other over the adjacent village of Wadabuna. The larger vessel was now directly over the onlookers, below the racing clouds. The craft remained until about 11:00, when a heavy downpour commenced.

At 6:00 the next evening the three UFOs returned. Gill exchanged waves with the beings on the larger saucer's observation deck, and then made random signals with a flashlight. The target ship responded by rocking back and forth "like a pendulum."

A faithful clergyman, Gill ushered his congregation inside for evening services. When they came back outside later no saucers were in the stormy sky, and none ever returned. Gill was among 25 witnesses who signed a statement attesting to the lengthy sightings.

The Royal Australian Air Force stated that the bright objects had been nothing more than a peculiar alignment of the planets Venus, Mars and Jupiter. However, this notion has numerous flaws—any one of them fatal. From Earth none of these planets (or even all three in alignment) appears large enough to be only half covered by a clenched fist held at arm's length. None are visible below clouds. None sways back and forth in response to flashlight signals. Lastly, none has observation decks upon which stride waving humanoids (at least none that are visible from Earth.)

Gill carefully preserved his account's objectivity (and his own) by making no attempt to read religious implications into it, or to profit from it financially. [13]

14 From Down Under

A REPORT CARRIED IN the Tasmanian newspaper *Mercury,* told of a UFO report announced by the curious headline: "Helmeted Man Seen by Object." It was dated February 5, 1963. The article described an incident in which a high school teacher named Mrs. E.D. Sylvester and her three children saw a glowing, oval-shaped machine on the ground in a town called Norwood. A small, manlike individual was beside the luminous sphere and wore a shiny helmet with tanks resembling those of a scuba diver. Sylvester stopped her car about 200 yards from the scene and watched for 10 minutes. Remarkably, the newspaper did not report what happened after the 10-minute observation. [14]

15 Burning Sand

POLICE OFFICER LONNIE ZAMORA was not thinking about flying saucers on the evening of April 24, 1964. He was in a high-speed car chase on a highway traversing the desert outside Socorro, New Mexico. He was torn from his fixation on the fleeing car ahead of him by a blinding flash of blue-orange light and an explosion that sent his cruiser careening off the road, bouncing to a halt beside a ravine.

Zamora's first thought was that a nearby dynamite storage shed had exploded, but then he saw a large oval shape on the ground. Two figures in white overalls were next to the egg-shaped device. When one of them turned and saw the patrol car Zamora later said the ufonaut "seemed startled—seemed to jump quickly somewhat."

At first the policeman thought the craft was an overturned car, and radioed the sheriff's office that he was going to investigate an accident, but when he got out of his cruiser there was a deafening report and the object, its underside blazing, began to rise. Fearing another explosion, Zamora dove behind his car. He noticed a large red insignia on the side of the noisily ascending machine, which "appeared to go in a straight line and at the same height—possibly 10 to 15 feet from the ground—and it cleared the dynamite shack by about 3 feet. The object was traveling very fast. It seemed to rise up and take off immediately across country."

State Trooper M.S. Chavez now joined Zamora and the two lawmen examined the area of still-burning brush, finding a trapezoidal pattern of square impressions of what were evidently landing gear. They also found humanoid footprints. [15]

16 The Possession of Stephen

IT WAS 9:30 ON the evening of September 27, 1973 in Westmoreland County, Pennsylvania, and two young girls waiting for a ride spotted an outline moving in the border of a wooded area. Moments later the silhouette resolved itself into what the witnesses later described as an enormous (8-foot-tall,) white-furred gorillalike beast with glowing red eyes, holding a luminous sphere in one hand.

These girls were not the only ones to notice that something odd was happening in and around those woods that night. There were several reports of unidentified aircraft hovering overhead and directing a column of light into the trees. The Westmoreland County sightings were the first of a rash of reports of UFOs and mysterious apelike creatures throughout the East and Midwest.

The most remarkable of these encounters took place outside Greensberg, Pennsylvania when twelve persons saw a big red craft land in a pasture. A young man (who in his later recounting of this episode identified himself only as "Stephen") decided to investigate.

Taking his rifle, Stephen got into his car with two ten-year-old twin brothers and headed for the pasture. As they neared the landing site the car's headlights dimmed and went out, and the trio continued on foot. Topping a hill they saw the glowing, domed saucer floating just above the ground. The vehicle was about 100 feet in diameter, and produced a low humming. Nearby, but away from the saucer, someone or something was screaming hysterically.

One of the twins let out a yell as the light from the UFO illuminated a pair of huge forms loping towards them. Like the Westmoreland County creature, these beings were in excess of seven feet tall, but their fur was gray, and their glowing eyes were green.

Stephen fired two warning shots into the air, but the things kept coming. At close range he fired three more shots into the larger beast, which reacted merely by raising its hands and letting out a whining noise. The UFO then appeared to vanish, and the two creatures made their escape into the woods.

Later that night a choking, sulfurous smell made investigators dizzy at the landing site. Stephen, as if possessed, began growling like a dog, shaking and flailing his arms wildly. Finally he ran in circles until collapsing from exhaustion. [16]

17 Fishers of Men

WHEN CHARLES HICKSON AND Calvin Parker went fishing from a pier on the Pascagoula River in Pascagoula, Mississippi all they had in mind was hooking a few speckled trout and redfish. It was October 11, 1973. After a little while the men noticed a peculiar, circling blue light that steadily descended and came closer. The two shipyard workers were soon able to discern an oblong craft liberally bedecked with flashing, colored lights. It came to hover four or five feet above the river bank, a hatch opened and three small humanoids "glided" out. By this point Hickson and Parker were paralyzed, and taken onto the UFO by these beings, who seemed to "float" them aboard. The creatures had pincer-type appendages in place of hands. They stood about five feet tall, had no eyes, a thin slit for a mouth, and strange, cone-shaped protuberances where a human's nose and ears would be.

Parker lost consciousness while he and Hickson were subjected to thorough physical examination. After an undetermined length of time the men found themselves standing outside the UFO, which "made a buzzing sound and was gone." There were numerous UFO sightings in the area that night.

A close acquaintance of Hickson and Parker described his friends:

"They're just country boys. Neither of them has enough imagination to concoct such a tale, or enough guile to pull it off. They never read a science fiction story in their life. All they meant to do was go fishing."

The 19-year-old Parker later suffered a nervous breakdown. [17]

18 Missionaries From the Cosmos?

AN INCREDIBLE SAGA BEGAN near midnight January 29, 1965 in Monterey, California. Mayor George Clemins and several other witnesses saw a brightly colored sphere hovering low over Monterey Bay. The object drifted to the other side of the bay and faded from sight like a Cheshire Cat's smile.

Meanwhile, local resident Sidney Padrick was pursuing his hobby as a ham radio operator. Slightly after 2:00 a.m. Padrick shut down his apparatus and set out for a stroll before going to bed. He was on Manresa Beach directly opposite Monterey when a sudden loud humming presaged the appearance of a UFO he later described as resembling "two real thick saucers, inverted."

Padrick turned and ran, but an amplified voice from the craft announced, "Do not be frightened! We are not hostile!" The unconvinced ham operator continued to flee. The hovering machine next boomed, "We mean you no harm! You are welcomed to come aboard!" Although only slightly reassured, Padrick did stop running and looked back at the object. A door slid open and the voice urged him to come closer. Stepping into a small room, Padrick encountered a medium-sized humanoid with very light-colored flesh, a sharp nose and chin and very long fingernails. Padrick described the scene:

"They wore two-piece suits with no buttons or zippers that I could see. The bottom section actually included shoes. It looked like boots which continued right up to the waistline without any break around the ankles. Just like a child's snowsuit. They had soles and heels similar to ours. I could hear them walking with a 'thump-thump' sound on the rubbery floor. The collar had a very pretty design on it. It came down to a V in front, and the neckpiece, right around the neck, had a braid of some kind on it. Very pretty. It had colors that I had never seen before—more beautiful than ours. I asked him his name, and he said, 'You may call me Zeeno.' I didn't know it at the time that the word Zeeno was probably the word 'xeno,' which means 'stranger' in Greek."

Zeeno ushered his guest into a room "similar to a chapel." Padrick recounted what happened next:

"The color effect in that room was so pretty I almost fainted when I went in. I mixture of colors. I can't describe them. There were eight chairs, a stool and what appeared to be an altar. Zeeno asked, 'Would you like to pay your respects to the Supreme Deity?' I didn't know how to accept it. I'm 45 years old, and until that night I had never felt the presence of the Supreme Deity, but I did feel Him that night."

After taking him for a short flight in the UFO, Zeeno returned Padrick to Manresa Beach and released him. He quickly reported his experience to the Air Force, and was investigated and questioned at length. His family and friends regarded him as an honest man who was neither a UFO enthusiast or deeply religious. These factors lend credence to his account of this highly unusual, theistic saucer encounter. [18]

19 Through the Looking Glass

Thirty-year-old Betty Andreasson had quite a bit on her mind in January of 1967. Her husband had been critically injured in a car wreck in December, and her parents had moved into her South Ashburnham, Massachusetts home to help her and her seven children in any way they could. Nevertheless, her main support was her strong faith in Jesus Christ.

On the night of January 25 unseasonably warm weather had blanketed South Ashburnham in dense fog. The lights in the Andreasson home flickered and died, to be replaced by a soft pink glow that poured through a kitchen window. Betty's father peered into the backyard. Later, in a signed affidavit, he described what he saw:

"These creatures that I saw through the window of Betty's house were just like Halloween freaks. I thought that they had put on a funny kind of headdress imitating a moon man. The one in front looked at me and I felt kind of queer. That's all I knew."

At that point the entire family (except Betty) fell into a trance. She saw several small beings pass ghostlike through a closed door as they entered the house. Their flesh was gray, their eyes large, slanted and catlike. They had three fingers on each hand, and wore shiny, tight-fitting uniforms.

They telepathically told her that if she would accompany them she would be helping the world. She followed them to an oval vehicle in the backyard. Once aboard the craft Andreasson was subjected to a painful physical examination during which needles were inserted into her nose and naval. Next, she was led through a long dark tunnel that emerged into a room with a glasslike canopy. Her hosts placed her in this compartment, which then filled with a gray fluid that immersed her and, she assumed, protected her on a journey to another world.

After an undetermined length of time Andreasson was released from the bubble. Two tiny guides led her through more tunnels, and they eventually emerged into a strange, seemingly lifeless region illuminated by a shimmering red light. As they moved along a floating conveyor belt she was shocked to see animals resembling headless lemurs crawling on some of the odd, cubic structures on both sides of the track.

After passing through a round membrane, the woman found herself in a different landscape. This one was suffused with *green* light. They were now flanked by mist-shrouded lakes, and ahead of them towered a pyramid and a formation of huge floating crystals.

Suddenly there appeared before Andreasson and her two companions what she later likened to a colossal eaglelike bird, twice the height of a human. This creature radiated intense heat, and as the human witness watched, the bird disappeared. In its place was a small, dying fire. From the ashes crawled a fat gray worm.

Andreasson heard her name called out by a loud voice from somewhere to her right. It told her she had been chosen for a quest that was not yet to be revealed. When she declared her Christian faith the voice replied that this was why she had been selected. She was then returned through the realms of red and green and back to the chamber with the glass bubble.

One of the ufonauts who had accompanied her called himself Quazgaa. He told her they would impart to her specific formulae that would aid humanity, but only when humans began to "search within the spirit."

After the return trip the oval craft landed (or perhaps materialized) in the Andreasson backyard. It was still dark and the other family members were still in suspended animation. The ufonauts led them all to their beds, and then departed. In the morning Andreasson recalled only snippets of her incredible journey.

Apparently humankind has never learned to search within its spirit, because Betty Andreasson never again heard from her saucerians. It would be eight years before she came forth with her story. After reading about J. Allen Hynek's Air Force-sponsored UFO investigation, she went public with her fantastic tale. Interestingly, despite a total lack of physical evidence, through psychological examinations and voice stress testing, investigators concluded Andreasson was telling the truth. [19]

20 All in a Night's Work

MANY CONTACTEES EXPERIENCE PUZZLING physical maladies following their confrontations—severe headaches, ringing or buzzing in the ears, or amnesia. During the predawn hours of December 3, 1967, on the outskirts of Ashland, Nebraska, 22-year-old police officer Herbert Schirmer was nearing the end of his shift, but he was not thinking about that. There was something strange about that wintry night. The town's dogs howled continuously, and a bull in a corral fought madly to escape his enclosure. Schirmer stopped to check the corral gate, and after assuring himself it would hold he drove on.

Approaching the intersection of Highways 6 and 63 he saw what he at first thought was a truck stopped on the thoroughfare, but a closer look revealed something very different. Later, the patrolman recalled only engaging his cruiser headlights' high beams and seeing an odd shape with a row of flickering lights fly away. Going off duty at 3:00 a.m. he entered in his logbook, "Saw a flying saucer at the junction of Highways 6 and 63. Believe it or not!" When a 20-minute gap turned up in his police report, Schirmer agreed to time regression hypnosis, which revealed his forgotten adventure.

He remembered a craft flying from the highway to an adjacent field. He was also able to recall driving down a dirt road toward the UFO. It was metallic, silver, football-shaped and bedecked with flickering lights. It rested on telescoping tripod legs. At this point Schirmer thought better of his proximity to the machine and attempted to depart, but later referred to "something in my mind" that stopped him. This force also prevented him from drawing his revolver when several figures emerged from the craft and approached the patrol car. One of the beings raised a container and sprayed the car with a greenish vapor, then drew something from a holster and pointed it at the car.

There next came a bright flash and Schirmer lost consciousness for evidently what was only a few seconds, for he next remembers rolling down his car window, whereupon one of the ufonauts grabbed him by the neck and asked, "Are you the watchman over this place?" He next pointed at a nearby power plant and asked, "Is this the only source of power you have?" He apparently was the commander, and next asked Schirmer if he would shoot at a flying saucer.

"No, sir," replied the bewildered young officer. The crew leader then invited him aboard.

After walking to the device with his strange companion, Schirmer watched a circular hatch open and a ladder extend. The saucer occupants ranged in height from four and one-half to five feet tall, and wore tight-fitting, silver one-piece suits with the emblem of a winged serpent on the left breast. The suits covered everything but their wearers' faces, and had an antenna on the left side of the head. The crew's facial flesh was pale gray, with a flattened nose, an unmoving slit for a mouth, and slanted (not Oriental) eyes.

Schirmer described the commander as talking to him in broken English with a voice that was part oral, part telepathic and did not seem to originate from the mouth. He told the policeman the craft was a scout ship with a crew of four, which was based far out in space on a mother ship. The commander stressed that his race was not hostile, and realized Earth's inhabitants were not ready for widespread contact with saucerians. They therefore avoided all but the most occasional, isolated encounters. He emphasized this by explaining how, through ionization, ships like his could literally be knocked out of the sky by Earth's radar. When this happened the mother ship destroyed the stricken vessel before it hit the ground, avoiding hysteria.

After about 15 minutes the commander looked directly into Schirmer's eyes and communicated this thought:

"I wish that you would not tell that you have been aboard this ship. You are to tell that the ship landed in the intersection of the highways, that you approached, and it shot up into the air and disappeared. You will tell this and nothing more. You will not speak about this night. We will return to see you two more times."

Schirmer was then let off the craft and drove away in his patrol car, remembering only what he was permitted to remember. The landing site was soon located exactly where the hypnotized policeman had indicated. The marks of the tripod landing gear were plainly visible, and one investigator described how, "Patches of grass had been swirled and twisted into odd patterns, as if the vegetation had been under powerful centrifugal pressure."

Herbert Schirmer was an excellent young police officer. Not long after this incredible episode he was promoted to become the youngest police chief in the Midwest. He resigned after only two months. As explanation he offered:

"I simply was not paying attention to my job. I kept wondering what had really happened that night. My headaches were getting pretty fierce. I was gobbling down aspirin like it was popcorn. You can't be a good policeman if you have personal problems. So I quit."

As we will see, Herbert Schirmer's story was nothing new. [20]

21 Road Map to Another World

IN SEPTEMBER OF 1961 a New Hampshire couple, Barney and Betty Hill, were driving through their home state's White Mountains while returning from a Canadian vacation. They made it home several hours later than they had expected, and were unable to pinpoint why.

Over the next three years odd dreams and terrifying nightmares plagued the Hills, and the couple finally sought help from Boston psychiatrist Dr. Benjamin Simon. Through hypnosis Simon was able to discern the Hills had undergone what they believed was an encounter with a UFO. The military later admitted it had tracked this saucer on radar.

At slightly after 10:00 p.m. on the evening of the 19th the Hills had left a restaurant in Coleville, New Hampshire, just south of the Canadian border. They headed south toward their home in Portsmouth. Near the city of Lancaster they noticed a glowing aircraft that, although so distant as to appear as a mere dot of light, seemed to be pacing them. As it came steadily nearer, Barney parked the car, took his binoculars and walked into an open field for a better look. The strange saucer craft he saw panicked him, and he ran back to the car and roared away.

At this point both Hills noticed a strange beeping sound seemingly coming from their car's trunk. They then lost awareness, retaining no memory of turning off the main road and leaving their car in a wooded area. The saucer was there, and the Hills were taken on board by its crew, who subjected them to a thorough physical examination during which Barney had some kind of instrument strapped to his groin. Over the following months he developed a series of warts where the device had been pressed against his flesh. The warts formed a perfect circle. They became inflamed after Simon's counseling brought out the buried recollection of the abduction, and they had to be removed by electrolysis.

After being thoroughly examined by the saucerians the Hills had been released and returned to their car. After getting underway and hearing a second series of beeps their awareness began to return.

During the forced examination Betty had spoken at length with the ship's commander, and he showed her a star chart that outlined alleged trade routes and regions still under exploration. Following the hypnosis sessions Betty was able to sketch this map from memory.

The chart she drew showed a star formation unfamiliar to anyone who saw it. Assuming it was oriented to another world's view of the galaxy it is not surprising it showed an astronomical background unknown to its earthly viewers. A grade school teacher named Marjorie Fish undertook the tedious task of triangulating the map. Beginning in 1966 Fish constructed a three-dimensional model of the Hill map by using wooden marbles suspended from strings. She searched for the proper angle to pinpoint the star system of origin of the beings who showed Betty the chart.

In the summer of 1969 Fish found an alignment that resembled the map too closely to be a fluke, but she was unable to complete the interstellar cartography for a staggering reason. She could not place three particular stars in any way that would correlate. However when Gliese's updated *Catalogue of Nearby Stars* was released that autumn it listed one newly discovered star with the identification number 86.1. It also rectified inaccurate placings of two others, numbers 95 and 97, which had been shown in the wrong parallax positions.

When Fish consulted the revised atlas Betty Hill's map suddenly snapped into focus. It was indeed a star grouping that includes our sun when viewed from a position beyond Zeta One Reticuli and Zeta Two Reticuli. Although the data that clarified Betty's map first became available in late 1969, *she had drawn it five years earlier.*

At the time Betty Hill sketched from memory a star chart she claims was shown to her by UFO-borne humanoids there was no existing information on this planet that would have enabled her to do this. Her map could not have been faked by any conceivable earthly means.

There *are* discrepancies between the Hill map and some of the stars' precise locations. Two stars in particular are markedly closer together than Betty drew them. Yet we must take into account that she drafted her map literally years after she saw the original, at which time she had a great deal on her mind. In such a situation as she was when she briefly viewed the chart, it is indeed impressive she could recall *any* specific details, much less produce her reasonable reproduction.

The mere existence of this map is noteworthy. *Our* society's present-day aircraft and ocean-going vessels navigate via gyroscopes and computers rather than archaic tools like maps. A civilization able to traverse the interstellar void would surely employ more sophisticated means of course-plotting. Perhaps the Hills' saucerians showed Betty the chart for the specific purpose of adding credence to the couple's future account of their encounter. Some ufonauts (for reasons we will examine in later pages) seem determined to have us believe in their existence.

The Hills' was the first abduction of the modern flying saucer era to garner widespread publicity, and to this day it is regarded as the classic in its genre. However, the Hills were never able to convince Dr. Simon it had taken place. He suspected they did see a UFO, but that the kidnapping was a false reality. The dreams, particularly Betty's, made her think she had actually seen and endured the things she later reported. Furthermore, he felt that when she told her husband of the dreams that he too adopted them as reality. He essentially "caught" the whole abduction/physical examination fantasy from her. Close scrutiny casts doubt upon Simon's conclusions:

1. The Hills' severe emotional reactions to, and physical symptoms of, their encounter (especially Barney's peculiar circle of warts) were unlikely to have been caused by a dream-induced non-event.

2. How could Simon's dream/fantasy explanation account for the couple arriving home literally hours later than they should have?

3. In order to fabricate such elaborate, esoteric stories and relate them under hypnosis years later would require a seemingly impossible degree of concoction, memory and planning. It also would have indicated un-scrupulousness not characteristic of the Hills.

4. The Hills' actions subsequent to the kidnapping signified they had no motive to fabricate it. They told only a handful of friends, relatives, researchers and Simon. They only went public after a tape recording made without their knowledge at their September 1962 meeting with a UFO research group in Qunicy, Massachusetts was used for a series of articles in a Boston newspaper in the autumn of 1965. These articles (from which they derived no financial gain, and which were written and printed without their collaboration) were what made their story common knowledge, rather than any attempt on the Hills' part to publicize the encounter.

5. Upon arriving home at dawn on September 20, 1961 they found on the trunk lid of their car a number of bright, shiny spots that caused a com-pass to spin wildly, as if the rear of the car (from where they had heard the beeping sounds) had been exposed to a strong charge of magnetism and/or radioactivity. In addition to that the Hills later reported their watches stopped working after the abduction.

6. The star map Betty drew virtually precludes the encounter having been a dream. If it was, the fantastic accuracy of the map was pure coincidence. This would seem too remote a possibility to warrant consideration.

7. Finally, Simon himself found his star patients to be competent observers with above-average intelligence and no sign of psychosis.

These factors considered, the unbiased conclusion would appear to be that Bar-ney and Betty Hills' abduction and examination by ufonauts happened, in its entirety. [21]

22 Attack of the Elephant Ears

ON THE NIGHT OF April 21, 1955 a rural Kentucky family named Sutton endured a night of terror during which they were repeatedly besieged in their home by an undetermined number of "little men."

It began when a pie-shaped aircraft, spewing multi-colored exhaust, flew over the house and landed in a gully several hundred yards away. Soon, glowing humanoids were advancing on the family.

For the Suttons the odd behavior of their assailants made the occasion as confusing as it was frightening. At one point one of the beings, hands raised, approached the farmhouse. When two of the witnesses shot at it, it "did a flip" and fled back into the darkness, but returned moments later to peer through a window. Again the Suttons shot at it, but apparently missed. Another creature was knocked off the roof by a bullet, but rather than falling the ufonaut slowly floated to the ground.

The Suttons later described their attackers as about 40 inches tall with large, almost perfectly spherical heads, huge, elephantlike ears, and large eyes with no lids or pupils. Their eyes seemed very sensitive to light. They avoided well-lit areas of the house and yard, always approaching from dark areas. They wore shiny, aluminum-looking suits, and had very long arms with big, talon-equipped hands. When advancing they would walk upright like a human, but at the sound of a gunshot they would retreat on all fours at great speed, with the arms seeming to provide most of the impetus.

Just before the light of dawn the baffling antagonists withdrew, never to return. The 11 Sutton family members were left terrified, stupefied but unharmed. [22]

23 Checkup

ON THE EVENING OF October 27, 1975 David Stephens and Glen Gray were traveling a road about 40 miles from Loring Air Force Base in Maine when their car was "possessed by an unknown force." It was propelled at more than 100 miles per hour to a field 11 miles away in the town of Poland. A cigar-shaped form with flashing red, green and blue lights rose from the field in front of the horrified young men, and they drove away at high speed. After they had gone only a short distance a brilliant beam of light engulfed the car and they lost consciousness, reawakening just before dawn. Unhurt, they tried to drive away, but the car was again commandeered by something unseen and deposited next to a pond, above which three UFOs hovered. Momentarily the trio of cryptic flying machines simply dematerialized.

The men had no conventional injuries, but their hands and feet were noticeably swollen, their teeth were loose, and they were severely chilled. They also had a reddish discoloration around their necks. Under time regression hypnosis Stephens was able to recall the time he lost that night. He remembered a domed room and a humanoid.

"He was four and one-half feet tall, dressed in a long robe. His head was shaped like a big light bulb. He had slanted eyes, no hair and no mouth."

Stephens also recalled that four other saucerians had entered the room and placed his inert body on an examination table. A machine with a robotic extension for an arm collected blood, hair and tissue samples. It then injected him with a brownish fluid he was told was a sedative.

That same night a UFO closely resembling the one that abducted the two young men scrutinized nuclear missile-equipped Loring Air Force Base. [23]

24 Tranquilizer

Another notable European report is that of French farmer Maurice Masse. At dawn on July 1, 1965 Masse was preparing to plow the fields of his Valensole farm when he heard a strange sound and went to investigate. Exiting his garage he saw that some sort of flying machine had landed in his lavender field. Thinking it was a military prototype aircraft he strode purposefully toward it, intending to tell the pilots to touch down elsewhere. Yet as he drew nearer his error became apparent.

The car-sized device was oval and supported by six thin legs and a thick central column. Two "pilots" were in front of it, closely examining a lavender plant. They wore greenish outfits with small containers attached to their belts, were slightly over a yard tall, with oversized heads and tiny, lipless mouths. They wore no gloves or respiratory gear and had humanlike eyes and hands. When they noticed Masse one of them pointed a small tube at the farmer, completely paralyzing him.

While the strangers seemed to confer over him in gurgling voices, Masse felt an undeniable certainty that they meant him no harm. This conviction was only partly conveyed through their human-appearing facial expressions, which indicated benign curiosity with no hint of hostility. After what seemed about a minute to Masse his visitors entered their egg and seated themselves in its cockpit, facing him through the transparent canopy. They took off backward, facing the still-paralyzed man while flying in the opposite direction.

Slowly, Masse's muscular control returned and he was able to go home, but his adventure was not finished. For a period of weeks after his encounter excessive sleepiness plagued the former resistance fighter. Being unable to stay awake for more than three or four hours at a stretch was disconcerting and inconvenient for a man like Masse, used to working throughout the daylight hours. Gradually this odd symptom wore off. [24]

25 Hunted Hunter

THE AERIAL PHENOMENA RESEARCH Organization meticulously investigated the case of a hunter who reported a bizarre, nightlong engagement with a small band of UFO occupants who seemed bent on capturing him. The hunter, Donald Schrum, had become separated from the rest of his party in the mountainous region of northern California near Cisco Grove on the afternoon of September 4, 1964. As darkness fell, the sportsman lit several fires to show his position. Shortly he saw a lighted object in the sky and assumed it was a helicopter searching for him. When it halted and silently hovered a short distance away, however, he realized it was nothing familiar, and he climbed a tree for a better look.

The light approached and circled the tree, and momentarily the outdoorsman saw a bright flash and something fall to the ground from the flying machine. He next saw two figures advancing noisily through the woods from different directions. They were slightly over five feet tall and wore silver uniforms that covered their heads. Shortly a third arrived. This one behaved like a mechanical construct. It had reddish-orange eyes and instead of a mouth it had a slit that would drop open like the door of a mailbox.

According to the witness these creatures spent the rest of the night trying to get him out of the tree without climbing it themselves. The hunter was able to keep them at bay by shooting arrows and throwing bits of burning paper and clothing at them, from which they retreated fearfully.

The robot's mouthlike cavity would drop open and it would insert its "hand" into the rectangular opening, whereupon a puff of what looked like smoke would issue out and envelope the tree. When the mist reached him Schrum would pass out, but he stayed aloft by using his belt to tie himself to the tree.

When the man awoke at dawn after the last gas attack his antagonists were gone. Only the arrows and burned paper and cloth remained to testify to his nightlong ordeal. [25]

26 Were There Any Survivors?

ANOTHER BEFUDDLING AND DISCONCERTING case is one that directly concerned the military. Late on the night of February 28, 1959 U.S. Army Private Gerry Irwin was traveling on Route 14 near Cedar City, Utah en route to his barracks at Fort Bliss in El Paso, Texas. He saw a brilliantly glowing object pass from right to left through the sky some distance in front of him, descending behind a ridge.

Thinking he had seen an airliner making an emergency landing Irwin stopped and wrote on a slip of paper, "Have gone to investigate possible airplane crash. Please call law enforcement officers." Placing the note under a windshield wiper he then wrote, "STOP!," in black shoe polish on the side of his car and set off on foot into the Trans Pecos desert.

Soon a game warden did stop and find the note, which he took to Cedar City Sheriff Otto Pfief. The sheriff organized a search party that fanned out into the darkness. They quickly found the soldier unconscious on the desert floor, but no sign of an airliner or anything else. They transported him to a nearby hospital where a Dr. Broadbent examined him and noted his patient's temperature and respiration seemed normal. He appeared merely to be sleeping, but could not be awakened. He occasionally would mutter something about a "jacket on a bush." Broadbent concluded his patient was suffering from hysteria.

When Irwin regained consciousness three days later his first words were, "Were there any survivors?" Lacking any memory of what happened after he left his car

Irwin was still under the impression he had seen a plane crash. Moreover, he was certain he had been wearing a jacket when he saw the bright light, but definitely was without it when found by the search party.

After being flown back to Fort Bliss, Irwin was placed under observation at William Beaumont Army Hospital, and released with a clean bill of health after four days. He was returned to active duty, but with his security clearance revoked. After a few days he began having fainting spells and passed out Sunday, March 15 on an El Paso street. He was admitted to Southwest General Hospital in a condition similar to that in which he was found in the desert. He woke about 2:00 the next morning, once again saying, "Were there any survivors?" He became disoriented and confused when told it was March 16, not February 28.

After being returned to William Beaumont Hospital he was placed under psychiatric observation for a month. The testing indicated he was normal, and he was released April 17, but the next day an overwhelming urge compelled him to leave the fort without permission and return to the desert where he had seen the UFO. He found his jacket draped over a bush, removed a slip of paper from a buttonhole and burned it. At this point the young soldier seemed to emerge from a trance or state of shock. Having no idea where he was he eventually found his way back to the highway and returned to Fort Bliss.

After Irwin's return the Aerial Phenomena Research Organization began investigating the affair. On July 10 Irwin was readmitted to undergo tests concerning his mental condition. On August 1 he disappeared from the hospital and has not been heard from since. [26]

27 Keep it Quiet

AT PRECISELY THE SAME time Norman Muscarello was making his historic sighting in New Hampshire, two Texas peace officers were involved in an even more remarkable incident just south of Houston. Deputy Sheriffs William McCoy and Robert Goode were patrolling a highway in Brazoria County. Goode, who was driving, was suffering from an injury to his left hand. Earlier in the evening a pet alligator had bitten him, and the already-festering wound was giving him a great deal of pain.

The lawmens' attention was drawn to a bright purple light to the west, cruising over the oil fields. It turned toward the deputies, who could now see that a smaller blue object accompanied it. The purple UFO looked to be about 50 feet above the ground. As it and its smaller companion sped toward the cruiser Goode, who had his window down, felt a surge of heat hit his left hand and arm. He stomped the accelerator, and McCoy watched as the objects fell back, rose, flared brightly and winked out. After the lawmen made it to Damon, Texas, Goode noticed his gator-bitten hand (which had been exposed to the UFO's heat blast) was almost completely healed.

Wire services carried the story. Immediately low-flying, conventional-looking but unmarked light planes heavily patrolled the area of the sighting.

Two strangers later followed Goode into a neighborhood restaurant and described the UFOs perfectly without him having told them anything about the objects. They then advised him that should he encounter any other such devices he do whatever the crews instructed him and treat anything they told him as confidential. These strangers and unmarked aircraft were never identified.[27]

28 Spectrum

THERE WAS A HEAVY downpour on the night of October 12, 1963 as Eugenio Douglas drove his coal truck down the highway between Monte Maiz and Isla Verda, Argentina. A brilliant beam of light abruptly stabbed through the rain and gathering dawn, blinding Douglas and forcing him to brake to a halt. The light went out when Douglas stopped his truck, and the quizzical driver got a better look at what was shining the light. What he saw was a huge round object about 35 feet high. An aperture opened and three towering figures emerged. At least 12 feet tall, they wore odd headgear with antenna-like appendages. One of these beings fired a narrow beam of red light at Douglas, producing a painful, burning sensation.

Firing at the unearthly trio with his revolver, Douglas fled on foot into Monte Maiz, with the burning beam of ruby light still being fired at him. The terrified truck driver noted that the red ray seemed to be turning streetlights odd hues of green and violet.

A family named Ribas gave Douglas asylum in their home, where all the electric lights *and candles* glowed with the same green coloration as the streetlights. A family member drove Douglas to the local police station, where the authorities were swamped with reports reporting the area's lights' unexplained color change. At first the authorities attributed the phenomenon to some sort of malfunction at the local power facility, but this could not account for candle flames turning green.

A doctor who examined burns on Douglas' face and hands said they looked like the kind caused by ultraviolet radiation, but the victim was certain the ray that had scorched him was *red.* When investigators went to the spot where Douglas had been assaulted they found his untouched truck where he had left it, and 20-inch-long footprints that the rain soon obliterated. [28]

29 Starman Visits Brazil

FROM THE BRAZILIAN TOWN of Safrada Familia came another report of giant saucerians, also in 1963. This story unfolded in late August. Three boys, Fernando Eustagio, 11, his nine-year-old brother Ronaldo, and a friend named Marcos were on an errand to draw water from the Eustagio's well. As they walked into the garden they were startled by a large sphere hovering overhead. Through a transparent opening they could see several rows of "people" working at instrument panels. A door on the bottom of the huge ball slid open, two bright rays of light flashed downward and a slim, ten-foot-tall humanoid floated slowly to the ground as if supported by the light beams. The giant's head was encased in a transparent helmet, and he had a single dark eye in the center of his forehead.

His tall boots left lasting footprints because of a triangular spike on each sole. He wore a glossy, one-piece suit that inflated as he touched the ground, and a square box with flashing lights was attached to his chest. Arms outstretched, he walked with awkward, robotic motions to a large rock and sat down.

When the quizzical boys ventured closer he made as if to grab them. Fernando snatched a rock to throw at him, but was rendered immobile as the creature looked into his eyes. The colossus then rose, returned to his ship on the beam of light and flew away. After his departure the boys felt an undeniable certainty that he had meant them no harm, and that he would return one day. These beliefs about the strange creature were imprinted on the boys' minds despite his not having said a word or made any discernible effort to convey a message.

30 Another French Connection

THE CASE OF A French doctor who declined to be identified remains one of the most prominent in a small but well-documented canon of UFO-related healings that indicate an advanced medical technology.

The investigation of this early morning visitation to southern France is unique because of its lack of governmental and journalistic representatives. A highly competent and efficient research team, including an astrophysicist, psychiatrist and psychologist carried out a thorough, fruitful examination of the affair, unhampered by political considerations or sensationalism, all on the condition that the witness' identity remain strictly confidential.

Slightly before 4:00 a.m. on November 1, 1968 the doctor hobbled painfully to his infant son's crib to give the baby a bottle. Crippled by a severe foot wound in the Algerian war of independence, he had also seriously cut his leg while chopping wood three days earlier. Although he noticed the baby was pointing excitedly out the window, the doctor thought little about it. He assumed the bright flashes outside were merely lightning, for it had been raining hard all night. Upon closer examination, however, he realized the flashes were not coming from natural causes, but from two hovering disks.

The saucers were whitish-silver on top, and red on the bottom, sported both horizontal and vertical antennae, and probed the fog-shrouded ground with powerful, cylindrical beams of light. About once per second there would be an instantaneous, marked increase in the luminosity of the objects, and a flash of light would arc between them. Moving in unison they aligned themselves in the center of the onlooker's field of vision and began slowly to advance on his window. While still approaching, the disks' beams converged on a single spot on the ground. Their antennae touched, the flashes stopped *and the two UFOs merged into one.* This single saucer came yet closer, and its near edge began to rise until the shaft of light, still emanating from the underside, shone directly onto the entranced witness. Finally, with a loud report, the device flew away, leaving a strange afterglow that slowly dissipated.

The physician immediately wrote down everything he had seen, and sketched the objects. He then woke his wife to tell her of the visitation, while excitedly striding back and forth. It was not until after his wife exclaimed, "Your leg!," that he too realized he was not limping. The ax wound on his leg was completely healed. Within a few days his land mine-mangled foot also returned to normal. The plot was not yet through twisting, though.

On November 8 the doctor experienced severe abdominal cramps, and a strange reddish discoloration in the form of a perfect triangle appeared around his navel. The next day this manifestation appeared on the baby's stomach. A psychosomatic explanation for this rash was elusive, for there had been no visible triangles during the sighting, and a dream the doctor had, associating a triangular emblem with a flying saucer occurred on the night of November 13, *after* the sighting and the appearance of the rash.

Although the physician was not bothered by his leg injuries after that unforgettable night, the red triangles persisted. They intermittently appeared on father and son, remaining for days at a time, as recently as 1986, when the phenomenon was photographed.

Another time-honored demonic indicator is uncontrolled levitation. The long-suffering physician and his wife subsequently were plagued by this manifestation, and another traditional symptom of satanic possession and/or persecution—telepathy. [30]

31 Heroes

EASILY THE MOST NOTABLE case of UFO healing would be the one from Petropolis, Brazil in the mountains west of Rio de Janeiro. It was the evening of October 25, 1957, and a daughter of the town's wealthiest family was dying slowly and in agony from stomach cancer. A beam of blinding light suddenly shone through a window, illuminating the entire room. Looking outside, the girl's brother was first to see the hovering saucer. A hatch opened and two small (slightly under four feet) individuals disembarked. They had shoulder-length, reddish-blond hair and bright green, Oriental-looking eyes.

Approaching the bed they laid out an array of surgical instruments. One of them placed his hand on the forehead of the sick girl's father and telepathically received (it would seem) all data of his daughter's malady. The otherworldly surgeons then flashed a "bluish-white light" onto the patient's stomach, illuminating it internally so that the malignancy was plainly visible.

The ensuing surgical procedure took about 30 minutes. Afterward one of the ufonauts handed the father a metallic "hollow ball" containing 30 small white tablets. He informed the man (again telepathically) that the girl was to take one daily. Without fanfare the saucerians re-boarded their craft and zipped out of sight.

By Christmas the young lady was diagnosed as being totally free of cancer. [31]

32 Lost Child

IN HIS BOOK, *INTRUDERS*, UFO investigator Budd Hopkins expertly chronicles the ordeal of a young woman he identifies with the alias Kathie Davis. Using time-regression hypnosis Hopkins established her memories of repeated abductions by ufonauts. These beings seemingly timed their temporary kidnappings to coincide with their victim's monthly ovulations. The saucerians apparently removed ova from Davis on numerous occasions. In another instance, when she was pregnant, her fetus was aborted.

The visitations started in the early 1960s when she was a small child, and continued as least as recently as 1986. At times the encounters included her mother, sister and two small sons being approached by small, gray-fleshed creatures with huge heads and tiny mouths.

The most dumfounding episode of the case happened late on the night of October 3, 1983. Davis awoke inside a UFO where she was shown a small girl who looked to be about four years old. The child's appearance was an ominous combination of human and saucerian features. The oversized head, wide forehead, pointed chin and tiny facial features were apparent to a lesser degree than in the creatures with whom the haunted young woman had become unwillingly familiar. The youngster also had a sparse hair growth, in contrast to the uniformly bald ufonauts.

These physical characteristics led Davis to believe the little girl was hers, raised from a stolen ovum. When she expressed a desire to keep her "daughter," her captors replied this would be impossible. They told her, chillingly, "You wouldn't be able to feed her."

33 Ufological Homicide

ON THE AFTERNOON OF June 16, 1980 Trevor Martin was re-loading his truck in his father's coal yard in Todmorden, West Yorkshire, England. He was horrified to find the corpse of an elderly man atop a heap of coal.

"It was just lying there in plain sight. I didn't know whether the man was dead or alive, so I called the police and an ambulance. I was very frightened. I didn't want to be out there by myself. The body gave me a very eerie feeling. I have no idea how the man got in the yard, but I know one thing for absolute certain—there was no body on that coal pile when I loaded my truck earlier in the day."

It turned out to be the remains of Zygmunt Adamski, 56. He had lived with his invalid wife Lottie in the nearby town of Leeds, where they had settled after fleeing the Nazi invasion of their native Poland more than 40 years earlier. Pathological examination revealed Adamski had died of a heart attack. He had chemical burns from an unidentified substance on his scalp, neck and back of his head.

The victim had disappeared five days before his body was found. On June 11 he had set out on foot to buy a bag of potatoes at a nearby shop. Despite a thorough search and broadcast appeals, no one could be found who had seen the ex-miner after that date. His widow told police her husband seldom drank, was not a gambler, had no known enemies, and had never in his life been to Todmorden.

Three times the coroner postponed the inquest so more evidence could be gathered. There was none to gather, and the case remained open. The spooky affair took an even stranger turn when one of the first two police officers who had arrived at the coal yard mentioned having seen a flying saucer in the vicinity earlier in the day. UFO investigators questioned him under hypnosis, and corroborated his claims, but after this the West Yorkshire Police Department refused to release his name or allow him to be further interviewed.

When the press released the bare supposition that there may have been UFO involvement in the killing there were ripples of international interest. If nothing else this could explain the peculiar placing of the corpse. How it had gotten atop an unstable pile of coal was a total mystery unless it was *lowered* there.

British UFO Research Association representative Walter Reid issued this statement: "There is no obvious explanation why the body was on the pile of coal. It would rather seem that it was literally dumped there from above."

There was no solving the case, and the following autumn it took another dramatic twist. Alan Godfrey had been the other officer of the pair that were first to arrive to investigate the coal yard. On November 28 he came forward with a shocking tale that seemed to substantiate the flying saucer aspect.

At 5:15 on the morning of June 17, Godfrey had driven to the Todmorden council estate, where he saw what he at first thought was a bus. Moving closer, he realized the object was floating about five feet over the ground. It had a row of portholes and a bright blue light. He tried to alert headquarters, but his cruiser radio and walkie-talkie were suddenly inoperative. Remembering his police training, Godfrey commenced sketching the craft. By the time he finished his drawing the UFO had disappeared. The young man was undecided whether to make his sighting public, but when four constables in neighboring Halifax released their report of a similar object, Godfrey submitted his account to his superiors.

Investigators noticed a 15-minute gap in Godfrey's report. This prompted an official request from his superiors for Godfrey to submit to time-regression hypnosis to reveal anything possibly buried in his subconscious. During the videotaped session he recalled being dazzled by a blinding light. When he regained his senses he was in an unfamiliar room and lying on a table. Looming over him was a man about six feet tall, bearded, wearing a skullcap and a black and white uniform. At this point in the regression session panic seized the hypnotized policeman. He cried:

"They're horrible…small…three to four feet. Like five-year-old lads. There are eight of them. He's touching me. He's feeling at my clothes. They have hands and heads like a lamp. They keep touching me…they are making noises. Joseph; I know him as Joseph. He has told me not to be frightened. They are robots! They're not humans! They're robots! They're his. They're Joseph's robots! There's a bloody dog! It's horrible! About the size of an Alsatian!"

Officer Godfrey's reaction to the hypnosis was so intense that the hypnotist felt obliged to bring his subject back to full awareness. His sense of panic was overwhelming, causing everyone in the room to feel the urgency Godfrey was experiencing. At a later session Godfrey recalled being examined by a machine, but balked when asked to describe it. "I haven't to tell you that! I haven't to tell you! Every time I think about it I get a pain!"

The last thing he remembered before finding himself back in his patrol car was the ufonauts removing his shoes and socks and examining his feet. When a newspaper reporter named John Sheard interviewed Godfrey he was told, "I'm just an ordinary bloke doing an ordinary job as a small-town bobby. Do you imagine being associated with flying saucers makes my life any easier? I've never read a science fiction book in my life."

There are several possible explanations to be drawn from this episode, and as many explanations as there are theories. The most likely may be that the saucerians seized Adamski, intending only to perform medical and scientific tests on him. Unfamiliar with the frailties of humans they unintentionally killed him. When it came to snatching Officer Godfrey they presumably were gentler, or perhaps the strapping young policeman, due to his youth and better physical condition, was a stronger specimen. At any rate it does appear that the case of Zygmunt Adamski may well have been the first documented study of a ufological homicide. [32]

34 Communion with Whom?

IN HIS BOOK *COMMUNION* author Whitley Strieber details an often-terrifying lifelong association with UFOs and their occupants that at times resembled outright demonic oppression. Although Strieber endured numerous abductions, the first two he remembered clearly and recounted took place on the nights of October 4 and December 26, 1985. The ordeal began with a mechanical construction leading a delegation into the victim's locked country cabin. This robot was followed by a line of short, heavyset individuals with huge, mesmerizing, upward-slanting eyes. After a physical examination, which included the momentary insertion of a long needle into his skull behind an ear, he was released. He was left with the impression that nothing out of the ordinary had happened that night except that he had seen a barn owl peering at him through a window. Strieber desperately wanted to believe this even when he found a small scab behind his ear.

Under hypnosis, Strieber later recalled these abductions and being told by one of his kidnappers, "You are our chosen one." When he complained they had no right to be using him for experimentation one of them told him emphatically, "We *do* have a right!"

These ufological adventures began in his childhood, when he occasionally would awake in the morning with grass and leaves in his bed, indicating he had had an unremembered nocturnal adventure. When he was 12 he once spent a night outside in a tent with his sister and two friends. He saw what he later recalled as a skeleton on a motorcycle ride across an adjacent vacant lot. His sister saw it too, but her recollection was that of a green fireball instead of a skeleton and motorcycle. At some point during this eerie rendezvous he was clinically examined by something resembling a gigantic praying mantis.

Strieber also recalls a 1957 train ride from Chicago to Texas during which he believes ufonauts forced him to eat some rather strange substances. Afterward he was violently ill, and saw the train speeding through the night from a position high above it. He came away from this ordeal with the persistent memory of seeing and hearing a lone wolf howling in a forest clearing. He believes this was another screen memory deliberately planted to camouflage less desirable (but real) events.

By the time he enrolled in the University of Texas at Austin the young man was being repeatedly plagued by "missing time" episodes. In 1968 he took off on a frantic, month-long dash across Europe in what evidently was a desperate but vain attempt to escape his pursuers. His memories of this trip are incredibly bizarre, confused, contradictory and interspersed with more missing time periods. He recalls being taken to a strange arid region with a tan sky and no night. He visited a "university" his keepers told him was millions of years old. While at this place he encountered several unfamiliar types of beings plus some human-appearing individuals, one of whom photographed him with a Bell & Howell movie camera.

The following December, Strieber found himself in London with no idea how he had gotten there.

His ongoing ufological saga became downright terrifying in 1979, when he and his family were living in Cos Cob, Connecticut. They were awakened one night by piercing human-sounding screams that seemed to be coming from above their house. This incident was repeated in 1986 in Provincetown, Massachusetts. During that period the family were tormented by a "white thing" that would silently enter their home at night and awaken them by poking and prodding them.

Strieber noted that when his "visitors" take him for brief periods, their purpose seems psychological in nature. Visitations of longer duration apparently concern physical examination and analyses. In his numerous contacts his wife has been only peripherally involved. However, when she was hypnotized for questioning about one of the intrusions, her first words after coming out of trance were, "Whitley's supposed to go. They came for Whitley!"

One night when he was lying in bed, working on the manuscript he planned to title *Body Terror,* his wife, although sound asleep, suddenly blurted out in an unfamiliar baritone voice, "The book must not frighten people. You should call it *Communion,* because that's what it's about."

Lengthy mental testing has indicated Whitley Strieber is psychologically normal.

35 Intersteller Leprechaun

In April of 2007 Russian scientists began releasing information on what they called the "Uralian Alien." This was a tiny humanoid found in the summer of 1996 near the town of Kyshtym in the Ural Mountains. After assisting in carrying out a series of five laboratory studies on the being's biological material in the Moscow-based Institute of Forensic Medicine, the coordinator of the Kosmopoisk Research Center, Vadim Chernobrov, made this sensational statement: "A gene discovered in the DNA samples doesn't correspond with any genes pertaining to humans or anthropoid apes," he said. "No gene samples available at the laboratory match the gene. The experts in DNA research haven't come across any creatures with such an elongated DNA molecule."

The creature was alive when discovered by an elderly woman who named it Alioshenka, but died soon afterward. An investigator with the police department in Kyshtym, Major Vladimir Bendlin, investigated the being's death. A urologist at a local hospital, Dr. Igor Uskov, was amused when Bendlin told him the police needed him to examine the corpse of an alien. When he saw the cadaver, Uskov's first impression was that it was a human fetus about 20 weeks old that either had been miscarried or illegally aborted.

Yet after the hospital's chief of morbid anatomy, Dr. Stanislav Samoshkin, autopsied the body he announced it was neither human or of any known animal. In his opinion it was an entirely unknown life form.

"The creature was not by any means a human being. The human skull consists of six bones. The skull of that creature was made up of 4 bones," he said. "There were other differences in the skeleton structure. Those anomalies didn't look like any congenital malformations known to date."

Ufologists who examined the case believed the creature was an extraterrestrial, but some clergy who looked into the affair later suspected it was a demon. Soon after being tested by the Institute of Forensic Medicine the cryptic cadaver disappeared, and despite a $200,000 reward being offered for its recovery it has not been found. At this point there commenced a series of happenings that reminded many of the Curse of the Pharaohs.

The woman who had found the tiny stranger was killed in a hit-and-run traffic mishap just days before a team of researchers arrived from Moscow. Academician Mark Milkhiker arrived in the Urals and commenced a meticulous examination of the area where the dwarf was found. He was abruptly taken seriously ill and rushed to a Moscow hospital where he died of a heart attack. In 2007, a mysterious disease that his fellow physicians were unable to diagnose paralyzed Chernobrov from the waist down.

Could the churchmen have been right about the Uralian Alien's point of origin? [33]

Homes Away From Home

Part 3

1 The Men in the Moon

POSSIBLE BASES FOR UFO activity are a subject overshadowed by the UFOs themselves, they deserve serious study in their own right. A few ufonauts have mentioned bases here on Earth. Mother ships have been referred to and perhaps seen occasionally. Lunar bases, however, are perhaps the most intriguing possibility. Cryptic lights, domes, geometric designs and unnaturally straight lines of unknown origin have been spotted. [1]

The late author and investigator of the paranormal, Frank Edwards, proposed that the 1960s government/military obsession to reach the moon was due in part to high-level suspicions that saucers were using it as a base for their operations. During this time the head of the Army's space development program, Major Patrick Powers, enigmatically told *Family Circle Magazine* that the first men to reach the moon would have to be prepared to fight for the privilege of landing. Predictably, Powers would not elaborate on this singularly remarkable statement, but its implications appear obvious and, on close examination, not particularly far-fetched.

After developing a set of 35mm photos he had taken through his 16-inch reflecting telescope on the night of November 26, 1956, astronomer Robert Curtiss of Alamogordo, New Mexico was staggered by what he saw. He had unwittingly photographed an enormous white cross northwest of the Fra Mauro ring plain near Parry Crater. Each arm of the cross was several miles long, of precisely equal length, and intersected at perfect right angles. There was no conventional explanation. After Curtiss made and distributed prints of this oddity to various astronomical authorities, none were able to satisfactorily explain it. Most confessed to being stumped.

One expert, however, asserted that the cross was not unusual at all. "Just a case where two mountain ridges cross each other at right angles." This individual may have been an authority on astronomy, but his knowledge of *geology* was lacking. It is impossible for two mountain ridges to intersect. The geological processes creating the second mountain ridge would have destroyed the one that was already there. Besides, it certainly did not look like mountains. It looked like landing strips, but there the enigma remains. [2]

The supposition that something strange might be happening on the moon was nothing new. As far back as 1821, mysterious lights were observed in the crater Aristarchus. In 1835, famed astronomer Francis Baily announced he had seen a brilliant light shining steadily in this crater. Two other astronomers, named Temple and Denning, claim to have seen this light twice—once on June 10, 1866, and again on May 7, 1867. On March 3, 1903, observatories in Marseilles reported a bright flickering light in Aristarchus. These sightings could have been of volcanic origin, especially since Soviet scientists announced in 1958 and 1961 that spectrograms had revealed to them the presence of hydrogen and carbon gases near the crater. [3]

Yet this possibility is debatable because other reports seem to be at odds with it, claiming that events have taken place in this crater that would preclude the possibility of volcanic activity. On the night of November 27, 1963, scientists using Lowell Observatory's 24-inch refracting telescope observed dark red lights that at first were several miles from Aristarchus. Hours later they were sighted on the crater's rim. If these lights were of the same lights (they looked identical) the volcano theory is dashed. It is an indisputable fact that volcanoes are stationary. [4]

Aristarchus was the scene of another enigma on the night of January 23, 1880, when a French astronomer named André Trouvelot and his assistant saw a narrow line of brilliant light stretched like a taut, illuminating wire completely across the crater. [5]

The late John O'Neil, a highly respected employee and science editor of the *New York Herald Tribune,* regularly scanned the night heavens with his personal telescope, which permitted very high magnifications. On the night of July 29, 1953, O'Neil was moon watching through a 90-power eyepiece when he saw the shadow of what looked like a colossal bridge on the Sea of Crises.

Increasing the magnification to 250 the quizzical newsman was able to make out clearly the gigantic construction. It was over 12 miles long and, incredibly, had been constructed in less than a month. Less than 30 days earlier O'Neil had observed the same area and had seen no sign of construction. There was no way such an engineering feat could have been constructed on Earth using human technology.

O'Neil published his finding, and received immediate corroboration from Drs. H.P. Wilkins and Patrick Moore, two of the world's leading authorities on the moon. Both men reported seeing the bridge, although neither could offer any logical explanation. [6]

Such lunar activity was not new. From 1869-1871 Britain's Royal Astronomical Society observed and catalogued over 100 mysterious groups of lights in and near the Sea of Crises. Geometric arrangements such as rectangles, triangles and straight lines were repeatedly spotted. Just before Christmas 1871 the cryptic lights abruptly ceased to appear. [7]

In 1912, American astronomer F.B. Harris reported seeing a tremendously huge black object passing so closely over the moon's surface that its shadow was clearly visible on the lunar plain. Harris estimated the thing at roughly 50 miles across. [8]

On March 30, 1950 noted English astronomer Dr. Percy Wilkins spotted something large, oval-shaped and glowing hovering low over the floor of the busy Aristarchus crater. American astronomer, Dr. James Bartlett, Jr. saw the same or a similar object three months later. [9]

On November 20, 1966 America's lunar satellite Orbiter II photographed a group of eight artificial-looking promontories from 29 miles above the Sea of Tranquility. Since the photos were taken from directly overhead the spires' shapes and heights had to be estimated from their shadows and from the sun's elevation above the horizon. NASA scientists came up with a figure of 50 feet in diameter at the base of the largest, and a height of 40 to 75 feet.

Soviet technicians disagreed with this rather general estimate, and reckoned the objects ranged in sizes from "similar to an extremely large fir tree" to "the size of a 15-story building."

NASA filed the photographs without further speculation. It did not fit into the long-range projections of the space program to have physical evidence that could not be explained. The very existence of such a situation would cast aspersions on their scientific ability, and indeed on the entire space program. [10]

On February 4, 1966 the Soviet probe Luna IX had landed on the Ocean of Storms, photographing a series of unnaturally straight lines. The rocks comprising the lines were all exactly the same size and laid out at precise intervals. After the probe took its first set of pictures something caused it to shift position slightly. Following this displacement a second series of photos was made from this different vantage point. The changed angle enabled the Russians to construct a three-dimensional stereoscopic display of the same lines.

One of the engineers working with the project, Dr. A. Bruenko, made this statement:

"With the stereoscopic effect we can affirm that the distance between the stones one, two, three and four is equal. The stones are identical in measurement. There does not seem to be any elevation or height nearby from which the stones could have been rolled or scattered into this geometric form. The objects as seen in three dimensions seem to be arranged according to definite geometric laws."

To most interested parties, East and West, the formations looked suspiciously like aircraft runways or direction markers. Regardless of what their function may have been these rocks did not occur naturally in this formation. This leads to the unavoidable conclusion that someone laid them out in this configuration.

The only known forces on our planet at this time capable of such a feat were the United States and the Soviet Union. Both were mystified. The implications are mind-boggling. Regardless of who *did not* do the deed, the fact remains that someone did. Whatever it was that moved the Soviet probe those few inches on the Ocean of Storms paved the way for another world of speculation. [11]

2 Child of Venus

WHEN RENOWNED ITALIAN-BORN ASTRONOMER Giovanni Cassini turned his telescope on Venus early on the morning of January 25, 1672 he was more than slightly astounded to note that our sister planet had suddenly acquired a very substantial moon. It was about one-fourth the size of the planet, large enough that its phases were clearly visible. Cassini studied this newly discovered satellite about 10 minutes, taking notes, but decided against making this monumental finding public until he could study it further. Here is where he ran into a problem. The next time he turned his telescope toward the tantalizing Venusian orbiter he found it had vanished as mysteriously as it had appeared. It took him 14 years to rediscover it.

At 4:15 on the morning of August 18, 1686 Cassini finally got another another fix on the prodigal. Writing furiously he took notes the whole 15 minutes he watched the immense object. He published his sighting this time, but this was a mistake because the discovery again disappeared. This set a pattern that would hold for the next 200 years. The body would make titillating, fleeting appearances, greatly exciting the scientific community, and then drop from sight for years at a stretch.

Venus' nomadic offspring turned up in 1740, 1759, 1761 and 1768, and then vanished for more than a century. It re-appeared for a month-long stay in 1886. American astronomer Edward Barnard had been an avowed skeptic of the Venusian "moon," so he was predictably shocked to observe it himself in 1892. This turned out to be the last sighting. When the itinerant satellite took off this time it did not return. Yet.

There is no reason to assume the saucers, whatever their motives or source(s,) are in our solar system to observe Earth alone. If a gigantic interstellar ark were to park in Venus orbit it could be visible to Earth-bound onlookers. If this construction were big enough it might be mistaken for a moon when viewed from Earth. Because of the planet's broiling temperature a surface base would not be practical, and an orbiting station would be the best option. At the completion of each mission the installation would depart, accounting for the irregular sabbaticals.

Currently we may be in between visits, or if the unknown spacefarers wish to remain undetected, they may have discontinued their trips in this type of vehicle. Perhaps they realize our technological level has reached a point where it would be impossible for them to avoid our recognizing them for what they are—interstellar explorers? No longer can they expect to be mistaken for a natural moon. [12]

3 Deep-Sea Fishing

LUNAR AND VENUSIAN BASES are certainly a riveting possibility, but just two of several. Herbert Schirmer's UFO crew showed him an image of a huge mother ship and told him there are numerous installations on Earth, including one off the coast of Florida in an area often referred to as the Bermuda Triangle. [13] This region is notorious for being the site of numerous disappearances of ships and aircraft. The sea here is extremely deep in places, and even a fairly large base might be difficult to detect if it were at a sufficient depth.

The notion that spacecraft have been carrying away the airplanes and ocean-going vessels (some of which have been huge) that have disappeared in the Triangle has been advanced by some as the only possible solution to the perplexing, without-a-trace vanishings. Meticulous investigations have eliminated many other theories such as space/time warps and primordial, still-operating power sources left over from the lost continent of Atlantis. The Sherlock Holmes axiom that one must "eliminate the impossible; whatever is left, however improbable, must be true," has come to the support of those espousing a ufological explanation for the disappearances.

There were wireless operators who claim to have heard Navy Lieutenant Charles Taylor, commander of the famous five-plane Flight 19 that vanished over the Triangle on December 5, 1945 call over his radio just before contact was lost, "Don't come after me! They look like they are from outer space!" [14]

When the diesel-powered launch *Nightmare* was returning from a fishing excursion late one night in September 1972 it passed between Featherbed Banks and Matheson Hammock on its way to Bermuda's Biscayne Bay. At this point its compass swung a full 90 degrees from its previous indication north, and the boat's light dimmed to blackness. The helmsman steered westward toward the lights of his destination, Cocoanut Grove, but instead of churning at full power the launch moved sideways, northward.

For two hours the three men aboard the vessel helplessly watched as the shore lights eased to the south. They also noticed a huge dark object hovering at least a mile away to the west. It was so big it blocked their view of the stars. As they watched it they saw a bright light fly into this darkened area, hover momentarily, and then vanish. Next the black mass also vanished, having the apparent effect of releasing the force dragging the boat off course. *Nightmare's* electrical equipment commenced functioning again and the ship regained full power. The nightmare was over.[15]

There have been other cases in this region of large, unlit hovering objects arresting the forward progress of ships and disabling their generators, and then releasing them. One might wonder how many times these dusky aerial behemoths *have not* let go. Fairly numerous reports of UFOs entering or emerging from the ocean in the Bermuda Triangle could indicate the presence of an undersea complex in deep water. Perhaps to keep an eye on nearby Cape Canaveral.

4 Thermostats on Zero

Following the alleged crash of a flying disk on the Norwegian island of Spitzbergen in 1952 the Norwegian Air Force assigned a Lieutenant Tyllensen as a special observer in the country's farthest north, where saucers had been quite busy. Tyllensen later made this illuminating report:

"I think the Arctic is serving as a kind of air base for the unknowns, especially during snowstorms when we are forced back to our bases. I have seen them land and take off on three separate occasions. I notice that, after having landed, they execute a speedy rotation around their disks. A brilliant glow of light, the intensity of which is variable with regard to speed of landing and takeoff, prevents any view of the things happening behind this curtain of light and on or inside the disk itself." [16]

A UFO base hidden in a place like the Arctic barrens might not be as hard to keep hidden as one would first assume. A 1970 report from the United Nations stated that four-fifths of the Earth's surface was inadequately surveyed or explored at that time. [17] A base could be secreted in a desert, rain forest or remote island and we easily could be unaware of its existence.

A peculiar report from Greenland in the 1960s announced the discovery of a gigantic object buried deep beneath the glacial ice caps. Whatever it was/is, it allegedly was broadcasting a powerful, undecipherable radio signal at regular intervals. This tantalizing dispatch was never documented, and despite the paucity of data it is tempting to consider that this could be a navigational beacon for spacecraft approaching a polar base.

During the late 1950s, numerous American and Russian scientists operating out of newly established Antarctic research stations reported what looked like huge artificial structures under the ice sheets. In one instance Soviet personnel claimed to have seen a huge shape "too geometrical" to be a natural formation. Many observers have reported the craft seen in the UFO-laden skies of Argentina's cold southern regions approach from or depart toward the south. [18]

5 Cosmic Colossus

A You Tube report from the summer of 2018 chronicled a video clip of a planet-sized UFO moving through deep space. The You Tube channel reported it noticed the object during research of the website of the NASA stereo mission. The conspiracy theory channel UFOmania shared the clip online and said the UFO appears to be encircled by a force field. Some theorists opined that the thing could be a mega-ship from deep space or a permanent space station ala` *Star Wars.* One user claimed the gargantuan thing had been under observation for at least a year and appears to be launching missiles.

Echoes From Antiquity

Part 4

1 What Goes Up...

MANY INVESTIGATORS HAVE LOOKED into what appear to be reports of UFOs in antiquity. A literal reflection of ancient ufological contact may have been the 1920s phenomenon called Long Delayed Echoes (LDEs) in which something would mirror radio transmissions back to their sources. The anomaly manifested itself to ham operators worldwide. Usually the delays between when the broadcasts were made and when they returned were only a few seconds, but there were instances of signals returning *days* later.

After the 1920s these boomerang signals became extremely rare. Decades later, however, Scottish astronomer Duncan Lunan examined the old LDE records and made a startling discovery. Using dots to represent the delays between transmissions and returns Lunan constructed a graph. To his astonishment the dots formed a star chart.

"The dots made up a map of an easily recognized constellation. The constellation Bootis in the northern sky. The curious pattern of delayed echoes was actually a pattern of star positions."

Applying his method to other LDE records he found the star Epsilon Bootis central in all the resulting maps. At a distance of 203 light years, Epsilon Bootis could hardly have been where the signals had ricocheted from, but could somebody have placed a satellite near Earth to give us a clue as to another civilization's whereabouts?

Lunan's findings gave fresh impetus to the search for LDEs in the 1970s, but success was elusive. Perhaps whoever had been responsible for the returns had given up on us and departed, only to have us decipher their code later. Despite their unmistakable depictions, Lunan's star charts are not perfect representations. They show the Epsilon Bootis constellation as it appeared 13,000 years ago. According to Lunan some extraterrestrial race sent explorers to our world 13,000 years ago. These pathfinders apprised the primitives they encountered as far too backward for the establishment of any mutually useful interaction, and went home.

Before these spacefarers left Earth, however, they may have placed a sophisticated communications device in a distant orbit. They programmed this machine to activate itself at a future date when its makers calculated we would be technologically capable of inadvertently contacting the beacon. This time was the 1920s. After a predetermined period of data-gathering and attempts to let us know of its existence (via the LDEs,) the satellite either shut down or left. [1]

2 Forgotten but Not Gone

CERTAIN ROCK CLIFFS IN Peru were partially melted in the geologically recent past, leading to suppositions of a prehistoric nuclear war. [2] Ancient cave paintings throughout Western Europe depict flattened shapes that could have been drawn by UFO witnesses of today. The walls of a cave outside Niaux, France are adorned with a drawing of a domed, saucer-like object trailing a dotted line that presumably marks a flight path. [3]

3 Clue From the Scriptures

MANY REGARD THE APPARITION chronicled by the Old Testament prophet Ezekiel as ufological. His excellent, detailed description of the vision does seem to conform to many contemporary UFO sightings when one keeps in mind that Ezekiel was using the vernacular of 593 B.C. to describe the event. The prophet's reference to "wheels within wheels" sounds like he was describing his first-ever glimpse of whirling propellers (a helicopter-style landing apparatus?) However, the truly tantalizing part is Ezekiel's account of the appearance of four multi-winged creatures with round feet.

In 1968 Austrian-born NASA engineer Josef Blumrich embarked on a project to debunk the idea the vision was ufological. As one of the architects and builders of the massive Saturn V rockets used by the Apollo space program, he had an excellent grasp of spacecraft design possibilities. To his surprise he found the prophet's recounting of what he saw that day almost 600 years before Christ was adaptable to a fairly large landing module, presumably launched from the fiery object Ezekiel saw hovering overhead.

The "living creatures" with wings and round feet interpolate into a feasible quadrupedal landing gear with shock absorbers and helicopters. Theoretical mechanical arms attached to these protuberances would have enhanced the misconception of animated beings. This is especially probable since the prophet had definitely never seen a flying machine, let alone landing gear.

Blumrich postulates that the images of a bull, lion, eagle and man could have been mechanical apparatuses. Similarly, a person of 200 years ago might, if suddenly confronted by a modern automobile, refer to its headlights as "eyes" or "spectacles." He calls on a second possibility to account for these "faces." They may have been painted-on artwork, like that which graced the noses of World War II bombers. If so it was a saucer fad strictly of the past. No contemporary UFOs seem to be so adorned.

Blumrich further suggests that the first meeting between Ezekiel and these Biblical spacefarers was coincidental. When the craft touched down near the group of captive Hebrews, the prophet, who assumed he was witnessing a supernatural event, drew attention to himself by not fleeing in terror like the others. Instead he reacted with supplication and livid excitement, greeting and conversing with the crew. His rare approachability and obvious intelligence perhaps prompted the ufonauts to seek him out repeatedly as their contact (and, as it turned out, chronicler.) [4]

4 The First Race

THE LONG-DEAD MAYAN CIVILIZATION of Central America recorded its history in a voluminous work called the *Popul Vuh,* which somehow managed to survive to the present age. This saga mentions a cryptic "first race" which possessed all knowledge and "…examined the four corners of the horizon, the four points of the firmament and the round circles of the Earth."

Round circles? How could predecessors of the ancient Mayas have known they lived on a gigantic sphere unless they were far more advanced than centuries of cultures that followed them? Maybe these elders never died out as did so many of their successors on that continent, but instead withdrew in some fashion and continued to develop their technology. If they could explore the entire planet in misty antiquity, imagine what they would be capable of now.

The Mayans' highly regarded first race might even still be with us, occasionally hurtling overhead in their silent saucers on missions beyond our still-primitive comprehension. [5]

5 Campaigns

BOTH ALEXANDER THE GREAT and Charlemagne reported huge "flaming shields." In Alexander's case they dove on his columns of troops and mounts, disastrously stampeding elephants as the Greeks moved to invade India.

More than 1000 years later Charlemagne's embattled forces were saved when fiery disks swooping from the heavens frightened away a huge Saxon army. After the Saxons' departure the craft flew away, their presumed mission accomplished.
6

6 Ring of Honor

SOME BELIEVE THE HUGE, circular stone monument on southern England's Salisbury Plain, Stonehenge, to be associated with the saucer phenomenon in prehistory. They point out that because of its precise astronomical alignments it must have been constructed (or its construction supervised) by someone with an advanced knowledge of astronomy. This would seem to rule out the thinly spread savages who populated the British Isles during the lengthy period it must have taken to erect the perplexing construction. This raises the suggestion that maybe it was built by or for saucerians, much as the Children of Israel fashioned the Ark of the Covenant according to specific instructions from Jehovah.

Noted astronomer Gerald Hawkins related in his book, *Stonehenge Decoded,* his discovery of an 18.6-year cycle in which at midwinter the moon rises over one specific stone. He also calls to mention a quote attributed to the historian Diodorus in 50 B.C.:

"The moon as viewed from this island appears to be but a little distance from the Earth, and to have prominences like those of the Earth, which are visible to the eye. The account is also given that the god visits the island every nineteen years, the period in which the return of the stars to the same place in the heavens is accomplished."

If Hawkins and Diodorus are correct that the ancients believed a god visited Salisbury plain every 19 or so years, this would at least provide a plausible religious motive to account for Stonehenge's construction. Might this deity have been a primordial astronaut returning every 19 (18.6?) years on a mission he never revealed to his faithful? Maybe he was involved in some prosaic, long-since-discontinued task—one he never dreamed would result in his being worshipped and having a perpetual shrine raised in his honor. After his work was completed and he ceased to return, the cult he unintentionally founded died out in his absence, but his memorial remains to confound posterity millennium after millennium.

This is remarkably similar to the experience of U.S. Army Air Force pilot John Thrum during World War II. Thrum was stationed on a remote island in the Ellis chain in the Pacific. The island's natives began to worship him. Basing their adulation on how his airplane gave him access to the heavens the primitive locals assumed he must be a deity of great proportions. To this day succeeding generations of islanders regard him as a god. [7]

7 Far Away and Long Ago

RESEARCHERS PICKING THROUGH SCIENTIFIC expedition records and examining old records from China's Payenk Ara Ulaa region have constructed a strong case for an ancient ufological incident in this remote mountain area.

Archaeologists combing local caves in 1938 were puzzled by the odd stone disks they kept finding. With a diameter of 30 inches, and two inches thick they resembled oversized phonograph records. Each had a double-spiral groove containing carved hieroglyphics.

There were also orderly rows of graves containing the spindly skeletons of what the scientists assumed was a species of extinct ape. The skeletons averaged about 5'6. These peculiar, totally unexpected artifacts understandably befuddled expedition members. The modern flying saucer era had yet to dawn, so the researchers made no attempt to connect these remains with 10,000-year-old tales of strange beings "landing in their craft" and attempting to establish a permanent enclave in this warm, sheltered valley.

Archaeologist Chi Pu Tei and his assistants could not conceive any conclusions or theories to account for what they found. They took careful notes and brought some of the granite disks back to the Peking Academy, where they eluded analysis for 24 years. In 1962, Professor Tsum Um Nui of Peking's Academy of Prehistoric Research revealed he had deciphered the writing on one of the plates. According to Um Nui it was the record of a flying machine that landed (or crashed) "about 12,000 years ago." When the craft's occupants emerged they were so hideous-looking that the local people attacked them. The strangers attempted to hide in caves, but were hunted down and exterminated.

Chinese scientists released tantalizingly little more on their findings, but it *was* revealed that the disks contained cobalt. Whether it was naturally present or had been artificially introduced via some metallurgical process was not divulged. However its mere presence raises a couple of very significant possibilities.

As a non-rusting metal with magnetic properties, cobalt could have been blended with the disks (or they could have been deliberately carved from rocks already containing it) in an effort to create a permanent record. The hieroglyphics might be a type of binary code such as that on the Voyager deep space probe, intended to show the point of origin of another civilization. The cobalt-laced grooves may contain a magnetic audio recording telling of a group of cosmic pilgrims whose attempt to migrate to a new world was aborted by the savagery of its natives.

Strange wall paintings also adorn the caves. There are drawings of the night sky with odd circles among the stars. Furthermore, the thin-boned skeletons are consistent with beings from a light gravity planet smaller than Earth. In any case the expedition members' assumption that the bones were those of apes seems utterly untenable. Apes do not bury their dead, and why would the ancient Chinese locals have gone to the bother of interring animals?

If Chinese ufologists ever join forces with scientists of other fields to seriously, meticulously study the strange plates found while China was preoccupied with the Japanese invasion, a revelation of historic proportions may tardily manifest itself. [8]

8 Dragons Over Europe

SPECTACULAR CAVORTINGS OF STRANGE aerial things were all the rage in medieval Europe. They were generally accorded religious significance, so priests, monks and other clerics recorded their appearances. On the evening of January 1, 1254 Benedictine monks at St. Albans in Hertfordshire witnessed a "large, round silver disk" passing over their monastery.

In April 1561 saucers and spheres performed a veritable air show as they gamboled over Nuremberg, Germany. Five years later residents of Basle, Switzerland were terrified by the multitude of black globes that suddenly appeared over the city. After a short period of chasing each other through the thin Alpine air they turned blood red and faded from sight.

British astronomer Edmund Halley, who was first to time the visits of the brilliant comet that bears his name, observed a number of UFOs over England in March of 1716. One of the nocturnal objects was so luminous that Halley was able to read by its light for two hours as it hovered over London.

These samplings must be considered a minute sampling since the vast majority of Europeans during the Middle Ages were illiterate. Only incidents witnessed by members of the upper classes, government officials or clergy were recorded. The fact that even the number of *chronicled* sightings is fairly numerous evidences the magnitude of UFO activity in European skies during past centuries.[9]

9 Mother of Many

LEGENDS RECOUNT HOW A goddess-like woman called Oryana who descended from the heavens aboard a golden conveyance founded the once-teeming primeval metropolis of Tiahuanaco, perched on a plateau high in the Bolivian Andes. She gave birth to 70 children, and then flew back to the stars, leaving her offspring to build and populate Tiahuanaco. The city was somehow constructed of stone blocks weighing up to 100 tons (*100 tons!*) at an altitude so lofty that heavy physical labor is virtually impossible.

By the time the conquering Spaniards arrived, Tiahuanaco had been abandoned and in ruins since prehistory. The local natives had no use for the ghost city, and did not connect it with themselves or their ancestors.

Who was Oryana? Was Tiahuanaco a seeded colony of non-humans? Statues found among the ruins depict human-looking individuals, but of races not indigenous to that part of the world. How did ancient South Americans learn what people from unknown continents look like?

Misty legends are admittedly flimsy hypothesis-building material, yet *something* gave rise to this impossibly situated city and the curious lore associated with it. In any case the Andean region of prehistory evidently saw a most remarkable chapter written and lost. [10]

10 Tales—Some Older than Others

THE COLLECTION OF OLD *Tales* was complied in the 4th Century A.D. by Chinese historian Wang Chia. Within this compilation of then-ancient folklore was mention of the appearance on the South China Sea of a brilliantly illuminated ship one night 4300 years ago. The vessel could fly, and was enormous. Locals called it the "Ship Hanging Among the Stars," and it took two men, Hou Yih and Chang Ngo, on a flight to the moon. After hanging around for 12 years this boat to the moon departed forever. [11]

11 You Take My Breath Away

ANOTHER INTRIGUING REPORT FROM past centuries comes from Bristol, England in 1200 A.D. An anchor dragging from an airship got hung up on a gate outside a church. When a humanoid crewman slid down the line to free the grapnel he was detained by a crowd of quizzical humans and sadly drowned in Earth's unpalatable atmosphere. [12]

12 Out of the Darkness

THE HOPI TRIBE PRESERVES an ancient legend that they migrated to the American Southwest from a "Red City" somewhere to the south. This move is supposed to have been guided by a group of beings called the Kachina clan.

These flesh-and-blood creatures instructed the Hopis in the occult. After re-settling their charges in their new homes and versing them in nefarious theology, the Kachinas forever departed, leaving with these words:

"The time for us to go to our far-off planets and stars has not yet come, but it is time for us to leave you. We will go by our powers to a certain high mountain, which you will know, where we will await your messages of need. We are a spirit people, and we will not be seen again by you or your people, but you must remember us by wearing our masks and costumes at the proper ceremonial times. Those who do so must be only those persons who have acquired the knowledge and the wisdom we have taught you."

Could the Kachinas have been a group of saucerians (of evidently questionable motives) who felt a need to be deified and worshipped? Everything in their actions and, especially, their parting statement points toward it. Furthermore, the occult angle may have indicated a very significant ufological aspect. [13]

13 Rediscovery

IN 1929 A MYSTERIOUS map turned up among relics from the Topkapi Palace in Istanbul. Dated 1513 it is known as the Piri Re'is map in honor of the 16th Century cartographer Admiral Piri Re'is. With sobering accuracy it outlines all the continents of our planet. The Antarctic is drawn with a precision not conventionally possible until the mid-20th Century. The southern polar land mass is depicted as how it would appear were it totally free of ice, and in a way now known to be accurate. The map shows mountain ranges that were not known to modern science until 1952. There is no way of knowing how old the map was when it was dated in 1513, but even had it been brand-new then (or even when it was re-discovered in 1929) it still would have been absurdly ahead of its time.

The chart either had to have been produced by someone with access to technology far in advance of anything then supposed to be available on Earth, or it is the most incredible coincidence in all of human history. It appears impossible for someone to have drawn the map without using extensive aerial surveying, and Admiral Piri Re'is compounds the mystery via a notation he left on the chart. This note reveals he copied it from older graphs dating from the time of Alexander the Great.

How could anyone in Alexander's day even have known of Antarctica, much less drawn it with such precision? The only plausible explanation is that in forgotten antiquity somebody with the ability to fly carefully mapped our world, and fragments of the work of these ancient surveyors have somehow survived.

Either those cartographers were members of a dead, fantastically advanced terrestrial civilization (unlikely, since had it been contemporaneous with Alexander it would not be forgotten,) or they were from somewhere beyond this planet, and their mapping, perhaps accidentally, fell into the hands of Earthmen.

The possibility of fraud can be entertained only if it can be proven that the Piri Re'is map was not, in fact, exhumed in 1929. This has not been done. [14]

UFOs in antiquity are perhaps even more plausible than they are today. The human race was spread much more thinly, and advanced visitors would have had less difficulty remaining undetected. Illiteracy was the rule, making written accounts less likely, and oral renderings were typically subject to exaggeration and distortion. For centuries in the Middle Ages any European claiming to have seen what today would be called a flying saucer ran the horribly real risk of being burned at the stake for religious heresy. All this makes it understandable that the vast bulk of ancient reports were made by learned, influential men like Ezekiel, Alexander and Charlemagne. At least we have these descriptions of what evidently is not an exclusively modern phenomenon.

Is It All in the Mind...or on the Ground?

Part 5

1 Mind Games

THERE ARE MULTITUDES WHO are firmly convinced that UFOs exist nowhere outside a few fervent imaginations, tired, sick or sham-inclined minds. This point of view cannot be ignored, since hallucinations can appear as concrete reality to those experiencing them. This sort of mental aberration can be induced by not-necessarily-prolonged periods of isolation, tension and fatigue. Excellent examples of what such stresses can do are found in the logbooks of the participants in a transatlantic yacht race.

The race discussed here took place in 1972. The 55 mariners sailed a demanding 3000 miles from Plymouth, England to Newport, Rhode Island. The winner arrived in 20 days, while the last participant, plagued by navigation errors, took 88 days. Each kept a daily journal covering events occurring during the voyage, and these log entries record some eerie experiences.

One sailor, 26 days out, saw "…what looked like the reflection of a window moving about 20 feet below the surface. It passed me three or four times." Another yachtsman, sailing alone, was certain he saw his father-in-law at the top of the mast. Later that day he saw his wife, then his mother, and finally his daughter lying on a cabin bunk.

One man, only five days into the race, "…awoke from a dream with someone shaking my shoulder, telling me to get up and go on deck as there was shipping about, and not to forget to drop my wife off at Lugo, Spain." He did not recognize the specter, but had the distinct impression it was a friend. Another contestant heard shrill cries of, "Bill! Bill!," coming from the boat's rigging.

Sleep deprivation plagued nearly all participants, and in some caused the distinction between sleep and wakefulness to become blurred. One wrote, "My mind was completely separated from my body. I just used my body to get me around the boat, and eventually there was no difference between sleeping and waking...almost like being drunk or high on pot."

Still, not all reports of UFOs of varying appearances come from witnesses under duress. The craft in a formation that passed over Edgerton, Wisconsin during the predawn of 22 July 2022, drew mixed metaphors. They were described as silver balls, boats, barges and glowing triangles by sober, clear-minded, rested onlookers.

Nevertheless, UFO reports coming from persons under psychological and physical strain must be regarded as highly suspect. These visual and audible hallucinations were undoubtedly real to those who experienced them, and certainly some saucer sightings do come from persons under similar duress. Such sightings obviously have to be deleted from the cases to be studied in any serious saucer investigation. If all sightings were of this genre there would be little trouble in going to the trouble of reading (or writing) this book, for all case histories easily could be explained away. This has never been the case. Too many reports come from sober, clear-minded witnesses under none of the types of pressure that would influence their descriptions. Those many UFOs sighted by multiple witnesses who provide identical descriptions present yet more cases to be seriously considered.

Saucer sightings made by persons suffering from mental disorders also must be dismissed. Temporal lobe epilepsy and certain forms of schizophrenia produce vivid delusions affecting all five senses. Should someone afflicted by such maladies undergo a hallucinatory episode which he sincerely perceives to be a UFO encounter it would be quite real to him and he easily could pass a polygraph test given to authenticate his "saucer sighting."

It is impossible to accurately estimate how many erroneous reports of this type are made, but the very nature of psychiatric sickness gives it a small place in ufology. Percentage-wise there are far too few mentally ill people or substance abusers in the general population for them to be considered a predominant cause of the phenomenon.

UFOs' predilection for nocturnal touchdowns in isolated, thinly peopled locations also argues against a psychological explanation. Few witnesses per landing provide correspondingly few opportunities for psychosis to be involved.

A related possibility concerns the physical planet on which we live. Mother Earth emits natural radio waves of between one and 30 hertz. These faint, extra-low frequency transmissions are compatible with those produced by the human brain, which itself is electrical in nature. Certain natural manifestations (lightning, aurora borealis, etc.) could conceivably affect our planet's normal transmissions in such a way as to trigger temporary, non-psychotic mental aberrations in individuals who are somehow more electrically/mentally receptive to this type of occurrence.

In a similar vein, modern reports of flying saucers could be tied to military transmitters used worldwide to communicate with atomic submarines. These radios use extra-low frequencies because they penetrate underwater, and in some cases these bottom-of-the-scale waves might literally be contacting peoples' brains, causing them to see and hear things that are not there.

2 Knowledge on a Platter

SWISS PSYCHOLOGIST CARL JUNG believed all of humanity possesses what he called the "collective unconscious." According to Jung this is a world-pervading non-physical encyclopedia of the sum total of human knowledge. He suggested that universal symbols (apparently the mental equivalent of computer chips) are contained in this unfathomably vast storehouse. He called these symbols archtypes.

Jung thought archtypes appeared spontaneously to individual humans, causing dreams, visions and real-looking images. He called one of these images the mandala, a disk-shaped symbol representing totality or completion. Jung proposed that the mandala might appear as a solid, saucer-shaped object in the sky, projected by the minds of persons craving peace and order.

3 Yellow Brick Road

BRITISH UFOLOGIST JENNY RANDLES referred to a quasi-mental deviation she called the "Oz Factor" as a possible cause for some UFO sightings and encounters. She described this as "…a sense of timelessness and sensory isolation" in which "…the witness feels the UFO has temporarily sucked him into a kind of void where only he and the phenomenon co-exist." This would take place in someone whose state of consciousness is somewhat below normal waking reality, and would cause him or her to misinterpret some commonplace object (the planet Venus, for example) as paranormal.

This erroneous impression supposedly can become strong enough subjectively for the affected person to develop psychokinetic ability, even enabling him to photograph the thing he thinks he sees *as he sees it.* Presumably this means that Venus, if photographed by somebody under the influence of the Oz Factor, would appear on film as having an elongated or saucer shape. Randles does not discount the possibility of otherworldly visitation as well, however.

4 What's Good for the Goose...

THE FLYING SAUCER QUESTION was still new and therefore of extremely widespread interest in the spring of 1950. American newspapers generally were of the opinion the craft were military prototypes being developed both from proliferating post-war technology and that captured from the Germans at the end of World War II. A discovery made on an abandoned farm outside Glen Burnie, Maryland bolstered this notion.

In May 1949 the U.S. Air Force department created to investigate UFO reports received a letter from a man in Maryland who claimed to have purchased stock in a small firm called the Gray Goose Corporation. This company, headed by a self-taught aeronautics engineer named Jonathan E. Caldwell, had been a little operation manufacturing novel types of aircraft. Caldwell's ignorance of how to run a business led him to financial ruin and prompted the Maryland attorney general to investigate the Gray Goose Corporation.

By 1940, Caldwell, alarmed at the authorities' interest in his dealings, had fled to points unknown and could not be located. Because some of them closely resembled the saucers he had been hearing and reading about so much lately the investor figured the Air Force would be interested in the strange flying machines Caldwell had designed and built. A joint team of Maryland state police officers and Air Force personnel set out to search Caldwell's manufacturing plant, and their Gray Goose chase ended at the forsaken farm.

The site yielded two weather-ravaged devices that had been used as prototypes. One was a small helicopter whose bottom half looked conventional enough, but above the cockpit there was fastened a large tripod supporting a 14-foot-diameter disk from which protruded propeller blades. The other machine was spool-like in appearance, with two circular sections separated by the cockpit. The upright spools had short props projecting from their upper rims.

The number of years it had obviously taken for these peculiar aircraft to fall into such an advanced state of disrepair and inoperability argued against any connection with the UFO phenomenon. The saucers had made no notable appearances until 1947, and by that time the Gray Goose Corporation was long since history and its unorthodox designs forsaken junk.

The investigators also managed to track down a man who claimed to have worked for Caldwell as a test pilot and to have flown the flat-topped helicopter in 1939 or 1940. He reported the craft never made it more than 40 feet off the ground, and could stay aloft for only a few minutes at a time. It was clear the Gray Goose machines' flight capabilities were far too limited for them to have performed the aerial acrobatics typifying the flying saucers. [2]

There was also the U.S. Navy's experimental V-173 "Flying Flapjack." Saucer-shaped, it might, if witnessed by those unaware of its development, have precipitated UFO reports, but it was quickly rendered obsolete by the military's proliferating jet technology. It did not fly after 1948. [3]

Despite the impracticality of prototypes and weather balloons (another favorite of debunkers) as blanket solutions, they do result in great numbers of saucer reports annually from witnesses who are honestly mistaken. Migrating geese, satellites, sun dogs, temperature inversions, ball lightning and that old deceiving enchantress Venus have spawned masses of false sightings, and always will. The fact is, the vast majority of UFOs *are* misidentified, known tangibles. Nevertheless it beggars credulity to rationalize that terrestrial aircraft, balloons or other such items that frequently generate reports of flying saucers also abduct humans, cause massive power failures, explode like nuclear bombs, or carry strange, sentient-appearing but plainly nonhuman entities. Human fallibility cannot be the overriding explanation.

5 High Voltage

Finally we come to the most convincing misleader. A natural phenomenon that, to someone not versed in the natural sciences, would appear to be "unmistakably" a UFO.

In areas with a great deal of surface vegetation the Earth continuously emits ions that accumulate on insulated wires such as those used to carry electrical power. These ions can gather in dense clouds with a density of from 1000 to 1,000,000 times above normal. Should these ion clouds condense further they may form a type of plasma that behaves in a fashion UFO researchers would find familiar. A terrestrial ionic plasma of this type is characterized by a powerful electric/magnetic field that may ionize and recombine air molecules so that light, weightlessness and radioactivity are produced, enabling it to achieve great speeds and make seemingly impossibly tight right-angle turns. Because of its natural magnetism it may "lock onto" and literally be pulled along by a metal object such as a car or airplane, appearing to follow the vehicle. Since UFOs are sometimes reported to cease trailing an automobile and shoot skyward when the car passes under an overpass, this could be caused by the overpass severing the magnetic connection and essentially "releasing" the plasma.

Furthermore, this type of ionized cloud may follow the Earth's magnetic fields at great speed, and would be attracted to the high-voltage lines from which it developed, explaining the many UFO sightings made in the vicinity of such wires. Because of their electrified nature plasmas could also cause temporary overloads in electrical circuits, causing power failures. Through subsequent dissipation of its voltage a plasma may instantaneously dissolve, appearing to dematerialize.

This sort of electrical apparition easily could be photographed and appear as a solid, mysterious object.

However there are far too many saucer encounters involving factors not characteristic of plasmas (such as the great number of sightings over water and deserts) for them to be the sole cause of all sightings. Plasmas could hardly produce UFO occupants, disembodied voices or the solid-appearing-and-feeling vehicles so often reported by witnesses. Thus, clouds of rogue electricity are also unsuitable as a blanket explanation.

6 P.T. Barnum

LASTLY, FRAUD IS ON the minds of enough "witnesses" to make it a definite reality. Many convincing-sounding stories have come from charlatans seeking notoriety and financial gain. These knaves have photographed tossed Frisbees, drawn pictures of "UFO occupants" for reporters, and used blowtorches to scorch circles in the grass of cow pastures in order to simulate landing sites.

These publicity hounds' lust for a few moments in the limelight and the chance to profit from their deceit places another snare before serious investigators trying to decipher a mystery of still-unknowable importance, but once again there is the problem of numbers. There are far too few hucksters to account for the entire matter. Many reports come from persons disinterested in publicity, and innumerable sightings are left unreported by witnesses specifically to *avoid* media exposure. Fraud, too, is inadequate as an overall explanation.

What Have We Learned?

Part 6

1 Say No Evil...Even if It's True

ON JUNE 21, 1947 what is generally regarded as the first significant sighting of the modern UFO era took place over Puget Sound, an inlet on the Washington coast near Tacoma.

State employee Harold Dahl was on harbor patrol when a ragged formation of round, white flying machines dropped from the clouds. They were large, perhaps 100 feet in diameter, and commenced circling a sixth craft that hovered motionless at about 1500 feet. This UFO abruptly dropped to about 500 feet. Dahl could see a dark opening on the underside. Bright flashes of light intermittently issued from this aperture.

After about five minutes one of the higher, circling machines descended to the lower one and came to rest on top of it. After several more minutes the sphere on top detached and began to rise. Dahl construed this action as an evacuation of personnel from the lower UFO, and that it was about to crash. Fearful it would fall on him he yanked his launch around and fled into a small bay just as a burst of metallic fragments spewed from the still-hovering machine.

Moving away slowly on a low trajectory it continued to expel slag-like particles that gave off steam as they hit the water. After another violent emission the presumably lightened device rose and rejoined the higher formation, which then departed seaward at high speed. Dahl's young son was with him in the boat, and was slightly wounded by the last slag burst. The boy's dog came off even worse—the shower of fragments killed it.

The following morning an odd, black-suited personage visited Dahl. After driving up in a brand-new Buick the man recounted a detailed description of the previous day's adventure as if he had been present. He also threateningly "advised" Dahl to not discuss his encounter.

Some of the slag samples were analyzed at the University of Chicago, and were found to be of volcanic nature. At this point Dahl and his boss Fred Crisman (who was involved in the investigation and had vouched for his employee's veracity) both did a sudden about-face, recanting their accounts and claiming they had found the fragments on nearby Maury Island and had turned them in to add veracity to their hoax. If this was the case, what was it that injured the boy and killed the dog?

On July 21, U.S. Army Intelligence began to look into the increasingly puzzling affair, but a series of thoroughly suspicious occurrences short-circuited the investigation. The slag samples were being flown to Hamilton Air Force Base in California, but were lost when the plane carrying them crashed.

There were those who believed these samples were worthless counterfeits anyway. Pioneering ufologist Ray Palmer was also participating in the inquiry, and later claimed to have had a cigar box containing the original samples. He said the box was stolen from his Chicago office and replaced with fake look-alikes. In the midst of all this cloak-and-dagger activity Harold Dahl suddenly vanished, never to be heard from again.

Fishily, Crisman (who had been a pilot in World War II) was unexpectedly recalled to active duty and stationed at a remote base in Greenland, making him virtually inaccessible. With the mystery's two central figures gone, the investigation ground to an inconclusive halt, which would seem to have been the intention of the black-garbed individual who approached Dahl so promptly after the initial sighting. These ominous-looking "Men in Black" (MIB) would become a persistent, permanent element of ufology. [1]

During the 1976 probe into a UFO abduction in Maine a hypnotist named Dr. Herbert Hopkins was working on the case as a consultant. Late one night he received a phone call from someone claiming affiliation with a New Jersey-based UFO investigating organization. The caller wished to meet with Hopkins to discuss the kidnapping. Despite the late hour the doctor unhesitatingly told him to come on over, and only later did it dawn on him how odd was this instant acquiescence to meet with a total stranger late at night. Nor did he give a second thought (until later) to his guest's arrival only seconds after the phone call.

The visitor was dressed as if in mourning. His shoes, suit and tie were tar-black. His unnaturally pale face and head were utterly hairless, lacking even eyebrows and eyelashes. He wore red lipstick. Later, Hopkins could not understand why none of this struck him as unusual at the time. He gave his guest a detailed description of the abduction and subsequent investigation. After awhile the stranger began to slur his words, and his movements became slow and uncoordinated. Rising unsteadily he announced, "My energy is running low. Must go now. Good-bye."

Only after the man went reeling out the door did realization of the visit's strangeness hit the stunned doctor. Hopkins later learned the research group his visitor had mentioned was nonexistent.

Although this individual *was* dressed in black, he was not a run-of-the-mill "Man in Black." MIB usually travel in threes, wear sunglasses, have Hispanic or Oriental features, and try to intimidate UFO witnesses and researchers into keeping quiet about their experiences and findings. [2]

Perhaps Hopkins' mystery man was on some sort of fact-finding mission.

The MIB are a perplexing enigma within a riddle. Those attempting to unravel the UFO mystery also feel the need to figure out who these beings are, as well as their true objectives. If they truly wish to hinder research, they may be doing a better job than we realize. Even when their threats go unheeded, the mere existence of these somberly clad people has the effect of distracting ufologists from their work. Interestingly, despite all the menacing adjurations of the MIB, no cases in which they have actually used violence are on record (notwithstanding the fact that no one can account for the whereabouts of Harold Dahl.)

Persistent suspicions that MIB are government agents participating in a federally sponsored UFO coverup are difficult to substantiate. The bizarre appearances and antics of these characters seem too weird for them to be feds, unless, of course, they have planned it this way to help allay suspicion. [3]

There *were* an inordinate number of sudden deaths among those involved in the Puget Sound case. Two Air Force officers, named Davidson and Brown, who were gathering data on the incident were killed in a plane crash while leaving Tacoma. Another investigator, Tacoma newsman Paul Lance, died unexpectedly soon afterward.

Private pilot Kenneth Arnold's sighting of a formation of gleaming metallic, crescent moon-shaped UFOs hurtling over the Cascade Mountains three days after Dahl's encounter, was the first widely reported spotting of the modern era. Arnold, too, participated in the Puget Sound investigation, and narrowly avoided dying young himself when his plane's engine cut out without warning over Oregon. Arnold's cool head and flying ability brought him down safely, but what was going on?

The MIB could not be conclusively linked to these tragedies, but suspicions tend to linger. Those who believe the government is responsible point to instances in which MIB-like characters claim to be with such organs as the Air Force or Central Intelligence Agency. No CIA agent would freely identify himself as such, and an imposter in military uniform is easy to expose. Surely if the Feds are attempting to keep a lid on the UFO mystery they would be more efficient and believable.

It is also noteworthy that in most cases in which persons sight flying saucers the MIB do *not* appear afterward. This inconsistency makes their true motives and identity even harder to establish.

In the summer of 1968 author Brad Steiger received a complaining phone call from a journalist friend whose attempts to investigate that year's far-reaching UFO flap had dead-ended because all the witnesses had been intimidated into silence. The man accused Steiger, his fellow writer and UFO investigator John Keel, and

Steiger's Florida-based collaborator Joan Whritenour of threatening people to keep them quiet about their ufological experiences—very effectively, it appeared.

Steiger instantly realized that either somebody was spreading lies about him or his friends, or they were being impersonated. He knew *he* certainly had not participated in this improper and highly uncharacteristic activity. He also knew for a fact that neither he or Keel had even been in the areas in question at the time the threats were made.

On the very afternoon he phoned Steiger the irate newsman had had a chance encounter with three odd-looking individuals and had witnessed their attempts to extort silence from a UFO sighter. Arriving at a farm to interview the couple living there he saw he had been preceded by three MIB who were "chattering at the farmer and waving a copy of this magazine in their hands and warning the man how Brad Steiger was warning all UFO sighters not to talk."

The reporter described the trio as short, deeply suntanned and wearing black suits and dark glasses. [4]

It could be that the majority of saucer sightings are staged in order to spawn any number of incorrect theories. Perhaps those witnessings that are followed up by the black suits are accidental and might lead to hypotheses that are on the right track. If so the MIB may be sent to head off this result by frightening observers into keeping quiet.

Of course this notion may be 180 degrees wrong, and the MIB might want the sightings *to be remembered.* They may insure this by telling the witnesses to forget what they saw, effectively employing reverse psychology.

The Men in Black and their motives are merely two of the unnumbered question marks riddling the WHAT and WHY of the flying saucer phenomenon. We will now explore some of those other question marks presently unknown. [16]

In 1960, NASA and the military announced Project Saint. This was a program in which specially equipped satellites would track and hopefully identify unidentified Earth orbiters. However, after the project's formation was revealed to the public the authorities fell silent on the matter, keeping any information they may have gleaned totally to themselves. [17]

The early days of manned space flight held several jolts for the infant space ministries. On May 15, 1963, while astronaut Gordon Cooper was making his fourth pass over Hawaii aboard his capsule Faith VII his radio transmission was abruptly drowned out by the powerful broadcast of a guttural voice speaking rapidly in a language that has never been identified.

The space channels being highly directional, the voice could only have come from a specially equipped aircraft circling or hovering directly over the dish antenna…unless it came from outer space. NASA had little to say on the matter, which would hardly seem expected had the interruption come from a familiar, easily identifiable source. Cooper also reported being accompanied by a glowing green object as he passed over Australia the next day. [18]

Unexplained "bogies" approached both Gemini IV and Gemini VII, and in the case of Gemini IV they came so close to the capsule that astronauts White and McDivitt feared they would have to take evasive action. [19]

Apollo XII was trailed by a UFO that temporarily knocked out the capsule's radio link with Houston. [20]

Skylab II had a 10-minute visit from an object that, for the whole time it was visible, was brighter than any of the planets or stars then in view. The astronauts estimated it loitered somewhere from 30 to 50 miles from them, making it impossible to identify. [21] The government had nothing to say.

High-level interest in saucers *has* been evident on occasion. The celebrated contactee of the 1950s and 1960s, Howard Menger, lived in High Bridge, New Jersey, an area frequented by UFOs. He claimed his "brothers from outer space" were mentally preparing him for some crucial task they had not yet revealed to him, that he frequently met with them in front of flabbergasted witnesses, and that he was from Saturn.

For several years he basked in the spotlight as Earth's foremost contactee. Then, on a television talk show in the early 1960s he dropped an interstellar bombshell.

It was all hallucinatory, metaphoric, erroneous and in general non-extraterrestrial. Later, in letters to publisher Gray Barker, who had printed Menger's book *From Outer Space to You*, Menger revealed it had all been a farce contrived by the Pentagon to learn how the masses would react to "confirmed" alien contact.[22]

If Menger was telling the truth about this governmental plot it would seem the powers-that-be take the saucers quite seriously. In January 1953 high-ranking members of the Central Intelligence Agency held a conference in Washington, D.C. to discuss the sudden proliferation of civilian saucer investigation organizations. The CIA feared these groups might become too influential with the populace should UFO sightings continue, and that these bureaus might begin to use their newfound political pull for subversive purposes. Although no overt CIA action against these organizations appears to have been taken, it was not long after this that media coverage of saucer news began to taper off, and for the first time the soon-to-be-familiar cry of "Cover-up!" was heard. [23]

In his book *The Gulf Breeze Sightings* contractor Ed Walters of Gulf Breeze, Florida describes a series of visits he received from silent, round UFOs that resembled gigantic, animated Christmas tree ornaments. He took a number of Polaroid photographs of them. Early on the morning of January 13, 1988 he had an unexpected visit from a pair of armed strangers claiming to be from "Air Force Special Security Services." One of them, calling himself "Agent McKathy," brandished a document with the heading *Material Seizure Warrant*, but did not let Walters read it.

The agents demanded the "photographs and negatives" Walters had made of the UFOs (where did they get the idea Polaroid cameras produce negatives?) When he told them he had already sent the photos to the *Miami Herald,* the two left, vowing to return if it turned out Walters had lied about the snapshots' whereabouts. Unless the strange duo were imposters it would appear our armed services (in ufological matters at least) are behaving in the brusque manner of a military dictatorship. Why? And if these men were phonies, whom did they actually represent?

American UFO theorist Tim Donovan also espouses the extraterrestrial hypothesis, and alleges heavy government involvement with aliens. Donovan cites data from a government informant codenamed "Falcon," featured in the October 1988 television special *UFO Cover-up? Live*. This program disclosed that President Harry Truman established an agency called Majestic 12 (Mj 12) in 1947 as a policy-making body to deal with what it believed were alien visitors.

Three of these creatures were allegedly held by the feds from 1947 to 1988. One was part of an exchange program in which humans voluntarily boarded saucers and traveled to the ufonauts' home world in the Zeta Reticuli star group. Furthermore, there are the decades-old rumors of several refrigerated corpses of saucerians killed in the famed Roswell, New Mexico crash. Donovan believes the 1947 crash was staged by the ufonauts to make them appear vulnerable and non-threatening, thereby avoiding a disruption of our society while paving the way for eventual overt contact. Some of this is consistent with ufological information from other sources, specifically Zeta Reticuli being the point of origin of at least some of the saucers. Betty Hill pinpointed this star system as her abductors' home.

Such governmental interest is nothing new. In November 1961, Air Force Intelligence initiated two secret projects, code-named Moon Dust and Blue Fly, to locate, impound and deliver to the USAF Foreign Technology Division any UFO that could be taken intact. It has been whispered that these UFO catchers had some success, but if so they were careful to not record (much less publicize) it. [24]

It is noteworthy that during the 1960s and 1970s the Air Force's Directorate of Operational Intelligence carried out a program to develop anti-UFO weapons. [25] Apparently something had convinced the flyboys that UFOs are not only real, but also a potential threat. Donovan is of the opinion that the government's long-suspected suppression of saucer reports stems from a fear that disclosure would compel a revolutionary overhaul and outright overthrow of current values and institutions. Judeo-Christianity and democracy would, in his opinion, be doomed by this revelation.*

* See Appendixes I & II

When author John Fuller investigated the 1965 Exeter sightings, Richard Hall of the National Investigations Committee on Aerial Phenomena, told him of the cover-up:

"The Air Force is constantly trying to knock down all UFO reports. They've clamped down the lid and issued denials of reliable sources repeatedly. This is our big battle. For instance we've got information to contradict the Air Force denial here. It's a nine-page report by the Oklahoma Department of Public Safety, outlining a sighting by the Carswell Air Force Base radar, and the reports are still going on. Reports from all over." [26]

2 Explorers

WHEN CONSIDERING THE STICKY questions of what the UFOs are and where they originate, the conclusion that comes quickest to most minds is that they are artificial interplanetary craft piloted by obviously intelligent beings more technologically advanced than us. They presumably would be coming from worlds at least marginally ecologically like ours, and their general motive for visiting would be the eternal quest for knowledge, so similar to what is now driving us into the cosmos in our simple, rickety spacecraft.

These conclusions were the first ones put forth by modern ufologists, who pondered the question from a viewpoint provided by strictly human logic. To mankind's brain UFOs being interstellar vehicles is the obvious answer because it is based on human motives, and is therefore easy to understand. Virtually anyone can grasp it, and there are also many indications seeming to support it.

In numerous instances saucer beings seem to have trouble breathing and/or appear intoxicated. Often these symptoms are alleviated by a pill the strangers take, or they subside on there own as if the saucerians were conditioned to acclimate to our atmosphere. [5]

Respiratory problems would be expected from someone used to breathing another planet's air, and if such a planet's atmosphere were more oxygen-rich and with less nitrogen than ours, then its inhabitants would indeed appear drunk after a brief time of inhaling Earth's air. Placing a human in an atmosphere with too little oxygen and too much nitrogen would definitely produce inebriation.

Skeptics who take for granted the distances between stars are too great to be traversed overlook our inability to see the technological future. What is impossible today could be possible next week, and commonplace a century from now. Any rookie physicist can take his calculator and mathematically "prove" it is impossible for bumblebees to fly. With this in mind why should it defy this thing we call "logic" that travelers from the stars could reach our planet?

In January 1950 *True* magazine published a well-researched investigative article titled *The Flying Saucers Are Real!* by retired Marine Corps Major Donald E. Keyhoe. His aviation background and high-level contacts in the military insured that his work had a great deal of informative quality, giving him high standing in journalism. His opinions were taken quite seriously.

Keyhoe's article was a far-reaching sensation. His research had led him to conclude the UFOs were interplanetary alien craft, and that the Air Force was attempting to hush up saucer reports. He based his case on the Air Force's chaotic attempts to investigate the phenomenon via its recently disbanded Projects Grudge and Twinkle, and on how none of his heretofore cooperative, highly placed sources would discuss UFOs with him. Keyhoe outlined his belief that the military was trying to cover up something of great importance for fear of a potential *War of the Worlds* replay causing widespread panic. [6]

If Grudge and Twinkle *had* yielded substantial information that their sponsors were keeping to themselves this data seems never to have reached Keyhoe. He did hint in his article that his conclusions were based on circumstantial evidence, and that the sources that confirmed to him the existence of UFOs were unnamed. [7] Then, two months after printing Keyhoe's piece, *True* released another ufological expose`. This one had concrete documentation.

This article was written by Navy Commander Robert B. McLaughlin, a guided missile expert, who wrote of a strange experience he and a team of engineers had while launching a high-altitude research balloon at White Sands proving grounds in New Mexico. On April 24, 1949 the group, as a precaution, had lofted a small weather balloon to determine wind patterns. As a technician trained his theodolite on the balloon something cut across his field of vision.

It was a white object, elliptical and over 100 feet in diameter. It was traveling five miles per second (18,000 miles per hour) at an altitude of 56 miles.

McLaughlin flatly stated his belief that what he had seen "was a flying saucer, and further, these disks are spaceships from another planet." A group of well-trained, well-equipped and experienced military technicians and engineers made very credible witnesses, especially when it was revealed the Navy had approved McLaughlin's article for publication. Correspondingly, his clearly stated opinion on the matter carried weight, and on May 11, 1950 the previously missing piece of evidence—a clear photograph—came to be. [8]

It was about 7:30 in the evening when a farmer named Paul Trent heard his wife scream outside their McMinnville, Oregon home. A metallic, pie-shaped aircraft was cruising slowly overhead. Trent grabbed a camera and snapped two shots of the saucer silhouetted against the overcast sky. The Trents showed the pictures to a few friends, and about a month later allowed them to be printed in a local newspaper. For decades the snapshots and negatives were subjected to intense scrutiny and progressively more sophisticated computer analysis. These examinations consistently indicated the photos to be likenesses of a flat-bottomed flying disk approximately 100 feet in diameter, three-quarters of a mile from the camera.

However, this wealth of evidence did not convince everyone, and debunkers soon counterattacked. Donald H. Menzel was a professor of astrophysics at Harvard University when he embarked on his anti-UFO campaign in the early 1950s. Viewing ufology as nothing more than a study of superstition, and every sighting as error or fraud, Menzel assumed the role of champion of rationality in an era faddishly obsessed with something that did not exist.

He was particularly vindictive toward the "Lubbock Lights," formations of soft blue-glowing objects that regularly patrolled the skies over Lubbock, Texas in the summer of 1951. Texas Tech University Freshman Carl Hart, Jr. took several high-quality photographs of these objects on August 30. The Air Force analyzed these ordinary 35mm negatives and declared them genuine. Menzel had something to say about that.

Five days before Hart took his pictures three college professors had spotted a group of lights that twice passed overhead at extreme speed. Menzel argued that craft traveling at the velocity reported by these academians would have been moving much too fast to have been captured by Hart's humble Kodak. However, the objects seen by the professors were in several ways dissimilar to Hart's. The teachers' flight of UFOs whizzed over in a ragged pack at great speed, but those of five days later cruised slowly in an orderly, easily photographed V-shaped formation.

Menzel nevertheless dismissed all the Lubbock sightings as reflections of ground lights on temperature inversions "probably just over the heads of the observers," and *Look* magazine printed his opinions in its June 1952 issue. [10] Prior to that, *Life* magazine had featured in its April 1952 edition an article by a team of researchers and writers who advocated the extraterrestrial explanation.

Public interest in the subject reached its greatest intensity in the midst of all this pseudoscientific jousting when the storied 1952 summer UFO wave rocked the nation. Reports skyrocketed from the usual 10 to 20 per months to 68 on the night of August 13 alone. [11]

Americans wanted to be told what was happening, but nobody could prove or disprove much of anything. It was a frustrating situation that has persisted through the decades. The enigma, like the phenomenon from which it springs, endures. Meanwhile, Keyhoe's charges of a military cabal to keep the public ignorant of the UFO situation (or at least of its magnitude) was substantiated by the sudden implementation of Air Force Regulation 200-2, prohibiting personnel from divulging ufological information to the public. Later, the Joint Army-Navy-Air Force Publication of 1966 made public revelation by military personnel of any saucer contact/sighting described in its pages a crime within the military. [12]

Considering the priority and resources the services were placing on keeping a close eye on the Soviets at this time, however, it is questionable whether any conspiracy by the armed forces to squelch UFO reports could have been as far-reaching and effectively imposed as Keyhoe seemed to think. Not impossible, perhaps.

Nevertheless the relative paucity of saucer information to reach the public after the early 1950s (indicating *some* sort of censorship) gave rise to civilian-run investigating organizations. The Aerial Phenomena Research Organization, the Civilian Saucer Investigation, and the National Investigations Committee on Aerial Phenomena (of which Keyhoe was a member) all set out to dig up, investigate and publish UFO news wherever they could.

The extraterrestrial advocates were buoyed by an October 1958 event when radar tracking sets at Cape Canaveral, Florida began picking up strong radio transmissions from some unidentified device traveling toward the moon from the Earth. The signals could not be identified or translated, and whatever was sending them was alternately decreasing its speed, and then accelerating in a way then impossible for terrestrial spacecraft. First detected about 3000 miles out from Earth, it was tracked through several velocity changes before it abruptly changed course away from the moon and hurtled off into deep space. For three more hours this cryptic beacon continued to radio its nonsensical broadcasts back to Earth, where teams of befuddled aerospace technicians listened as the airings slowly faded into the distance. [13]

In December 1957 Dr. Luis Correlas of Venezuela's Communications Ministry photographed something closely following Russia's Sputnik II satellite. Then, in January 1960, two large unidentified satellites turned up in polar orbits. They were much bigger than anything so far launched by the U.S. or USSR. A few weeks later the National Space Surveillance Center found another enigmatic something-or-other in orbit. [14]

In those days the scarcity of manmade satellites made keeping track of them a fairly simple task. Yet none of these unidentified orbiting objects was ever explained, and both superpowers spent a great deal of time wondering how the other launched and maintained these mysterious machines. What if neither the Russians or NASA placed these chunks of gleaming metal in the heavens? Someone else must have.

When the Soviets shot Sputnik II aloft carrying the first living creature sent into space by humanity, the dog Laika, the capsule got more and closer scrutiny than expected. On December 18, 1957, 16 days after launching, Corrales was tracking

Sputnik (and its by then-dead occupant) from Caracas. After making a time-exposure photograph of the capsule, Corrales discovered it had a traveling companion. Sputnik's path appeared as a straight white streak on the photo, and alongside this white line there was another. The trail was only one-seventh the length of the capsule's, and showed a clearly defined course change where the object had veered away from Sputnik, and then returned to its side.

Scientists who examined the photo and its negative released this statement:

"It cannot be a double exposure, for the stars would have also registered double images on the film, and they did not. It cannot be an internal reflection, for the path is not the same as the one left by Sputnik. It is not a scratch on the film, for examination under magnification reveals it is a precipitation of the emulsion on the photographic material, which is accomplished by light alone. The camera photographed something that we cannot identify…if the luminous trail running parallel to the satellite's trail is the path produced by another body, and if it became luminous during a short period of time, we would be making a hypothesis hard to prove. [15]

The possibility that unidentified satellite probes are monitoring us is undeniable. At an extremely high *Trojan* orbit (approximately 240,000 miles) a transmitting beacon would be at the same distance as the moon. This would free it from the orbit-destroying gravitational tug-of-war between Earth and moon that limits the life spans of *our* artificial satellites. It would be able to circle us at an undetectable distance for centuries.

If a bug from beyond has been overhead for ages it must have kept a rather boring vigil before the early 20th Century. Nowadays, however, it may be hard-pressed to assimilate and report on the deluge of sundry transmissions saturating the space around our busy little world. If its makers are as impressed as we are with our technological advancement they may decide the time to introduce themselves is imminent, and our ongoing attempts to find someone "out there" to talk to may be rewarded.

A foretaste may have been received by English television viewers September 14, 1953 when the logo and call letters of TV station KLEE spontaneously appeared on screens throughout the British Isles. The station was unfamiliar to those watching, and several quizzical Britons photographed their televisions during the odd broadcast.

When the British Broadcasting Corporation (BBC) heard of the occurrence and commenced investigating, it learned that KLEE had been a station in Houston, Texas. Under certain freak conditions video transmissions have been known to travel such abnormal distances, but the most shocking part of this incident was that KLEE had gone off the air in 1950. At the time its powerful signal blanketed Britain, KLEE had not made a broadcast in three years. The possibility of an elaborate (and seemingly pointless) hoax was ruled out by the fact that it was technologically impossible.

At the conclusion of the fruitless official inquiry, a BBC official told reporters:

"We are confronted in this instance with a set of circumstances which are at variance with the accepted knowledge of television transmission. It is unthinkable that these signals could have been circling the Earth for the time since that station last broadcast them. It is physically impossible that they could have been reflected to us by chance from any celestial body at such a vast distance. That leaves us with one possibility, however bizarre, that these signals were transmitted to us purposefully and intelligently from a source and for a purpose.

In the autumn of 1985 a couple of Stanford University research scientists demonstrated a technique they called "remote viewing" (also known as "scannate") for the federal Office of Science and Technology. The method involves using psychics to pinpoint the locations of nuclear submarines worldwide. The psychic (referred to as the "viewer" in this Washington, D.C. experiment) not only managed to locate several subs and give their coordinates (all were great distances from Washington,) but also detected a saucer craft hovering above one of them. The military's officially long-dormant interest in UFOs began to reawaken. In February 1987 the Army, Air Force, National Security Agency and the Defense Intelligence Agency jointly formed the Unidentified Flying Object Working Group. [27]

From the beginning the outfit was extremely clandestine. When its leader, Army Colonel Harold Phillips, finally took a call from a determined reporter he flatly denied any knowledge of its existence. Military concern over UFOs was nothing new, of course, but beginning back in the autumn of 1975, mysterious aircraft began showing an uncomfortable interest in the Air Force's caches of nuclear weapons, particularly those in Canada and the northern U.S. This resulted in a series of Security Option Three Alerts at northern tier bases. In some cases unidentified helicopters buzzed arsenals. [28]

An alarmed North American Air Defense Command (NORAD) distributed an aptly titled brief *Suspicious Unknown Air Activity*, to its unit commanders, informing them of these elusive night fliers, and giving what few details were available. All preparations and reactions proved futile except for the quest to keep the public uninformed of all the frenzied activity in, around and above the most sensitive atomic armories in the north.

None of the intruders were ever identified or brought down despite the best efforts of the world's most sophisticated defense network. After eight months of this maddening cat-and-mouse the bogies disappeared, as unidentified and untouched as ever. It was almost as if somebody had been ascertaining our military capabilities and inabilities...or *showing us.*

The armed forces, fearing an imminent, very real war of the worlds, quietly commenced mobilizing. However, this time at least, the reconnaissance (?) flights were all that showed, and nothing menacing ensued. One cannot, in fact, help but wonder how the populace might have reacted to an interstellar invasion. [29]

Donovan points to how for centuries dictators have taken advantage of public fear of an outside threat in order to seize or consolidate power. In this case a worldwide saucer panic could conceivably give extremists the vehicle with which to take charge on an unprecedented, international scale and set up a totally secular, fascist government.

Donovan notes the skeptical reaction of ufologist Jerome Clark, head of the Chicago-based Center for UFO Studies, to the widely reported autumn 1989 report of a landed UFO with occupants in the city of Voronezh, Russia. If this sighting was farcical it could have been an example of a fading authoritarian regime, hoping to reverse growing trends toward independence and democracy, staging a saucer incident in hopes of playing on xenophobic fears of extraterrestrials in order to rally the populace around a dying central government.

The case for governmental cover-up is strong. As far back as 1952 the head of the Office of Scientific Investigation (a department of the CIA,) Edward Tauss, distributed an internal memorandum containing this illuminating passage:

"As long as a series of reports remains 'unexplainable' (interplanetary aspects and alien orientation not thoroughly excluded from consideration) caution requires that intelligence continue coverage of the subject...It is strongly urged, however, that no indication of CIA interest or concern reaches the press or public, in view of their alarmist tendencies." [30]

It could be that alarmist tendencies are not entirely inappropriate in dealing with UFOs. Late on the night of April 22, 1976 policeman George Wheeler was watching a huge saucer from his patrol car outside the hamlet of Elmwood, Wisconsin. He was describing the craft as "...bigger than a two-story house" over his car radio to a dispatcher when a blue ray shot from the object and engulfed the car, blowing out its electrical system and knocking Wheeler unconscious.

He spent the next six months in and out of hospitals, seeking relief from excruciating pain in his head, arms and legs, and insisting to doctors that he was suffering from radiation poisoning. They could find no trace of radioactivity in their agonized patient, nor could they diagnose the cause of his constant pain. Neither could they explain why, six months after the UFO zapped him, Wheeler collapsed and died. [31]

Donovan postulates that all civilizations eventually metamorphose into totalitarianism ala *Brave New World*, but that an extremely advanced level of technology (not yet attained on Earth) will be required for it to become worldwide and permanent. He outlines a scenario in which outworlders implanted Christianity centuries ago in order to suppress authoritarianism for as long as it takes for our technical development to reach a level where an all-powerful worldwide government is feasible. Without being technologically capable of exercising total control over everyone and everything, dictators have so far in Earth history been premature and temporary.

Christianity is antithetical to the totalitarian, power-oriented spirit, thereby long helping to stifle it. Donovan construes this as evidence in favor of his theory. He believes aliens wish to remain unknown for the time being because we are still too primitive for their master plan to be implemented, but that by the mid-21st Century the applied sciences will have advanced to the point that a central fascist government will be capable of ruling *every human* via high-tech surveillance and resultant overall control. By this point democracy and religion will have out-lived their usefulness, and be forcibly discarded. Extraterrestrials will introduce our planet into the ranks of the galaxy's superworlds, in which humanity itself, through ultra-technology, will become god.

As for Christianity being antagonistic toward science on occasion when it contra-dicted accepted doctrine (e.g. Galileo and Darwin) the church still did not impede science and invention. These, in fact, generally flourished in the Christian West, beginning in the Medieval period. It could be that this hypothetical guiding/con-trolling influence has been methodically explaining itself to us for ages. A human cannot effectively, directly communicate with a much lower life form such as a mouse. Apart from the colossal difference in intelligence, there is the mismatch in life spans. A mouse three years old is as rare as a man of 100.

Let us picture a setting in which a theoretical lab technician decides to explain to his experimentation rodents something fairly complex even by human standards, and that these are specimens drawn from an exceptionally gifted strain of mouse, capable of keeping written records and passing oral descriptions on to its proge-ny. By the time one group of mice begins to grasp one part of the intricate matter their master is teaching them, they would be dying of old age. Still, they would have passed their findings and conclusions on to the next generation, which, armed with this head start, would carry its ancestors' academic quest closer to clarification. Each crop of offspring would die being more knowledgeable than its sires, with the dynasty gradually working toward total comprehension of the sticky problem.

After 15 or 20 years a final class of researcher rodents would achieve mastery of the formula their predecessors had attacked. Yet it would be the very same human lab technician who initiated the teaching process who would still be hov-ering over them, patiently, unerringly guiding them to enlightenment.

In this script we are the mice, and the task we have been laboriously undertaking for ages is solving the saucer enigma. Let us hope that learning the identity and motive(s) of the mysterious lab technician is at least part of the solution. Donovan believes we are due to find out within the next few decades. His scenario allegedly reveals how through the centuries extraterrestrials have occasionally used their advanced technology to perform events that to us appear as godlike and miraculous. We have attributed these events to divine entities, thereby bolstering religion and retarding fascism from becoming too widespread. This genre of performance may have been exemplified by the spectacular series of "miracles" at Fatima, Portugal in 1917.

On May 13, Lucia Abobara, 10, Francisco Marto, nine, and seven-year-old Jacinta Marto were playing in a field outside Fatima when a bright flash of light in the cloudless sky startled them. They saw a brilliantly illuminated sphere hovering over an evergreen sapling. Within the transparent globe was an entity wearing a glowing white robe, and whose features shone with a blinding light.

"Don't be afraid. I won't hurt you," the elemental said in a low, feminine voice. "I come from heaven. I come to ask you to come here for six months in succession at the 13th day at this same hour. Then I will tell you who I am and what I want, and afterward I will return a seventh time." She reminded them to say their rosaries and pray for world peace. Then the sphere and its ethereal occupant soundlessly floated away. [32]

For never-explained reasons Francisco saw the globe and its inmate, but unlike the two girls he heard nothing. The three ran home and told their families of their encounter, but the adults shrugged it off as just another attention-getting ploy from this precocious trio who for months had been reporting sporadic visits from angels.

The entreaty to pray for peace was very significant at this time. Nations were using such terrifying new weapons as airplanes, tanks, submarines, machine guns, long-range artillery and poison gas to butcher millions of young men on flaming battlefields stretching from the North Atlantic to France to the Russian steppes to East Africa. Could this mystical chapter being written in sedate, neutral Portugal have been aliens using their superior ability to appear in a dazzling display of godlike majesty? Were they strengthening Christianity to prevent wartime stresses in neighboring countries from precipitating a total breakdown of Western values and a widespread emergence of totalitarianism? If so, all the ufonauts needed for this ploy to succeed was for word of its unfolding to spread. It did.

Despite the incredulity the children encountered within their own families, word of their strange encounter got around, and a group of about 50 curious and devout townspeople accompanied the youngsters to the field on June 13 for their next scheduled audience with "The Lady." The onlookers saw nothing out of the ordinary as the children knelt and spoke to something invisible, but did notice a distinct buzzing sound consistent with modern, low-flying UFOs.

On July 13, the blind and crippled in the considerably larger crowd begged the children to ask for a miracle of healing. Lucia did so and later reported the Lady told her:

"Continue to come here every month. In October I will tell you who I am and what I wish, and will perform a miracle so that everyone will have to believe. When you see a night illuminated by an unknown light, know that it is the great sign that God shall give you that He is going to punish the world for its crime. To prevent this I come to ask for the consecration of Russia. If they will listen to my requests, Russia will be converted and there will be peace." [33]

The Lady also told the children a secret (presumably a prophecy) that they took to their graves. When questioned about it Lucia would only say that it would "…be good for some. For others bad."

No information could be obtained from the entity on August 13 because Lucia, Francisco and Jacinta had been taken to nearby Ourem and imprisoned by a high-ranking government official determined to prove the whole affair was a hoax. Even when threatened with death the children refused to recant their claims of celestial visitors.

Back at Fatima a crowd estimated at 6000 saw a brilliant flash of light in the sky, then watched a small, transparent cloud drift down to momentarily rest atop the evergreen. Simultaneously the onlookers' faces were bathed in multi-colored light.

By the time the children were found and freed it was August 19. They immediately returned to the field and spoke briefly to the Lady in what was evidently a rather uneventful meeting. The September 13 rendezvous was also rather low-key. When the children went into their trance the sun dimmed noticeably.

The next month, however, saw an overwhelming multitude (estimates claimed 70,000) attend. The Lady's earlier promise of a miracle was on everybody's mind. Scores of newsmen carried cameras, including an assortment of simple, hand-cranked movie cameras. However the low clouds and pounding rain were not conducive to photography.

The trio of young prophets and their parents, surrounded by a sea of umbrellas, waited by the little evergreen. Shortly after noon the children suddenly gaped at something in the heavens only they could see. The Lady was there, and she held an infant in her arms. She told the youngsters she was called the Lady of the Rosary. She also said the European war would soon end. At this point the throng suddenly shrieked in horrified fascination as a gigantic silver disk dropped from the clouds and descended toward the mass of humanity.

Halting its descent the object commenced steering an erratic, bobbing course just under the cloud ceiling. All the time the saucer spun at an incredible speed while changing colors. Dropping yet lower the UFO passed barely over the heads of the terrified, praying pilgrims. A peculiar, cobweb like substance drifted down throughout the spectacle, but dissolved instantly upon landing. Observers as far as 25 miles away later claimed to have seen the disk as it performed its air show.

A huge gap appeared in the overcast and a bright light that most in the crowd at first took to be the sun shone through the opening, but it quickly became evident this was not the sun. Among the onlookers was Professor Almeida Garret from Coimbra University. He described the circular shape as:

"A disk of very definite contour. It was not dazzling. I don't think it could be compared to a dull silver disk, as someone later said at Fatima. No. It rather possessed a clear, changing brightness, which one could compare to a pearl. It looked like a polished wheel. This is not poetry. My eyes have seen it. This clear disk suddenly began turning. It rotated with increasing speed. Suddenly the crowd began crying with anguish. The 'sun,' revolving all the time, began falling toward the Earth, now reddish and bloody, threatening to crush everybody under its fiery weight." [34]

A polished wheel? Shades of Ezekiel!

A blast of heat erupted from the hole in the clouds and swept over the crowd, instantly drying tons of rain-soaked clothing, and the saucer ascended into the overcast. The show was over. Many blind, lame and otherwise handicapped persons later claimed to have been healed, and the entire Fatima episode was duly accorded the status of a truly miraculous appearance of the Virgin Mary. Yet, close analysis throws doubt on this conclusion.

Lucia had been having sporadic visits from strange apparitions for a full two years before the dramatic climax in the autumn of 1917. In the summer of 1915 she and her friends were approached by a glowing, transparent entity who asked them to join him in prayer. In keeping with their strict Catholic background the children complied until the figure, who resembled a boy of about 15, slowly faded into nothingness. More such encounters followed until the culminating appearance of the Lady, who, significantly, never claimed to be the mother of Jesus.

This sequence of events closely resembles the experiences of contemporary con-tactees, who generally are repeatedly visited by ufonauts in preliminary, tentative contacts long prior to being fully inducted into their ufological situations. Assum-ing Lucia's specters were saucerians, they seem to have tailored their likenesses to appear as angels and saints to their young, credible spokesperson, particularly regarding the Catholic faith, to which she was devoted.

There is virtually no chance that Fatima was a series of true acts of God. Consider the following: It is very difficult to make sense of the vague statement, "If they listen to my requests, Russia will be converted…" It seems unlikely this unnamed "they" ever heard any requests from the Fatima apparition simply because even if the Lady did make any requests that the children understood (which does not appear to have been the case—no records of clearly stated entreaties seem to have survived,) to whom were they to have been delivered, and by whom?

It seems a reasonable assumption that the spectacular Fatima events must have been heard about in Eastern Europe, but considering what was happening there at that time it seems the affair had no effect. The revolution was underway, the European war had gone badly for the Russians, and the members of the last Tsarist dynasty, the Romanovs, were soon to be executed as their regime crumbled. All this was a distant cry from Christian conversion. Besides all the bloodshed in itself being decidedly un-Christian, it had the final effect of putting Holy Russia out of business and spawning the Communist Soviet Union. No Christian influence there. Despite word of its occurrence and relevance presumably having arrived in some form in the area in question the Fatima extravaganza was, in most un-Christlike fashion, a complete failure if the "conversion of Russia" truly was its aim.

The second part of the statement is equally noteworthy. The Lady said, "...everyone will have to believe." Everyone will *have* to believe? An unshakeable tenet of Christianity is that belief in and acceptance of the Lord's gift of salvation is the quintessential act of freewill. Nobody *has* to believe. Nobody can be forced to become a Christian. Whatever the Lady was alluding to could not have been Christian salvation, and it is difficult to imagine what else a true messenger of the Creator would have had in mind.

The healing blast of heat is another problem. There is no biblical precedent for it. During His earthly ministry Jesus Christ never used heat in His innumerable healings. It has, however, been observed and felt in association with healings by modern UFOs.

Most telling against a theistic explanation for Fatima, however, is that the Holy Trinity apparently was never even mentioned by the entities. The children and others in the predominantly Catholic throngs of onlookers predictably assumed the Lady to have been the Virgin Mary (complete even with a "Baby Jesus" at her last showing,) but she never directly identified herself as such. Why? She instead called herself the "Lady of the Rosary," a name not found in the Holy Scriptures. If she was indeed Mary the mother of God why did she not identify herself as such instead of using an evasive alias?

The entire Fatima experience smacks of having been a gigantic put-on by some-one who felt a need to give humanity's religious convictions a widespread boost, and it is here that Donovan's theory would apply. The First World War helped sire totalitarian movements. By 1917 the ETs may have begun to fear the upheaval might imperil traditional western values, as was already happening in Russia. Fear of a potential international Communist takeover (technologically premature totalitarianism) could have spurred the aliens to action, prompting them to ap-pear in godlike splendor at Fatima. Their emergence in sedate, neutral Portugal meant that the hordes of witnesses the event required would be in no danger of becoming incidental victims of the world war. Although the observers were at a safe distance from combat, their presence and vast numbers would insure the incident was reported to the whole world. Also the government and, especially, the press, less encumbered by war concerns and coverage of combat than the belligerent nations, would be able to devote greater attention to the goings-on outside Fatima.

Although the extraterrestrials' theoretical master plan for Earth would feature the eventual worldwide triumph of totalitarianism (a similar situation is outlined in the Revelation of St. John,) 1917 was far too early. Technology had a long way to go before it was possible for every human to be totally controlled by a central authority. Something had to be done to stop this from happening. Ergo, out-worlders may have staged Fatima to give a revival to dictatorship-stifling religion.

Although it is *this* writer's fervent belief that Christianity was not implanted by ufonauts, and Jesus Christ was sent by the one true God as the savior of mankind, Fatima does appear to have been a production by somebody who wished to bol-ster religion, but whose imperfect knowledge of Christian doctrine and vernacular (or perhaps an unwillingness to brazenly claim to be Almighty God) seems to have led to the discrepancies between what happened at that Portuguese town in 1917 and what *should* have happened had those events been actual acts of the Holy Spirit. If Donovan is correct it appears the alien long-range plan just happens to be the same as the Lord God's.

Revelation portends the eventual emergence of globe-blanketing fascism, but in 1917 the time had not yet come. Donovan's hypothesis provides a plausible explanation for Fatima's events (which so far have remained confusing because of their extremely bizarre nature,) and for why they happened when they did. His is a secular viewpoint that provides possible illumination on an affair (Fatima) that has long been suspected of having a ufological connection, but as an event was so outlandish as to be incomprehensible. The actual reason that Donovan alleges was the purpose of the affair remained undetected by us—as would presumably have been the perpetrators' intention. There have been scattered Fatima-like phenomena since 1917, usually on a smaller scale, but always involving innocent, believing children.

From 1937 to 1945 a phantasm calling itself the Queen of the Universe manifested itself to four German girls. Living in the village of Heede, Susanna Bruns, Greta and Maria Ganseforth and Anna Schulte, all between 12 and 14, repeatedly communed with this wraith, who implored them to "Pray, pray, pray much, especially for the conversion of sinners." [35]

Nazi Germany was a prime example of what Donovan calls Premature Resurgent Holism (fascism,) and the Queen (another name not found in the Bible) could have been an agent sent by our guiding extraterrestrials to counteract the effects of National Socialism. German anti-Nazi factions did function during Hitler's regime. The clandestine student humanitarian organization called the White Rose, and the 1944 Cologne peace demonstrations played a part in damaging German morale and hampering the Nazi war effort. The influence of the Queen of the Universe and her proselytes may have been at least partly responsible for the collapse of the Third Reich and its technologically premature aspirations. After Germany's defeat the Queen ceased to appear. There were still plenty of sinners for the children to pray for after the end of hostilities, so why would she have departed unless her job was done? Perhaps after the threat posed by Hitler was removed she no longer cared about the salvation of the lost. Again, this does not sound like the actions of a genuine messenger from the Lord.

June 18, 1961 was a Sunday, and three young girls, Mary Mazon and Jacinta Gonzales, both 12, and Mary Gonzales, 11, were shooting marbles just outside the hamlet of Garabandal in northern Spain near the French border. They suddenly became aware of being watched by an "angel." He resembled a boy of nine or 10, wore a long blue robe, had a small face, black eyes and "fine hands and short fingernails." He radiated an aura of power, and the girls got the distinct impression he was very strong. A bright halo surrounded him, and as the entranced youngsters looked on, he faded wordlessly into nothingness.

Two days later the girls were terrified and temporarily blinded by a dazzling burst of light that erupted in front of them as they walked along a path outside Garabandal. Soon after this the three began going into long trances in which they would see and communicate with a divine lady. Kneeling with their heads thrown back they would stare bug-eyed heavenward for hours, completely oblivious to the crowds of faithful surrounding them. At times, evidently summoned by some unknown force, they would simultaneously awaken in their separate homes in the middle of the night and rush to rendezvous with the spirit. [36]

The girls experienced their most remarkable rendezvous July 2, 1961. It was about 6:00 p.m. when they met and entered their trance. They were later able to provide a detailed description of the lady's appearance.

She had long, thin hands, a long, angular face "with a fine nose," her lips were "a bit thin," and she was rather tall. Her dark brown hair was parted in the middle. To her right there hovered a peculiar "square of red fire framing a triangle with an eye and some writing." The children described the writing as "an old Oriental script."

Providing this description was accurate, the lady could have just stepped off a modern flying saucer. Her appearance was strikingly similar to many confirmed ufonauts as described by contactees unconnected with the Garabandal case, and the triangle imagery is another frequently reported ufological element. On October 18, 1961 the lady gave the girls a rather startling message:

"We must make sacrifices. Do much penance. We must visit the Blessed Sacrament frequently, but first we must be good, and unless we do this a punishment will befall us. The cup is already filling, and unless we change, a very great punishment will befall us." [37]

Again, despite the obvious sincerity of the children involved, Garabandal does not appear to have been a series of true acts of God. Although (like at Fatima) thickly couched in Catholic-sounding jargon, the lady's messages were vague and disjointed. Rambling admonishments about how "we must be good" gave listeners no specific instructions of the type typical of Old Testament prophetic instructions and warnings. The recipients of the Garabandal specter's words were at a loss as to what exactly they were being told to do, but the seemingly divine experience nevertheless boosted their Christian faith.

Donovan postulates that we are being watched by a galactic organization of advanced worlds whose representatives are slowly, furtively guiding us toward the eventual summit of supercivilization. In the case of Garabandal they may have become concerned that the right-wing policies of Spanish dictator Francisco Franco were about to spread, perhaps to Spain's then-politically unstable neigh-bor France. The Garabandal entity was perhaps an alien (or projection of such) on a mission to strengthen the influence of Christianity and head off yet another outbreak of untimely totalitarianism.

If this scenario is accurate it would appear much of the world was teetering on the brink of dictatorship during the turbulent 1960s. The Garabandal apparition was appearing as late as 1965, while similar manifestations turned up in Cairo, on the Philippine island of Cabra, at St. Bruno, Quebec, and Urupan, Mexico. It is impos-sible to estimate how many similar occurrences may have gone unreported. [38]

It could be the exact opposite is true, and Earth was (as many believed at the time) on the verge of international anarchy in the 60s. As a unifying force, Christianity would have served to prevent the total breakdown of centralized government. Whereas worldwide Caesarism would have been a too-fast progression toward the ultimate goal of supercivilization, arriving there *before* we are technologically ready, anarchy would have *halted* our natural advancement toward the pinna-cle—equally disruptive to the extraterrestrials' hypothetical itinerary.

Donovan's theory could also explain the saucerians' repeated warnings against nuclear weapons. If we are being groomed for admission into an alliance of planets, our world (and hopefully ourselves) must be deemed of some value to this theoretical organization. It could be that our ever-vigilant watchers, who are now warning us against nuclear proliferation for reasons that may not be entirely altruistic, did not anticipate our development of atomic arsenals. Earth would not be of much use to anyone from anywhere were we to reduce it to radioactive charcoal. Ergo, we are being cautioned against the bomb by extraterrestrials whose master plan requires we be saved from ourselves.

One day in January 1954, people across the American Midwest were startled by a flat monotone voice from turned-off radios stating, "I wish no one to be afraid, although I speak from space, but if you do not stop preparations for war you will be destroyed." [39]

A masculine voice claiming to be, "Nacoma from the planet Jupiter" came through clearly on the 75-meter band on August 3, 1958. Ham operators around the world monitored Nacoma's broadcast. For two and one-half hours a warning of impending doom, spoken in turn in English, German and Norwegian, blanketed Earth. A fourth, unknown language also came through, and was generally assumed to have been the speaker's native tongue. Curiously, the transmission was not issued in Chinese or Russian. It was the most powerful such broadcast ever received, and despite its length it could not be traced. The FCC emphatically denied responsibility. [40]

If Tim Donovan is right, UFOs are more crucially significant than we ever have dreamed, and should we someday be presented with a membership application from a galaxy-wide federation, liberty and religious freedom will likely be the admission price.

If an outside ufological force is capable of inserting information and images into the human mind via a beam of electromagnetic energy without the person being aware of it, many sightings could be hallucinatory. A third party at such an event would be blind to the spectacle being focused upon the witness.

This appears to have been the case with the children at Fatima, Garabandal, Heede and elsewhere. They would gape in wide-eyed stupefaction for hours at what, to others, looked like empty sky. The occasional widely shared vision provided provide credibility to the childrens' claims.

Furthermore, the use of children as mouthpieces fits nicely into this script. Logical-minded adults are unlikely to suspect such young, inexperienced minds of having the guile to pull off such a convincing hoax. Therefore, the affair's apparent authenticity is reinforced.

Such activity would be a relatively simple matter for the highly advanced out-worlders Donovan believes have been manipulating us for centuries, and the proliferation of contactees could be yet another clue. The earliest known contactee was one William Denton of New England. Beginning in 1866, Denton claimed to be in telepathic communication with extraterrestrials who later flew him and his family to visit Mars and Venus. These saucerians rode craft constructed of aluminum. This was 20 years before the process for producing commercially marketable aluminum was developed. Denton described his friends as resembling ordinary humans. In general his experiences closely paralleled later cases. [41]

During the 1950s UFO contactees George Adamski, Truman Bethurum, George van Tassel, Ruth Norman and George King founded the Aetherius Society, Unarius Foundation and similar organizations. Gabriel Green, founder of the Amalgamated Flying Saucer Clubs of America, Inc., ran for President in 1960 and 1972. He also sought a California senate seat in 1972. Green garnered 171,000 votes in the 1972 senate race. [42]

These people claimed to be in telepathic and/or physical contact with benign beings, usually from other planets in our solar system—planets we subsequently discovered to be lifeless. These entities described the worlds from which they hailed as celestial Edens from which all serpents were banished, and that if the contactees spread the space peoples' cosmic gospel, Earth would also be transformed into a utopian paradise.

Although highly visible, these organizations were never taken seriously by a significant percentage of the American population, and by the 1960s the friendly neighbors from Venus, Mars and Saturn began to drop from sight. Unidentified Flying Objects commenced carrying less-benevolent passengers who were no longer particularly interested in the improvement and well being of humans. Reports of forcible abductions and medical/scientific experimentation began to multiply.

In his 1963 book *Flying Saucers and the Three Men*, ufologist Albert Bender chronicled how he abruptly shut down his international flying saucer research bureau in 1953 because he was pressured to do so by a band of saucerians who were supposedly headquartered at a base in Antarctica that Bender claimed to have visited. They had come to collect a rare substance from Earth's oceans. This mission would be completed in the early 1960s, Bender was told, and then he would be free to publish his fantastic story. Perhaps *those* ufonauts left. [43]

It was at this time that prominent Austrian psychoanalyst Wilhelm Reich began espousing a theory that UFOs are piloted by hostile extraterrestrials bent on robbing our planet of a precious substance he called "orgone." Reich described orgone as a life-giving energy found in our water, air and organic material. He was of the opinion that the saucers use orgone as fuel much as we use petroleum, and that orgone's "blue color" accounted for the blue lights often associated with UFO sightings. He further suggested alien spacecraft expel orgone in its used state, which he called "deadly orgone." According to Reich this waste matter causes illness in humans and desertification of Earth's surface. [44]

The extraterrestrial hypothesis has also been proffered to explain the saucer phenomenon not only in its modern form, but to account for the numerous sightings of ancient flying objects. In some cases these devices may have landed personages who did much more than merely communicate with primitive humanity.

Saucer investigator and prolific author John Keel theorizes that the almost-forgotten dynasties of god-kings who ruled major civilizations virtually worldwide from 5000 B.C. to 1000 B.C. could have been alien. Osiris and Isis in Egypt, Quetzalcoatl in Mexico, Oannes in Babylon, and the Wondjina in Australia all appeared suddenly and were granted absolute power by early peoples who were awed into reverence by these beings' displays of superhuman powers, discernment, wisdom, military and leadership skills.

Not all these god-rulers were humanoid. Oannes is said to have been an amphibious beast who emerged from the Persian Gulf to instruct the local savages in matters of agriculture, science, art, religion, mathematics, architecture and the written word. He never ate or drank with his subjects, and at dusk he would return to his watery abode, not reappearing until daylight. [45]

The late author and paranormal investigator Ivan Sanderson was an ardent believer in undersea civilizations whose inhabitants, it would seem, feel a need to remain hidden from us. These creatures apparently check up on us on occasion, perhaps from the periodically reported saucer-subs seen erupting from or splashing into the world's oceans. [46]

Oannes' teachings must have had an enormous impact. Those he enlightened went on to found, maintain and expand the highly advanced Babylonian empires of Hammurabi and Nebuchadnezzar, but what was he? He did not arrive in a fiery flying chariot, as one might expect of an ancient astronaut posing as a deity. He simply swam ashore, and later departed in the same manner, which obviously was not intended to attract a great deal of attention or awe.

Oannes could have been a very mortal representative of a technologically superior civilization that felt obliged to point our backward ancestors in what it perceived to be the right direction, and as unobtrusively as possible. Perhaps he never actually intended to be worshipped, but his influence was so great that his pupils could not resist according him veneration. Maybe there was an unseen, submerged craft dropping him off in the mornings, and awaiting him in the evenings. Perhaps he never ate or drank with his charges because he was from another world and could not digest Earth's foods.

In any case, if helping humanity toward a more exalted plane of sophistication was in fact the aim of these beings it does not appear to have gone according to plan. Ever since we began banding together in large numbers (which was largely a result of the influence of the god-kings) we have been killing each other off at a ghastly rate.

Realization of their unforeseen complicity in this state of affairs, and of their inability to undo it may have brought about the end of the god-ruler dynasties. They departed, never to return (at least in such a fashion.) By 1000 B.C. they were gone. [47]

If Keel's theory is correct, and it was extraterrestrials who taught and ruled our distant forebears and are now responsible for the UFO phenomenon, theirs is a mixed blessing. Besides steering us on a course that eventually led to modern medicine and food-producing techniques, they accelerated us to our present status of being martially capable of almost instantaneously destroying our world. It is a lesson in the value of non-interference.

Now that the god-kings are gone we have the more immediate matter of deciphering their motives and makeup in our modern world. Yet again we ask—What are they?

Keel contended that the saucers are primarily of electromagnetic nature, but artificial. He believed they are manipulated by a "Great Intelligence" with such total control over the electromagnetic and radio spectrums that it can control "patterns of frequency" in order to change from its normally invisible, energy state to appear to us as any physical being or conveyance it chooses.

Expanding this hypothesis to an international level, Keel outlined a scenario strikingly similar to the theistic concept of divine guidance. He noted how the multitudes of molecules in a drop of water are unaware of being scrutinized through a microscope, nor are they cognizant of anything outside their miniscule, wet world, which obviously is only a very minor part of an infinitely greater whole. 48 Perhaps Mother Earth is an enlarged version of that drop, and some lab technician is peering through a lens at us. What might be his motives?

Bud Hopkins believes that the intrusive ufonauts he investigated in the Kathie Davis case may be members of an otherworldly race that is crossbreeding with humans to make it possible for emissaries to live here, presumably secretly. Considering the remark made to Davis indicating these creatures are incapable of taking nourishment from any earthly substance, they may be attempting to produce hybrids who would not require noticeably foreign sustenance. Such a being conceivably could live among us unnoticed.

A second hypothesis presented by Hopkins is that this is a race in the midst of a severe genetic crisis, and is crossbreeding with humans in a desperate attempt at self-preservation through the infusion of fresh bloodlines. This possibility is supported by an image Davis was shown during one of her abductions. She saw what she was led to believe was an infant of her captors' race. It was emaciated and apparently dying, and Davis got the impression that what was being done to and with her was part of a large-scale operation to head off extinction.

The crossbreeding scenario is most strongly supported by the famous Antonio Villas-Boas case from Brazil. Villas-Boas, a 23-year-old farmer, was plowing a field on the night of October 15, 1957 when an egg-shaped flying machine abruptly landed and blocked his path. The tractor's lights died and it lost all power. The panicky farmer bolted, but covered only a few yards before a trio of gray overall-clad ufonauts tackled him. They wore helmets that covered everything but their eyes, and may have enabled the saucerians to breathe in an atmosphere toxic to them.

They dragged the kicking, gasping Earthman to their craft, stripped him naked and sponged him off with a clear liquid that may have been an antiseptic (or, as it turned out, aphrodisiac,) and took a blood sample from his chin. They then locked him in a room containing nothing but a couch, then pumped it full of "gray smoke" that nauseated and half-suffocated him.

The next act of this incredibly bizarre episode commenced with a door opening and admitting an exquisitely beautiful nude young woman. Her hair was blonde, but her pubic hair was red. Her arms were covered with freckles, her large blue eyes slanted outward, her flesh was very pale and her mouth was a thin slit. She had high cheekbones and was no more than four and one-half feet tall. When she embraced him he "clearly understood what she wanted."

During the ensuing sexual act her non-humanity was evident. Villas-Boas later complained of how "some of the grunts coming from that woman's mouth at certain moments nearly spoiled everything, giving the disagreeable impression I was with an animal."

Before leaving the room the woman pointed to her stomach, smiled and pointed skyward. Afterward the helmeted beings returned and gave the Brazilian his clothes, and then showed him around the ship before releasing him.

Villas-Boas was concerned that because he had no physical evidence his story would not be believed, so he kept it to himself for awhile. During the following months, however, he developed the full range of symptoms of radiation poisoning. Repeated medical examinations irrefutably established that his lost appetite, stabbing pains, burning eyes, headaches, persistent nausea and easily bruised flesh resulted from a hefty dose of radioactivity. It appeared it could only have been received during his otherworldly tryst.

Repeated investigations and interrogations by Brazilian military intelligence operatives found no flaws in his story. Somewhere, Antonio Villas-Boas may have a most unusual offspring.[49]

The noted phenomena researcher and prolific author Charles Fort was of the opinion that someone owns our planet and us along with it. Ivan Sanderson shared this belief. He suspected Earth is a farm and we are the crop. [50] This may have always been the case. The supposition that the beings who appeared to and were worshipped by early humans were extraterrestrials is nothing new, but their motives (especially their modern ones) remain elusive. These entities masqueraded as gods as centuries, and usually were not as benevolent as Oannes. They often demanded offerings and human sacrifices from their quivering disciples. They seemed to have a physical need for human beings, and the ancients were easily coerced into complying with the god-rulers' demands. [51] Yet as the ages passed, *homo sapiens* matured into more sophisticated creatures, and the cosmic ranchers may have felt it prudent to adopt a lower profile.

Possible indications of continued harvesting persist. In the mid- to late-1960s persistent rumors circulated on American college campuses that coeds were being systematically taken by saucerians, and the girls' relatives and acquaintances were simultaneously subjected to a long-range brainwashing technique that erased all memory of the missing students. [52]

Taking into account the huge numbers of persons who annually turn up missing in the U.S. alone, the possibility that not all of them are runaways or victims of foul play is not that incredible. Of course, all this takes for granted that UFOs are flown by sentient beings from another planet.

It may be notable that the saucers seem to have chronic mechanical problems. There are many cases in which they crash or explode—hardly the type of performance to be expected of machines manufactured by highly advanced technology. It is almost as if someone is trying to convince us that they and their vessels are physical matter from this present-day cosmos.

An English contactee, James Cook, claimed he was taken for a saucer ride on the morning of September 7, 1957. The crewmen were huge, about seven feet, and they told him their craft were only used near Earth because they could not operate in outer space. [53] There have been other such remarks by ufonauts, indicating their ships fly by "working against gravity." [54] There is no gravity to work against in the interstellar void, so how did they get here if they came from another planet?

Despite many seemingly obvious indications that UFOs are from other physical worlds, during the 1980s some leading ufologists began to suspect many sightings and contacts were being deliberately staged to mislead witnesses, who would then report and spread their incorrect assumptions. The extraterrestrial theory began to lose adherents.

It is undeniable that saucerians have always been fond of lying to the hapless humans they contact. When unsuspecting housewives, mail carriers, truck drivers or businesspersons see a gleaming astroship land and a singularly otherworldly being emerge and announce he/she/it is from Saturn or Venus or Ganymede or Zomdic, it is unsurprising the stupefied onlooker unquestioningly accepts this as the truth (particularly if the witness is unfamiliar with astronomy, as is usually the case.)

When experts later point out the impossibility of these points of origin, the contacted person is branded a liar, drunkard or schizophrenic. Thus the credibility of a sincere eyewitness is destroyed because he or she merely passed along what turned out to be lies from a deceitful ufonaut. Perhaps this is done to create and sustain the air of confusion and contradiction which has always surrounded ufology and is (unrealized by us) an effective smokescreen hiding someone's true objectives. We have already examined some of these hypothetical motives, and will look at others later.

The late, renowned astronomer Carl Sagan, in an attack on the extraterrestrial explanation, calculated that there should be about a million civilizations advanced enough for interstellar travel. If each of them desired to look in on all the others just once every 10 Earth years, it would have to launch 100,000 spacecraft annually for this purpose alone.

Sagan said that for Earth to be singled out for continuing visits, it must be pretty unusual by intergalactic standards. He summed up this reasoning in one of his speeches:

"This goes exactly against the idea that there are lots of civilizations around. Because if there are lots of them around, then the development of our sort of civilization must be pretty common, and if we're not that common, then there aren't going to be many civilizations advanced enough to send visitors." [55]

Sagan's belief that although technologically advanced extraterrestrial life must exist, it is not responsible for the UFO phenomenon is dependent on two assumptions: that his calculation of approximately one million worlds capable of sending out the craft is at least fairly accurate, and also that each of them would even feel the need to visit *all* the others at least once every 10 years. There is no way of knowing whether these speculations are valid.

Of course there is the possibility that our attempts to decide the validity of the ET explanation via human logic may the wrong approach. How can we be certain our notion of logic even applies in this matter?

There remains the possibility that if the saucerians (or even just *some* of them) possess a different kind of intelligence than ours, perhaps a type totally incompatible with human logic, all attempts to communicate are futile until one side figures out how the other side thinks. Who can guess how long this might take?

Some scientists are beginning to suspect that some cetaceans such as bottle-nosed dolphins may actually be sentient beings whose minds function in ways so far removed from ours that their self-consciousness has gone undetected. We have always known they are intelligent, but could it be they actually *think*?

We have never recognized another kind of intelligence against which to compare ours, so it has not occurred to most of us that other thought-awareness patterns may even exist. If we could gain access to and translate a nonhuman intellect to our way of thinking, we might open a long-distance line to *somewhere.*

Along these lines there could be planets inhabited by intelligent beings with ancient civilizations that, despite their advanced social and mental states, have no way of contacting us. Because dolphins are physically adapted to a totally aquatic existence, they are incapable of using tools. They must tailor their existence to fit within the restrictions of their environment rather than alter their habitat to suit their wants and needs as we do. Our kind of civilization is impossible for them to develop. [56]

On a world where the only sentient species is fettered by such a restriction there could be beings with an average IQ of 1000 who are totally unable to rule their own planet or communicate beyond their immediate vicinity. If tool-using ability only infrequently occurs in creatures of advanced intellect, the relevance of extraterrestrial life to ufology would be drastically reduced.

Furthermore, if there *is* merit in the extraterrestrial proposition we had better consider the possibility that at least some of the saucers are piloted by hostiles. Suppose these unfriendly beings come from a world with a totally different concept of time. They could have a lifespan of thousands of our years. If they are plotting a takeover, they may be doing so in a manner that is gradual even by their standards in order to usurp Earth and her resources (which may include us) easily and in an undamaged, usable state. In this scenario the covert invasion could have started no telling how many centuries ago and still be in its primary stages. This initial probing may be hidden in plain sight.

During the 1970s, mysterious letters purportedly from the planet Ummo began circulating throughout Europe, particularly France. The missives were intricate and articulate, dealing with a myriad of cosmic concerns. The French became so caught up in the excitement of this apparently imminent contact with an extraterrestrial civilization that the government from the prime minister on down became deeply concerned.

However, nobody ever came forward to claim responsibility for the letters, which were all that ever materialized from Ummo, and the French Intelligence Service (FIS) was unable to track down the senders. The government eventually turned the investigation over to civilian ufologists. After equally fruitless sleuthing they announced to a disappointed public that everybody had had the wrong idea. Even if Ummo exists, they said, it might not be an extraterrestrial realm, but (along with all of ufodom) part of a far-reaching socio-psychological phenomenon of some kind. It was an intriguing proposition that quickly caught on internationally. [57] Those who accepted this view decided UFOs are nothing but an unusually enduring, far-reaching fad which humankind has embraced with remarkable tenacity. Everyone loves a good mystery, and especially its solution. Could someone with a desire to make skeptics of us all have arranged the Ummo craze in order to convince as many of us as possible that the saucers are not even real, much less from other planets? This would well suit the aims of somebody affecting a long-term surreptitious takeover. We are unlikely to remain vigilant for a threat if we do not realize it exists.

Furthermore, the endlessly diverse descriptions provided by witnesses of UFOs and their passengers could be false clues planted by the saucerians to confuse and distract us from a creeping menace. It is a fact that ufologists have spent so much time trying to determine what the saucers are and where they come from that relatively little research has been devoted to the possible motives for their visits.

Actor Stuart Whitman was in New York and temporarily imprisoned in his 12th-story hotel suite by the Great Northeast Blackout. While sitting idly in the darkness he heard "a sound like a whippoorwill" outside his window. Looking out he saw two glowing disks, one orange, one blue, hovering. A loud voice rang out, giving Whitman a message of how we could expect worse consequences than power failures unless we learn to behave:

"They said they were fearful of Earth because Earthlings are messing around with unknown quantities, and might disrupt the balance of the universe or their planet. The blackout was just a little demonstration of their power. They did it with almost no effort. They said they could stop our whole planet from functioning." [58]

Was the blackout truly meant to impress and intimidate us into ceasing our dealing with "unknown quantities?" Was the accompanying message/warning deliberately given to somebody who not only was a victim of the colossal power failure, but also was in a position of high visibility, so as to insure its delivery to a large audience?

Yet the warning was too general to be of much use. It mentioned nothing specific, just the ambiguous caveat to avoid something called "unknown quantities." If these were authentic instructions they were too hazy for us to know how to go about following them.

The motives of beings with a different kind of intelligence would most likely seem nonsensical or misleading to us. Although this is a definite possibility, it might instead have been yet another attempt to throw us off the right track (or keep us from finding it in the first place) to learning who the ufonauts are and what they want here.   It could be that by legitimizing the saucer phenomenon by officially acknowledging its existence we might pave the way for serious international cooperative study and investigation, recognize a previously undetected peril, find some way to counteract it and save unborn generations of humanity from worldwide slavery or genocide. By preparing for the worst, we cannot be unpleasantly surprised.

To his dying day J. Allen Hynek, chairman of Northwestern University's astronomy department and for years the Air Force's scientific consultant on ufological matters, tirelessly maintained that ufology sorely needs to be shorn of its crippling "lunatic fringe" reputation. Only in this way can the discipline receive the respect necessary for it to be adequately explored as a legitimate scientific discipline, and one of inestimable value.

The revamping of our outlook on the natural world necessary for such an overhaul admittedly will be difficult, yet do we dare to not undertake it? Dr. Hynek asked, "Where do we go from here?" Let us hope the answer is forward. It looks suspiciously as if changing our general attitude toward the study of flying saucers is a significant hurdle on the most desirable path to the future.

Whitley Strieber came to wonder if his whole conscious existence was a mere cover for some other, hidden life. He speculates that his cryptic guests may be humankind's adult stage, which we all achieve upon physical death, and that we who are still in the flesh are larvae. Another possibility put forth by Strieber is that his ufonauts may be a sentient hive species with a communal intelligence, in contrast to our individualized minds. This would make them mentally formidable collectively, but confused, lost and not very quick-thinking individually. During his encounters he sensed that his abductors feared him, or perhaps his primitive but quick to learn and independently react human brain.

He also believed his saucerians exist in some other reality, and that the forms (bodies) in which they appear to us are used as vehicles, much as we use scuba gear and pressurized space suits. Perhaps they come from a parallel dimension that occasionally intersects ours.

3 Here, There and Everywhere

In August of 1887 a pair of highly unusual children emerged from a cave outside the Spanish village of Banjos. Hand in hand, they wandered into a field where some farmers were working. The youngsters had green flesh, wore clothing made of an unknown material, and addressed the astounded Spaniards in an incomprehensible tongue.

The pair were sequestered at the residence of a magistrate named Ricardo de Calno, where they almost starved to death due to an apparent inability to ingest any food offered them…until they discovered beans, which they consumed frantically. Despite this nourishment the boy sickened and died within a month. The girl recovered and worked as a servant in the de Calno home. In time her verdant hue faded somewhat, and she learned a few words of Spanish. The story she told further confused the situation. She claimed to be from a land with no sun, but perpetual dusk. However, if one crossed a large river near her crepuscular home he would find himself in a region of bright light. If earthly laws of physical science apply in wherever it is these children called home it would seem they came from a high latitude on a planet not tilted on its axis. The whereabouts of this world remain a total mystery.

She further described how she and her brother had heard a deafening sound, and the next thing they knew they were in a field in a place called Spain. The lost young creature passed away after five years without being able to clarify her situation. No race on Earth has green pigmentation or lives exclusively on beans. If these children were not denizens of another dimension, caught in a spatial overlap, then where *did* they come from? [59]

Such anomalous appearances of sentient, nonhuman beings have been paralleled by scattered vanishings.

On the afternoon of September 23, 1880 a farmer named David Lang was pleasantly wiling away a few idle moments with his family on the porch of his farmhouse outside Gallatin, Tennessee. Rising from his chair, Lang set out across his pasture to bring in his horses. At this moment a buggy carrying his friend, Judge August Peck, appeared on the road leading to the Lang home. As Lang strode across the field he suddenly vanished in full view of his family and Judge Peck.

The investigation into this perplexing tragedy lasted several weeks, and was totally futile. There was no hole or cave into which Lang could have fallen. No conventional explanation existed, and another eerie event 11 months later deepened the enigma, and perhaps offered a clue to investigators of a later period. The following August, Lang's son and daughter were crossing the pasture. As they passed the spot where their father had dissolved into nothingness the girl impulsively called out, "Father, are you anywhere around?" To their terrified fascination they heard his voice, as if from a great distance, crying out, "Help!"

For the next three days Lang was heard but not seen, desperately calling for assistance. Nobody could tell from what direction his cries were coming, but it was clear they were growing fainter as if he was receding into a distance. By the end of the third day they were no longer audible. [60]

A few years later police near London were mystified by the disembodied voice of a missing girl repeatedly sobbing, "I can't find the hole!" [61] These unfortunates could have blundered into temporary dimensional intersections from which they could not escape, but as long as the two realms were in close proximity the missing persons' voices were still heard.

If these bisections also alter time, the 11 months between Lang's disappearance and his audible pleas for aid may have been only a few seconds to him. UFOs that vanish in front of eyewitnesses have also been pointed to as possible interdimensional vehicles.

When Captain James Howard was piloting a Boeing BOAC Strato Cruiser off the coast of Newfoundland on June 29, 1954 he was understandably entranced by the gigantic hovering contraption ahead that dwarfed his big plane. He reported the UFO to Goose Bay, Labrador's military airfield, and two F-80 Sabre jets rushed to investigate. The interceptor pilots reported that six small silver disks accompanied the large, dark aircraft. As the fighters closed on them the smaller objects lined up and entered the big machine through some unseen aperture. The UFO then dematerialized. [62] Could it simply have gone off our space/time continuum?

Since individual atoms are so widely spaced relative to each other it is theoretically conceivable that if we were to collide with matter whose energy patterns and/or atomic frequencies are markedly different from ours (perhaps stuff from another dimension) we would pass ghostlike through it. Perhaps at least some UFOs come from places where the still-intangible (to us) boundary between dimensions has been located, and to visit us they simply fly into and through it, departing in the same manner. To us they would appear to emerge, or vanish into, thin air.

Then there is the possibly related subject of black holes. A black hole is an ancient star that has expended its fuel reserves. With its nuclear furnace burned out, gravity forces it to collapse upon itself into an unimaginably dense mass. The gravitational attraction of this body is so powerful that not even light can escape it. There is no way of knowing what would happen to a cosmic traveler should he be sucked into this ultimate unexplorable. Death is only one possibility. He might find himself elsewhere in time, or in another dimension.

If physical, naturally occurring time portals do exist, black holes appear to be the most likely prospect. In some cases entire galaxies seem to be swirling in whirlpool fashion around gigantic black holes at their centers, and being steadily devoured by these lethal nuclei. If laws of relativity apply as supposed within these gravitational nether regions, hapless spacefarers pulled into a black hole would not simply be crushed, but rather hurled into a separate universe. From this alien region there would be no hope of return.

The existence of such a phenomenon has been confirmed. In May of 1994 scientists Holland Ford of John Hopkins University, and Richard Harms of Landover, Maryland's Applied Research Corporation revealed they had used the newly repaired and improved Hubble Space Telescope to isolate a spot in the heart of Galaxy M87 in the Virgo constellation (52 million light years distant) which presumably harbors a giant black hole. The astronomers focused their instrument on the center of the gigantic galaxy and found an unusual region 500 light years across that is behaving strangely. It is a disk-shaped gaseous cloud rotating at 1.2 million miles per hour around an invisible central point. Only a gravitational source of imponderable power can be holding the cloud together with it whirling at this velocity. Using spectrographic analysis, Ford and Harms were able to measure the mass of the unseen vortex as equaling 2.3 billion of our suns packed into an area only about the size of our solar system.

This carnivorous colossus will have already swallowed untold billions of stars, and the gas disk encircling it has already assumed a spiral shape uneasily reminiscent of water spinning down a drain. It is disquieting to consider how big and strong this black hole will be by the time it finishes consuming Galaxy M87, how far it will be able to reach out and grab hapless cosmic travelers, and to where and when it will fling them. [63]

Some flying saucers could be intra-universe survivors of a gravitational maelstrom, flung flotsam-like into our corner of deep space. Peculiar manifestations are definitely known to accompany gravitational disturbances.

Something brilliant lit up Russia's Tashkent region moments before the disastrous predawn earthquake of April 26, 1966. An engineer named Alexei Melnichuk was on a Tashkent street when the blinding light struck. He first heard a distinct rumbling, then, "I seemed to be bathed in a white light that extended as far as I could see. I was forced to shield my face with my hands. After a few seconds I took my hands away from my face, and the light was gone."

Seconds later the Tashkent fault slipped, and the ensuing tremor left the region in ruins. Many of the 200,000 homeless survivors who staggered from their wrecked residences were further shaken by the sight of "glowing spheres floating through the air like lighted balloons." [64]

UFOs appeared in large numbers over the rubble created by the Algerian quakes of September 1954 that left over a thousand people dead. [65]

Five peculiar "tadpole-like objects" cruised over the English towns of Nottinghamshire and Leicestershire as a major quake rocked them February 11, 1957. [66] Is it possible the physical disturbance of a dimensional maelstrom slinging luckless interstellar travelers into our locale could have jolted plate tectonics into violent activity?

Another novel, possibly related hypothesis embraced by some investigators in the 1980s concerns mysterious "Earth energies" which seem to emanate from our planet's crust through portals undetectable to conventional science. In 1974, scientists at the Centre National d'Etudes Spatiales in Toulouse, France released a report on their findings on the UFO-rich year of 1954. Project scientist C. Pohrer revealed that after reviewing 635 sightings he and his colleagues had realized a major fluctuation had occurred simultaneously with the saucer wave. According to this notion UFOs (or at least those in Pohrer's study) are caused by cryptic geologic/magnetic disturbances. [67]

This is in line with ancient occult beliefs that etheric fissures (necromancers call them "gateways") exist in Earth's crust and somehow create weak spots in our planet's psychic envelope, and that these apertures admit astral visitants. [68] Areas such as England's Sussex County, the Ohio River and Mississippi River valleys and the region surrounding Prescott, Arizona are settings not only for periodic UFO waves, but more definite preternatural events such as poltergeist manifestations, specters, possession and inexplicable disappearances of humans and animals. [69]

In August 1979, ground witnesses in London watched a Concorde supersonic jet passenger liner hurtle uneventfully *through* a huge, round reddish UFO that abruptly materialized in its flight path. [70] Whatever the object was, it was not solid matter. Or maybe it was, but *elsewhere*. It could have been a very material machine whose occupants were looking in on us from another dimension or era.

A visitor to Stonehenge once pointed his version of an Ankh, a loop-ended crucifix wielded by ancient, pagan Egyptian priests, at the ring of massive carved stone uprights. The resultant, instantaneous surge of pseudo-electricity that flowed up his arm knocked him unconscious. It took six months for him to regain full use of his arm. [71] An ethereal manifestation of some kind apparently is present at or around Stonehenge.

This enigmatic megalith is thought to have been built in stages from 3100 B.C. to 1100 B.C. If its generations of builders possessed some long-forgotten method of detecting Earth energies, Stonehenge and others of the numerous such monuments scattered throughout the world (virtually all of them are so old there are not even any legends to account for them) may originally have served as temples to what the ancients perceived as deities dwelling at these monuments' specific locations.[72]

A preponderance of these cryptic constructions is in Western Europe (particularly the British Isles.) On a November evening in 1976 local residents Ted Pratt and Joyce Bowles gave little thought to the many nearby prehistoric burial mounds and megaliths (chiefly Woodbury Ring and Danebury Long Barrow) as they motored on Chilcomb Road en route to Chilcomb, England.

Their car began to vibrate violently. It swerved off the road by its own accord, and its headlights and engine died. Through the windshield the startled couple spied a glowing orange aircraft, cigar-shaped, hovering over the road. They could see three individuals observing them through windows. One of these beings emerged and approached the car. He appeared human except for his eyes. They lacked irises or pupils. All the frightened humans could see were two solid pink eyeballs. The ufonaut wore a silver jumpsuit.

Bowles later recounted how, "He peered through the window at the dashboard controls." At that point the engine and lights came back on, and "...he and the cigar simply vanished." [73]

Was the UFO and its occupants extraterrestrial, attracted to that area by some power emanations their sophisticated instruments detected from outer space, or was everything Ted Pratt and Joyce Bowles saw that night a *manifestation of that power*?

In 1978, megalith researcher Paul Devereaux launched what he called his Dragon Research Project at Rollright Stones, northwest of Oxford. Employing psychics and dowsers Devereaux discovered that odd energy fluctuations and sounds beyond the range of human hearing begin at Rollright eight to 20 minutes before dawn, and stop abruptly one or two hours later. [74]

Geiger counters indicate the venerable stone circle has a slightly above-average radiation level, raising the question of whether it may sit atop a uranium deposit. Worldwide many areas that are more naturally radioactive than their surrounding countryside were/are considered sacred by locals.

Along these lines it may be significant that on separate occasions Project Dragon volunteers reported peculiar sightings on a road adjacent to Rollright. Researchers reported seeing a car, a large furry animal and a Gypsy caravan appear, and then suddenly dematerialize. This led Devereaux to hypothesize that the spot's elevated radioactivity may induce hallucinations. [75] This sounds plausible enough to explain a UFO sighting, but it does not clarify what caused Joyce Bowles' car to malfunction.

Most paranormal investigators suspect the megaliths are portals for Earth energy, but what if they are not conductors, but merely mark the locations of natural power sources? Innumerable unmarked outlets may exist worldwide, attracting saucers from beyond, or creating their images in persons' minds.

It could be that the dimensional possibility is connected with these poorly understood Earth energies, and the portals mark regular transit points between dimensions. French ufologist Jacques Vallee believes UFOs are indeed interdimensional vehicles visiting us from another space/time continuum. As we will see, this view, while it took quite awhile to catch on, is not new.

Before his 1959 suicide, acclaimed ufologist Dr. Morris K. Jessup was first to propose that saucers come from another dimension, and that they manipulate magnetic fields to traverse dimensional boundaries. He believed UFOs to be rimmed on their interiors with cathode ray generators. A crew theoretically could propel their ship by engaging the generators on the inner wall facing the desired heading. This would ionize the air and create a vacuum outside that section of the craft, which literally would be pushed along by the air pressure on the side opposite the vacuum. [76]

This process obviously is unsuitable to explain how a UFO could travel in the enveloping vacuity of outer space, but Jessup did not believe this mattered because he did not think this was where the saucers come from anyway. His research into the U.S. Navy's 1943 "Philadelphia Experiment" led him to conclude that ionization and strong magnetic fields could make dimensional transfers of matter possible.

In this remarkable test a destroyer was liberally equipped with both pulsating and non-pulsating magnetic generators in an attempt to envelope it in a powerful magnetic aura that would produce invisibility as predicted by Einstein's "Unified Field Theory." From the information Jessup was able to dig up, the sailors had some success.

When the generators were activated, a green haze formed around the ship, which then faded into invisibility along with its crewmen. It proved difficult to restore some of the men to normalcy, and a specially designed electronic gadget had to be used to rematerialize those whose state of transparency became so acute they could not be seen *or touched.* This restoration device was only temporarily effective in some cases, and men would continue to fade away for short periods at unpredictable intervals. Where did they go?

If Einstein was correct about space/time and energy/matter being essentially the same entity and transmutable under specifically created electromagnetic conditions, the invisible seamen may have been sent inadvertently to a plane of being wholly removed from ours. If the inhabitants of some continuum have learned to control electromagnetism to a sufficient degree they would not need to cruise lengthy stretches of the cosmos to visit us. They would simply pop in and out by manipulating magnetic fields. [77]

Jessup built and published a strong case for this revolutionary theory. Unknown to him, he was not alone in his support for it. At some point during the late 1950s someone mailed a copy of Jessup's book, *The Case for UFOs,* to the Office for Naval Research in Washington, D.C. The copy's margins were filled with notes (written in three hands) on UFOs in general, the interdimensional concept and, of greatest interest to the Navy, the supposedly top-secret Philadelphia Experiment.

The Navy brass summoned Jessup to Washington to see if he could identify the handwriting of those disturbing margin notes and thus shed light on who was privy to such highly classified military information. Jessup identified one of the handwriting samples as belonging to one Carlos Allende, who had been corresponding with him via mail. It was Allende who had first informed Jessup of the Philadelphia Experiment, claiming to have been one of the vanishing crewmen.

Allende appeared to have vanished yet again, for all attempts to track him down were futile. The two other persons whose notations were in Jessup's book remain totally unknown. It would appear some unidentified group was able to gain access to the Navy's classified invisibility experiments, and then fill the margins of a copy of The Case for UFOs with notes on flying saucers and the possibility of their being interdimensional vehicles, and on the confidential Philadelphia Experiment. In other words, to point out a connection and lead us to realize the experiment's potential for being our first step in learning how to travel from one space/time continuum to another. The unanticipated side effects on crewmembers of the subject destroyer prompted the Navy to abandon the project, however, and the mystery group's efforts went for naught. [78]

Unfortunately for Jessup, he was too far ahead of his time. The scientific/academic establishment of the 1950s was far from ready for the notion of parallel dimensions. This was especially true when applied to ufology. The few renowned scientists brave enough to express belief in the saucers took for granted they were astroships from another physical civilization in this dimension. The scientific community's blistering attacks on his ideas fatally depressed Jessup.

Pioneering ufologist Dr. Morris K. Jessup was found dead in his carbon monoxide-filled station wagon in Miami's Dade County Park on April 29, 1959. There was a hose connecting the tail pipe to the interior. [79] For a time it looked as if his theories had passed on with him, but the late doctor's beliefs were resurrected and re-examined decades later by a more receptive generation of researchers.

Some of them proposed that if the saucers are interdimensional they may become visible only while traversing the very narrow band of light sandwiched between ultraviolet and infrared. This presumably would mean our world is continuously swarming with UFOs that are unseen most of the time, briefly emerging into many-colored splendor when their travels along the light spectrum bring them into the realm of rainbows. [80]

In some cases the saucers may even be composed of pure energy. They could ordinarily be invisible to us, but capable of altering themselves to enter our material region, and in so doing they enter the band of visible light.

If some UFOs *are* composed of energy, this would explain the haunting sensation some close-up witnesses have experienced that the saucers themselves were living organisms rather than mere conveyances. Denizens discharged from these animated machines would be walking extensions of the craft.

4 Confusion

IN A FURTHER ATTACK on the extraterrestrial theory, Jacques Vallee notes the similarity between the appearances of contemporary flying saucer occupants and the fairies, leprechauns, elves and nymphs who haunted our world in earlier times. This leads to the suggestion that what we call the UFO phenomenon is actually something that has been with us for centuries, but until recently was in another guise.

He also points out that to gain complete knowledge of Earth's fauna, flora, climates, geography, languages, customs and mores, an advanced civilization would not need to make any landings. *Earth's* current technology is quite capable of learning all this and more from the data-gathering capabilities of a single, small artificial satellite. A race able to traverse the hard-to-fathom distances between stars would not need even to enter a planet's atmosphere to learn all it possibly could need to know about that world. Vallee (and an ever-increasing number of other researchers) also believes the landings are being staged in order to confuse and mislead us. [81]

The saucerians who contacted Herbert Schirmer informed him bluntly that they meant to bewilder us. During his hypnosis sessions he remarked, "To a certain extent they want to puzzle people. They know they are being seen too frequently, and they are trying to confuse the public's mind." [82]

Interestingly, these ufonauts took pains to convince him they were "from a nearby galaxy." Assuming they *were* from such a fantastic distance, their means of propulsion comes into question. Even with a *Star Trek*-style time/warp thrust it presumably would take ages to complete such a voyage. Even if it were undertaken it is taxing to come up with a motive. What possibly would make such a trip worthwhile? Whatever these visitors were after, it surely must have been available *somewhere* nearer to their home world.

It is highly unlikely these creatures were from another galaxy, but by claiming to hail from such a distant spot they conveniently made astronomical observation of it impossible. Our telescopes can reveal to us whether other stars in our sector of the Milky Way may be circled by habitable planets, but other *galaxies* are much too far away for us to make such a determination.

Schirmer's ufonauts did not want him (or anyone else on Earth) to learn their true point of origin, but when one asks where it might be (as we hopefully are in the process of learning,) a fascinating array of possibilities presents itself. Although most of the encounters with the 1896-1910 airship occupants involved familiar-appearing and familiar-sounding crewmembers, one witness, Judge Lawrence E. Byrne, who came upon one of the landed machines outside Texarkana, Arkansas, described the airmen as speaking "…some kind of foreign language, but judging from their looks I would take them to be Japs." [83] Interestingly, many modern ufonauts are described as Oriental-looking.

In the autumn of 1896, before the wave of airship sightings reached the West Coast, a small, swarthy, well-dressed man visited two prominent San Francisco attorneys, George Collins and William Hart. The man claimed to have invented a flying machine driven by compressed air. He wanted Collins and Hart to help him obtain a patent for his new aircraft, which he intended to use against the Spaniards in Cuba.

If this mysterious inventor ever told his name to either lawyer, it was never printed in any of the newspapers that carried the story. When the wondrous, cigar-shaped airships appeared in the California skies, their unnamed inventor immediately dropped from sight, never to reappear. Whoever was behind the far-reaching airship sightings went to great lengths, via two of the best-known legal advisors in the West, to make it all appear to be of earthly origin through an emissary who disappeared before he could be investigated. [84]

The "inventor" told Collins the airship was powered by compressed air, but told Hart it ran on gas and electricity. In some cases airmen told witnesses that steam propelled the mysterious machines. Practical aircraft driven by, stream, compressed air, or by electricity have never been developed—the requisite machinery and fuel are too heavy. Something else must have been running those strange craft.

Primitive dirigibles had flown in Europe as early as 1852, so they and their distinctive oblong shape were easily recognizable by the 1890s. It appears that perhaps some group from another place, time or dimension staged a nonviolent invasion, realizing the need to do so clandestinely in order to avoid mass panic. Thus they devised a plan to convince the populace that the weird contraptions coursing through Earth's virgin skies were prosaic and non-threatening.

It appears they succeeded. Onlookers predictably shrugged off nocturnal sightings of colored light-bedecked flying machines in high-speed transit through the heavens as "the airship." In actuality these devices often traveled at speeds not attainable by earthly aircraft until decades later.

The zeppelin-like craft seen in broad daylight likely were decoys, while the intruders' actual vehicles were obscured by darkness, and perhaps were the saucer-shaped objects familiar to modern ufology. In later years many UFOs were not recognized as such because of their resemblance to earthly aircraft.

A most peculiar airplane buzzed the airport outside the UFO-frequented city of Bahia Blanca, Argentina on the afternoon of July 22, 1968. Numerous witnesses described it as having a strangely elongated fuselage. It emitted no sound other than a faint hissing, and flew impossibly slowly, particularly in relation to its extremely short delta wings. By all laws of aerodynamics it should have dropped like a hammer. Instead it continued its leisurely circling of the field while all attempts to contact it via radio failed.

Observers watching through binoculars could discern no insignia save for four black squares (one much larger than the others) on the fuselage. At one point the plane, at an altitude of about 200 feet, rolled over and made an incredibly tight 360-degree turn. A few minutes later it zipped out of sight to the southeast. [85]

Not-quite-conventional-looking and oddly behaving aircraft have been reported more frequently than is generally realized. In 1957 a government official living on Long Island, New York stepped outside one night to see what was agitating his frantically barking dog. As he did so a huge, delta-winged jet whizzed overhead. Delta-winged (swept-back wings) planes were extremely rare in the 1950s, being limited to a few scattered prototypes, and this one was utterly silent and surrounded by a strange red glow. The befuddled bureaucrat reported the ghostly craft to the nearest Air Force base. The next day he received a return call from an officer who asked for additional details and revealed the UFO had been reported by several other local residents. [86]

The most notable of these quasi-planes would be the one reported by Canadian rancher William Hertzke. It was October of 1965, and Hertzke was crossing a pasture on horseback on the Circle J Ranch outside Calgary when he came upon a small airplane. It was approximately 16 feet long, and its delta wings spanned about 12 feet. The plane's exterior had an irregular "waffled" surface, and a transparent, apparently plastic bubble encased the cockpit.

Through this canopy a complex instrument panel was visible, complete with a foot-wide "television screen." There were two undersized bucket seats made of a clear, glassy material. The machine had no discernible jets, propellers or any other mode of propulsion, and bore no insignia. Hertzke was unable to locate the plane's crew, and his ranching duties left him no time to return for a later look. He did subsequently pass a polygraph test, answering questions devised by trained psychologists.

The craft was a riddle. It obviously was designed for occupants much smaller than adult humans. Its rippled surface was unsuitable for high-speed flight, but its delta wings were of a sort specifically developed for the greatest velocities. It evidently was propelled by some unknown means, since the wings were far too short for it to have been a glider. [87]

Many mystery planes' pilots exhibit a strange inclination to fly at night with their cockpits brilliantly illuminated by interior lights. This should completely blind the pilot to anything beyond his windshield. Yet if these unidentified fliers are flying blind they are doing a marvelous job of it, for they have been reported aloft in weather that would ground or send spinning to Earth virtually every known man-made flying machine. In fact, the anonymous aircraft that haunted Scandinavian airspace during the 1930s showed a marked *preference* for bad weather, usually appearing amidst raging blizzards (to dissuade pursuit?) and effortlessly circling towns, military installations and sea-going ships.

They often would cut their engines and nonchalantly glide through storms, and generally were much larger than any conventional aircraft of that time. In one case, five eyewitnesses reported an enormous, eight-engine plane. [88]

A newspaper dispatch dated January 22, 1934 chronicles a typical incident:

Pitea. The permanent curate in Langtrask has reported that he has been seeing mysterious airplanes in the area for the past two years. Last summer the ghost flier passed over the community 12 times, following the same route each time, southwest to northeast. On four different occasions the plane appeared at very low altitude, but no marks or insignia were visible. Once the plane's altitude was only a few meters over the parsonage. For a few seconds two persons were visible in the cabin. The machine was grayish in color, and single-winged.

The curate had not reported this earlier because he thought the flier had been reported by the coastal population. [89]

The moniker "Ghost Fliers" stuck, and the mystery quickly assumed international status. Late in December 1933 a ghost flier began patrolling the Norway-Sweden border. The 4th Swedish Flying Corps was ordered to Tarnably to investigate, with emphasis on finding the ghost fliers' base. They never did, and one cannot help wondering if these persistent reports from the sensitive border region were staged to lure the military there while some never-detected activity transpired elsewhere. [90]

Like the American airships of decades past, the ghost fliers often played dazzling searchlights onto the countrysides and towns they buzzed. Also, they rarely were seen on days other than Wednesdays and Sundays, the days most favored by modern UFOs. [91]

On the evening of Wednesday, January 10, 1934 there was a report of a pontoon-equipped ghost flier resting on the calm sea near the Norwegian island of Gjeslingen, remaining there quietly for about 90 minutes. It took off just before a naval vessel arrived. [92]

The ghost fliers' predilection for military bases and other sensitive installations prompted the governments of Finland, Norway and Sweden to organize a massive armed investigation. As the military moved into the heart of ghost flier territory, the reports dropped markedly. No large, well-equipped base and landing field (absolute necessities for the number and size of the planes spotted) ever were located.

Aircraft carriers still were experimental and extremely rare, and could never have launched (much less landed) many of the huge vessels seen hurtling through the northern heavens. The fliers' habit of cutting their engines and gliding for impossibly long distances raises the question of their true mode of propulsion. Predictably, no answer was forthcoming. [93]

In many instances there were nocturnal sightings of high-altitude, multi-colored lights. Ground observers assumed these were their faceless mystery pilots flying those omnipresent, not-quite-conventional-looking airplanes, obscured by darkness and altitude. It was a definite fact that in many of the "hard" sightings of unmistakably physical airplanes the craft sported red, white and green lights. It is unsurprising that when nighttime "soft" sightings were made of high-altitude red, white and green lights it was assumed they were affixed to the relatively standard-looking planes seen in daylight. [94] Perhaps the nocturnal lights were fastened to something else entirely, something totally out of this world. Perhaps the multi-engine planes seen during the day were decoys to lull quizzical Scandinavians into taking for granted the enigmatic lights they also saw in *darkened* skies were nothing new.

One of the very last notable ghost flier reports came from the crew of the fishing boat *Fram* as it departed Kvalsvik, Norway on February 11, 1937 (as usual, the mystery craft seemed to favor the dead of winter—another factor making pursuit difficult.) As *Fram* rounded a peninsula her captain spotted a large, pontoon-equipped plane on the water. Thinking the aircraft was in difficulties he changed course toward it to offer assistance, but as his boat drew near the aircraft (which was festooned with red and blue lights) it suddenly was enveloped in thick smoke. When the smoke cleared, the plane was gone. [95]

Scandinavia's skies have never lost their allure for unidentified flying objects, either. A You Tube report from September 17, 2018 reported two massive UFOs cruising over Sweden in broad daylight.

Both the American airships of the 1890s and the European ghost fliers of the 1930s were machines slightly ahead of their eras' technological capabilities. This had the effect of leading witnesses to believe they were seeing prototypes of flying machines still in their developmental stages, and that this accounted for their unfamiliarity. Had they flown already-perfected and familiar aircraft the mystery airmens' flights might have incited fear of an impending invasion from a hostile terrestrial power.

Whatever were the American airshipmens' motives, they carried out their mission as the Spanish-American war was looming, and as it was being fought. However via presumably planned encounters with usually human-appearing crews, and through highly regarded legal figures the populace were convinced the airships were not Spanish, and therefore non-threatening. With the ghost fliers this same end was achieved by appropriate timing.

Knowledge of Adolf Hitler's massive rearming of Germany led most to believe the strange aircraft were experimental German warplanes. By being perceived as unfinished mockups the odd airplanes did not appear mysterious. By the time World War II did erupt, the ghost fliers had long since vanished. Another course of action that allayed fear. Hitler never made any attempts to molest Sweden or Finland (both so favored by the ghost fliers,) and his Luftwaffe never flew any machines resembling those that frequented the prewar skies of his northern neighbors.

Throughout the ghost flier years wireless operators throughout Scandinavia picked up peculiar radio broadcasts, presumably from the ghostly airmen. These transmissions generally were received over the 900-meter band or from 230 to 275 meters, and the speakers had such poor command of the Swedish, Norwegian and Finnish languages that the messages were virtually nonsensical. [96]

The American airship and European ghost flier affairs smack of having been carefully contrived and executed deceptions. If only we could learn who in the universe was behind them. Furthermore, these ruses may be ongoing.

The Cash-Landrum incident is not the only case of military-appearing helicopters accompanying flying saucers. Flocks of eggbeaters, usually the large, double-rotor type, have appeared in conjunction with the more traditional, disk-shaped UFOs on numerous occasions, generally encircling the saucer. The seemingly obvious conclusion is that the armed forces are intercepting and dealing with the intruders, thereby reassuring a potentially jittery public that there is no cause for alarm. The problem here is that these helicopters have a knack for showing up in locales that are at great distances from military bases where they might be headquartered, and are beyond their flight range. Also, helicopters in these cases commonly congregate in numbers far greater than are housed at military bases.

When a blindingly bright object cavorted above Wanaque Reservoir in New Jersey on the night of October 11, 1966, it was nothing the locals had not seen before in this area of high UFO activity, but moments after it departed, seven unidentified copters arrived and circled the reservoir at very low altitude. Investigating police Sergeant Robert Gordon later remarked, "I've never seen seven helicopters at one time in this area before in all my life…and I've lived here for 40 years."

The two Air Force bases nearest the Wanaque Reservoir were in New Jersey—Stewart AFB and McGuire AFB. Neither had seven choppers available, and even if they had they never could have had them over the area in question so quickly. Besides, the Air Force was never even formally and directly informed of the Wanaque Reservoir sighting. [97]

With their relatively slow speeds and short ranges helicopters are poorly suited to intercepting UFOs, whose phenomenal velocities and distance capabilities would leave them far behind. These factors would instantly be obvious to the armed forces, who would not bother scrambling helicopters for a task for which they are totally unsuited. An incident during the Vietnam War would seem to absolve the military of suspicion of ownership of these machines.

At the height of the autumn 1973 UFO flap, Air Force Chief of Staff George S. Brown was quoted by the Associated Press and United Press International: "I don't know if the story has been told, but they (UFOs) plagued us in Vietnam during the war."

Brown had commanded the 7th Air Force in Indochina, and later remarked, "We didn't call them that. They could only be seen at night in certain places."

In one instance in the summer of 1968, near the demilitarized zone (DMZ,) UFOs were misidentified as enemy aircraft and, as Brown put it, "...set off quite a battle, with an Australian destroyer taking a hit."

Newsweek's war correspondent Robert Stokes reported in his magazine's July 1, 1968 issue on the squadron of weird "helicopters" that had haunted the airspace over the DMZ throughout June:

It was 11:00 p.m., and U.S. Army Captain Bill Bates sat in front of a radio set at his regimental headquarters at Dong Ha. Just then a Marine forward observer came on the air reporting he had spotted, through his electronic telescope, 13 sets of yellowish-white lights moving westerly at an altitude of between 500 and 1000 feet over the Ben Hai River, which runs through the middle of the DMZ. Bates immediately checked with authorities at Dong Ha to see whether there were any friendly aircraft in the area of the reported sightings. He was told there were not. Then he checked with the counterbattery radar unit at Alpha 2, the northernmost Allied outpost in 1 Corps. Within minutes the answer came back from Alpha 2's radar tracker: The "blips" were all around him, 360 degrees. By 1:00 a.m. U.S. Air Force and Marine jets were scrambling at Da Nang in pursuit of the unidentified objects. Forty-five minutes later a Marine pilot reported that he had just shot down a helicopter. But when an Air Force reconnaissance plane, equipped with infrared detectors which pick up heat, flew over the area, it could find no evidence of burning wreckage. All it could confirm, the pilot reported, was a burned spot.

Use of helicopters by Communist forces in Vietnam was extremely rare; the Reds did not have access to them. Also, these cryptic machines apparently never attacked American forces, as one would expect of craft piloted by the enemy. The unidentified choppers abruptly vanished at the end of June, thereby raising an-other question—why would the enemy stop using aircraft of such great potential value? It would appear the Communists had nothing to do with them.

On the other side of the world a similar case was unfolding. Soon after the disappearance of the Vietnamese mystery helicopters, an oval craft banded by red and white flashing lights turned up over the Rosecroft Racetrack outside Phelps Corner, Maryland. At least seven clattering helicopters were encircling it. Onlookers were baffled, but the chopper escort reassured them. With that kind of powerful "military presence" the UFO hardly could be a threat, could it? Yet even this apparent assurance of safety struck some as odd. Local resident Gwen E. Donovan watched the spectacle, and later said, "It struck me as funny because I have never seen so many in the sky at one time." [98]

Like the airships and ghost fliers of earlier years, the puzzling eggbeaters of the 1960s (and beyond) seem to have been props in performances given to simulta-neously mislead and reassure us.

The indefatigable John Keel called to attention the scarcity of reports of separate-ly observed UFOs with matching descriptions. He proposed that some, most or all such "hard" sightings may be decoys to camouflage the much more numerous sightings of distant, fuzzy lights, i.e., the "soft" sightings. [99]

The flying saucers humans have seen at close range, touched and occasionally entered could be temporary transmogrifications that are not created according to basic plans or designs, thus accounting for the widely divergent descriptions. If the disks, phantom jets and helicopters of today are performing the same hypothetical function previously acted out by the airships and ghost fliers, they seem to be doing the same old adept job.

When private pilot Kenneth Arnold made his sighting over the Cascade Mountains in 1947, the flying saucer era was thrust upon a world newly modernized by the technical strides spawned by the Second World War. The timing was pre-cise, and the unidentified flying machines were (again) seemingly just beyond our technological capabilities. While some said the saucers were prototypes of secret military projects, others, dazzled by the recent advances in the applied sciences, swore we were being visited by extraterrestrials. Yet others said it was all erroneous, hallucinatory or fraudulent. All were predictable conjectures. Yet amid all the confusion and controversy nobody seemed to take into account the possibility that *none* were 100% correct.

From a historical/statistical standpoint the years since 1947 have not produced a greater average number of annual sightings than in preceding years, but we are regarding these sky things differently. The sudden scientific and technological leaps of the 1940s spurred a few open minds to seriously ponder the previously scorned possibility that maybe we are not alone in the universe after all, and that perhaps somewhere there is a civilization more advanced than ours. It looks as if someone is taking great pains to convince us this hypothesizing is on the right track.

Abruptly our skies were again invaded by aircraft too advanced to be of terrestrial origin, and even though for a time in the late '40s most figured the strange devices cavorting over northern Europe were flown by Soviet test pilots, the blanketing of our world by news service communications insured this misconception would not last for long. When these super-aircraft were not used by Communist forces in the Korean and Vietnam wars it became apparent to the now-well-informed world that the Eastern Bloc nations were not responsible. Another façade was needed. Space aliens would be the latest pretense.

Machines only slightly ahead of our capabilities would no longer suffice if we were to be convinced the saucer pilots were representatives of some interstellar superpower. They would have to be able to travel unfathomable distances through the icy cosmic vacuum, and no vehicle of this sort had even been contemplated by earthly science. The incredible abilities of modern UFOs had the desired effect. Sure enough, most modern saucer enthusiasts assume the objects of their fascination are of physical, extraterrestrial origin.

The Herbert Schirmer case appears to support the likelihood of a staged encounter meant to bewilder and mislead us. If these ufonauts were as anxious to remain undetected as their leader indicated, why was not the entire episode erased from Schirmer's memory, rather than just a portion of it? The part the saucer commander was careful to preserve predictably led to the hypnosis session that revealed the whole episode. It appears to have been a cabal in which saucerians, by pretending they wanted to be forgotten, insured they would be remembered.

Two veteran police officers, Koos de Klerk and John Lockem, came across a large saucer in the middle of a highway outside Pretoria, South Africa at midnight on September 16, 1965. Seconds after the patrolmen arrived the craft violently blasted off via twin jets of thrust from its underside, ripping the asphalt roadway to pieces and setting it ablaze.

By landing and taking off where and how they did, and in front of law enforcement officers (highly regarded as witnesses,) whoever was flying this UFO made sure the visit would be both well remembered and thoroughly documented. Of course literally hundreds of persons (including reporters and their photographers) viewed the shattered, burned highway. [100]

The small community of Gulf Breeze, Florida was frequented in the late 1980s by a squadron of UFOs that seemed determined to have their existence documented, but did not appear to want this motive to be too obvious. The devices avoided camera-equipped news crews sent to check them out, and instead concentrated on local businessman Ed Walters. He periodically would hear a humming inside his skull, followed by a cryptic telepathic message that generally went, "Zehaas, sleep and know!"

Following this odd directive Walters would grab his humble Polaroid camera and dash into his yard, above which a huge, round, sparkling object inevitably would be hovering/posing. After Walters had snapped a picture or two his subject would dematerialize in a twinkling (not fly away) until the next photo session. Walters got dozens of hard-to-discredit prints in this fashion. This more firmly established the UFO phenomenon, as did numerous sightings made by other Gulf Breeze residents during this period. The entire episode helped to further, slowly familiarize us with the saucers without this intention being too obvious. [101]

Meanwhile, while they seem determined for us to believe in them, they also appear bent on keeping us from *understanding* anything concrete about them. Keel related in print the weird incident in which a destitute young woman of his acquaintance managed to take an expensive trip to the Bahamas, from where she sent him a postcard. Upon her return the only recollection she had of the entire journey was of debarking a jet at an airport where some "Indians" met her and took her baggage. The next thing she remembered was arriving home. [102]

If this peculiar adventure, complete with MIB-like characters, was some sort of ufological abduction her remembrance of the jet, airport and "Indians" may have been due to an inefficient application of the memory erasing procedure so often associated with close contacts. Or it may have been just another red herring to keep investigators running in confused circles.

The saucer people have claimed a bewildering variety of points of origin. Cuba, Kansas, Uranus, Clarion (a planet the saucerians claim is in our solar system, but is hidden from us by the sun) and a world called Lanulos have all been fingered as homeports by our enigmatic callers. This may point toward another weakness in the extraterrestrial theory.

In numerous instances allegedly ufological artifacts have been branded fraudulent because chemical analysis revealed them to be easily identifiable earthly substances. Researchers who take for granted the saucers come from some wholly unearthly world automatically discard any evidence found to be of terrestrial origin, but what if our visitors are from *this* planet?

The late saucer investigator/author Frank Edwards described an interview he conducted with a Canadian metallurgist named Wilbur B. Smith in November 1961. Smith told Edwards of a 3000-pound mass of "very strange metal" an organization called the Canadian Research Group recovered in the summer of 1960. At one point in the interview Smith described the giant hulk of metal thusly:

"We are speculating that what we have is a portion of a very large device which came into this solar system...we don't know when...but it had been in space a long time before it came to Earth. We can tell that by the micrometeorites embedded in the surface, but we don't know if it was a few years ago, or a few centuries ago." [103]

Smith also described a tiny (two-foot diameter) UFO that was attacked by a jet interceptor near Washington D.C. in 1952. A one-pound piece of the disk was shot off and later recovered by a search party. Analysis revealed it to be "a matrix of magnesium orthosilicate. The matrix had great numbers, thousands, of 15-micron spheres scattered through it." [104] It would seem this was part of a larger craft that had been in outer space quite awhile, but does this necessarily mean it was from another planet? Both these artifacts could have flown from Earth into space numerous times, thereby gradually amassing their impressive collections of micrometeorites. Finally—they were made of materials found on this planet.

A metallic disk that passed over Campinas, Brazil on December 14, 1954 spewed a stream of silver fluid resembling mercury. When a Dr. Risvaldo Maffie analyzed it he found it to be liquefied tin. [105]

The huge flying "egg" police officer Lonnie Zamora met in the New Mexican desert in the spring of 1964 left a melted substance that turned out to be silicon. [106] A UFO that exploded over Maryland in 1965 scattered fragments of terrochromium. [107] Nine years earlier the wreckage of a saucer that blew up in Brazilian skies was pure magnesium. [108]

The extremely tough strips of paper-thin aluminum dumped from a circular object over Chiba, Japan on September 7, 1956 were similar to the radar chaff used by military aircraft. Large quantities have been found in areas of heavy UFO activity. [109]

On April 18, 1961 a gleaming silver disk landed at the Eagle River, Wisconsin home of 60-year-old poultry farmer Joe Simonton. Four small, totally mute beings dressed in dark blue emerged. Simonton gave them some water, and as he looked on in amazement one of the saucerians went back into the craft, then returned and gave him four hot pancakes he made on what looked like a stove inside their ship. They then re-boarded the machine, which made a sound like "tires on wet pavement," and slowly flew away to the south. On nearby Interstate 70 a motorist named Savino Borgo saw the UFO as it departed. [110]

Eagle River and its general vicinity were among the few to undergo heavy saucer activity during the otherwise uneventful period from 1959 to 1963. It was also plagued with plane crashes and power and telephone failures. There were also four very strangely delivered pancakes. [111]

They proved to not be made from some exotic, impossible-to-identify other-worldly recipe, but from cooking oil, salt and corn meal. Discounting all such artifacts because they are composed of familiar, Earthly material may be acting on an entirely incorrect assumption. If UFOs are not extraterrestrial it is hardly surprising the souvenirs they leave are not either.

Some ufologists have proposed that the saucers come from an as-yet-undiscovered undersea civilization, or that Earth is hollow, and flying saucers come from the interior. Fervent believers in a hollow Earth go way back and have included such notables as Edmund Halley of comet-discovering fame, and, reputedly, Adolf Hitler. [112]

Paranormal investigator F. Amadeo Giannini, in his book, *Worlds Beyond the Poles*, claimed to have discovered evidence that polar explorer Admiral Richard E. Byrd had, in 1947, flown 1700 miles "beyond" the North Pole, and 2300 miles past the South Pole on a 1956 flight. Byrd's strange phrases about the "enchanted continent in the sky" and "the country beyond" led writer Raymond Bernard and magazine editor Ray Palmer to suspect there was a conspiracy to keep the public ignorant of some of Byrd's polar discoveries. They also claimed to have discovered recordings of radio messages from the admiral describing ice-free Antarctic regions with lakes, forested mountains and huge animals resembling mammoths.

A woman who did not identify herself wrote Palmer that in 1929 she had viewed a newsreel of Byrd's 1926 flight over the North Pole, in which the explorer "exclaimed in wonder as he approached a warm-water lake surrounded by conifers, with a large animal moving about among the trees." [113]

Being unable to find this newsreel did not put off the enthusiastic investigators, nor were they daunted by their inability to interview the controversy's central figure, as Admiral Byrd had died before Giannini published his book. This doggedness is not surprising. Belief in and fascination with a hollow Earth is too ancient to fade away easily. Besides, there were some later developments.

Cloud cover was uncharacteristically thin on November 23, 1968 as NASA's polar-orbiting ESSA-7 satellite photographed a gargantuan black area, resembling a hole, surrounded by Arctic ice caps. When the ATS-III satellite, in equatorial orbit, photographed our planet on November 18, 1967 from 47 degrees west, what looked like the sloping sides of an enormous opening were distinctly visible at the North Pole. An undated print taken from a height of 23,000 miles by NASA's 67-HC-723 satellite shows a similar depression. [114]

Also, Byrd was not the first polar explorer to report incongruities on our world's ice caps. Earlier expeditions by Sir George Hubert Wilkins, Rear-Admiral George Dufek and by Dr. Fridtjof Nanses encountered baffling air temperatures that rose the farther north they penetrated, polar bears and Arctic foxes migrating *northward* in winter, by abundant insects and by mysterious clouds of dust (from internal volcanoes?) [115] Still, these first-hand reports seem to have ended by the late 1950s. Could an internal civilization, for reasons known only to itself, have become alarmed by our looming proximity, and somehow sealed off their polar openings? Of course this script is quite incredible, but then few aspects of the UFO phenomenon are not.

Nevertheless, increasingly advanced technology applied to numerous, well-equipped expeditions has effectively dispelled the notion that our world has any kind of polar openings, or that its interior is anything but a geologic, thermal furnace.

Byrd's poetic radio messages could have been the result of him being captivated by the primordial, desolate beauty of the Polar Regions. UFOs coming from within our planet appears highly unlikely, but like most hypotheses it cannot be unconditionally disproved.

Somewhat along these lines it has been speculated that the entities behind the old beliefs in fairies, leprechauns, elves and gnomes may be behind the saucer riddle. These beings generally were considered to be subterranean dwellers.

Jacques Vallee believes UFOs are the most recent manifestation of an unknown, unrealized controlling force that has been with us all along, but in ages past was applied through belief in the little people. Credence is lent to this notion by the research of ufologist Leonard Keane into the case of contactee Betty Andreasson. Keane has found that the strange language Andreasson lapses into under hypnosis closely resembles Gaelic, the tongue of ancient Ireland. Gaelic is a dialect to which she has had no prior exposure. [116]

Keane also notes the high percentage of UFO encounters in which persons of Celtic ancestry are involved. The connection to the fairy legends of yesteryear is supported by scattered reports of *very* undersized saucers and occupants, such as a 1970 Malaysian case in which several youngsters watched a Frisbee-sized craft land, and three-inch-tall ufonauts debark. [117]

Even more notable is the mini-UFO encounter described by a young Seattle woman in August 1965. She awoke one night at about 2:00 to find herself totally paralyzed and mute. It was a hot night, and she had left her bedroom window open. As she lay in silent stillness she watched a gray, football-shaped little object float soundlessly through the window.

It lowered tripod landing gear, settled onto her dresser, and about half a dozen miniscule humanoids emerged and went to work on some kind of repairs to their ship. After a few minutes they re-boarded and zipped out the window, and the witness was freed from her paralysis. [118]

As recently as 1968, road builders near the Irish town of Ballymagroartyscotch had to re-route a highway around an ancient "Skeog" (fairy tree) because townspeople and contractors were fearful of the possible consequences of felling the tree. [119] Such old beliefs of underground-dwelling little people could have been an earlier blind. Maybe they were not people at all. If they were surreptitiously manipulating us, what were/are their motives, and where are they from? The dimensional idea again comes into play.

Noted physicist Dr. Barry H. Downing scrupulously outlines the theory of parallel dimensions in his book *The Bible and Flying Saucers.* He points out that our own space may be curved in either a negative or positive direction, or that it could have zero curvature.

If our universe resembled a closed curve it could have an "outside" (or perhaps "inside") universe co-existing in the same space. A sufficiently advanced technology might bridge the gap and visit the neighboring space/time continuum. With this in mind, Dr. Downing also points out that the occasionally reported "mother-ship" with smaller UFOs entering or leaving may actually be an interdimensional portal.

If our universe is not alone, if it is but one of many, others may not necessarily resemble ours. Co-existing universes may have but one or two dimensions as opposed to our three, or they may have multitudes. Some may have no such thing as time. The results of an intersection of one of these realms with ours are impossible to predict, but may be at least part of the saucer phenomenon. If nothing else, the hypothetically vast diversity of these possible regions could explain the seemingly illogical and incomprehensible actions of many ufonauts. Perhaps we appear as weird to them as they do to us.

UFOs' trait of changing colors could be connected with interdimensional travel. A scientist named Robert Lazar stated in a 1989 interview that he had just complet-ed a tour of duty at the military's secret installation (designated S-4) in Nevada. When he arrived in April 1988 he found the base "...takes up a whole range of mountains," and includes a row of mysterious hangars built to blend in with the Papoose Mountain Range south of Groom Lake, Nevada.

Allowed to enter only one small office he was one of 27 researchers who were outnumbered more than three to one by security personnel. Lazar was given more than 120 research papers to study dealing with "...propulsion and physics."

The documents outlined how the U.S. at that time possessed a number of un-earthly spacecraft, and helped prepare him for an eventual hands-on examina-tion of an exotic astroship. It was 16 feet thick and 40 feet in diameter with an "anti-matter reactor" and "gravity amplifiers" in its lower section.

As he put it, "The disk I saw up close was not made by the United States. It was definitely extraterrestrial. I don't think it crashed. It was in perfect operating condition.

"There's a [hollow] central column that goes right up through the center of the disk that's a wave guide: the gravity wave is channeled through there. The bottom of that connects to the anti-matter reactor, which is a half of a sphere on the floor of the craft."

In a later, videotaped interview (1991) Lazar described the machine as being powered by atomic fuel element 115. The highest such element known to earthly science is 106, and he stated that "...up around elements 113 and 114 they become stable again. This connection is bombarded with protons, whereupon it releases antimatter in what is called an annihilation reaction.

"Inside the reactor Element 115 reacts with a proton which plugs into the nucleus of the 115 atom and become Element 116, which immediately decays and releases, or radiates, small amounts of antimatter. The antimatter is released into a tuned tube which keeps it from reacting with the matter that surrounds it. It is then directed toward a gaseous matter target at the end of the tube. The matter and antimatter collide and annihilate, totally converting to energy. The heat from this reaction is converted into electrical energy in a near 100% perfect efficient thermoelectric generator."

This mode of propulsion, when used outside a planet's atmosphere, does not produce thrust or move the saucer at all. The best analogy of how its occupants visit fantastically distant points is to imagine a thin rubber sheet tacked by its edges to a tabletop. Place a pebble on one border of the sheet to represent a spacecraft, and then select a point on the sheet to symbolize a destination. Take that spot between thumb and forefinger and pull it to where the pebble sits. This is roughly how the ship's gravity generators warp the fabric of space to draw a location to a fixed point. When the generators are shut off, the UFO follows the rubber/space fabric back to its original position. There is no linear travel through the intervening void, only the hitching of a ride with warped space/time as it resumes its normal positioning.

Lazar claimed to have seen a saucer being test-flown, and he noted it could become invisible and its appearance could become distorted when it was visible. 120

Upon penetrating our dimension/time locality they may be decelerating from higher spectral frequencies, and this slowing is indicated by the visual color shifts from violet to blue to green to yellow to red to white. A UFO turning white would presumably mean it has achieved dimensional stability. Acceleration would be marked by a reversal of this sequence. Along these lines, UFOs may not even be matter, but energy or something else altered so as to appear material.

The dimensional theory could also offer a clue as to why the objects' abrupt accelerations, decelerations and direction changes evidently are not harmful to their occupants. This would definitely be the case with the human body, which would be plastered into jelly on the interior surfaces of any of our spacecraft making such sudden and extreme maneuvers. Saucerians that have been encountered by human witnesses do not appear to be so snugly constructed as to be immune from drastic G-forces.

If these are astroships from someplace besides our specific, physical universe, maybe they come from a place where our laws of physics do not apply, where there is no such thing as velocity/momentum. If the saucers, in some way still beyond our ken, continue to inhabit their native realm while they visit ours there may not be the slightest sensation of motion within their craft even during the wildest high-speed cavortings. If there is some method by which they can abide by their own, different laws of relativity while they are in our skies it would explain their being unfettered by the physical limitations binding us.

Many characteristics of UFOs, such as shooting through our atmosphere at supersonic speeds without producing sonic booms, performing feats of maneuverability and acceleration/deceleration that would destroy our machines and their pilots, and instantly dissolving into nothingness, seem to indicate they are paraphysical, or paranormal.

5 Revelation

ONE OF THE VERY first serious UFO investigators was parapsychologist Dr. Meade Layne. Beginning in 1947, Layne communicated with ufonauts (he called them "Etherians") through trance mediums during séances. [121] This activity is strictly prohibited by the Bible, which refers to it as dealing in familiar spirits.

The dead cannot return to this world in any fashion. It is totally inaccessible to them (Job 7: 9-10.) In cases of hauntings and séances, demons impersonate the dead so convincingly that attending friends and relatives are deceived into believing they are in contact with their departed loved ones.

The imposters generally give their listeners a hazy impression of being in some ill-defined but apparently tolerable spirit realm, and scrupulously avoid any mention of the Holy Trinity. This spreads a concept of an afterlife detached from Christian beliefs of heaven and hell, and leads the uninformed (and hence vulnerable) to the terribly false conclusion that acceptance of Jesus Christ as Lord and Personal Savior is unnecessary to avoid eternal damnation.

Layne's communing with his saucerians in this manner indicates this group of ufonauts was/is a satanic manifestation to be carefully avoided. Otherwise why would they need mediums and séances? Why not communicate in a more efficient, credible fashion?

In many UFO encounters involving multiple witnesses one individual lapses into unconsciousness (such as when Calvin Parker passed out during his abduction with Charles Hickson, who remained awake and lucid throughout the encounter.)

Could the comatose individual unwittingly be serving as a type of trance medium through which the entire event transpires?

In the late 1960s the U.S. Air Force Office of Scientific Research, aided by the U.S. Government Printing Office, and the Library of Congress, released *UFOs and Related Subjects: An Annotated Bibliography*. After reading numerous relevant books, articles and other publications, the project's senior bibliographer, Lynn E. Catoe, made this observation in the book's preface:

"A large part of the available UFO literature is closely linked with mysticism and the metaphysical. It deals with subjects like mental telepathy, automatic writing and invisible entities as well as phenomena like poltergeist manifestations and possession...Many of the UFO reports now being published in the popular press recount alleged incidents that are strikingly similar to demonic possession and psychic phenomena which have long been known to theologians and parapsychologists." [122]

Some of the effects UFOs and ufonauts have had on those who come into close proximity with them (precognition, levitation, instilling terror in animals, mind reading and promises of wealth and power) are also symptoms of demonic possession or persecution. [123]

Reports of hostile activity by UFOs could be connected with this occult scenario. The phantom "foo fighters" which frequently bedeviled Allied and Axis pilots late in World War II were sometimes more than a mere nuisance. Allied intelligence, while investigating the disappearance of 12 American heavy bombers over Germany early in 1945, received this chilling report from a Swiss informer: "A strange flying machine, hemispherical, or at any rate circular in shape, attacked them at fantastic speed, destroying them in a few seconds without using any guns." [124]

At about this same time another dozen U.S. four-engine bombers were lost over Wurtemberg when a peculiar, round, wingless and rudderless craft passed in front of them at extreme speed. Seconds later all twelve planes caught fire and exploded in midair. [125]

Suspicious plane crashes and disappearances involving UFOs were once relatively commonplace in the early days of powered flight when aircraft flying long distances had poorer communications with their bases than today. The June 11, 1938 issue of the *Chicago Daily News* covered the destruction of an Army bomber outside Delaware, Illinois. The paper described how nine men died in this "sudden crash in midair." [126] On December 3, 1953, four jet fighters and their pilots were lost outside Lawrenceville, Georgia when they hit something ground observers could not see because of heavy overcast, but personnel in the control tower at nearby Dobbins Air Base picked up the transmission of one of the terrified airmen as he cried out, "We can't miss it!" Seconds later all four crumpled, burning planes tumbled to Earth. [127]

In October 1955, two B-47 bombers were destroyed in similar mishaps in which they apparently struck (or were struck by) aerial objects that did not crash with them. One of the B-47s was over New Mexico, and the other over Texas. In both cases witnesses saw strange fireballs near the doomed planes immediately prior to their crashes. [128]

The most puzzling (and unsettling) case of an assault on a conventional aircraft by an unidentified flying assailant would be the one described by ufologist Jerome Clark in *Flying Saucer Review*. Clark had found a 1939 newspaper article written immediately after an incident in which an Army transport plane left the Marine Air Station in San Diego, headed for Honolulu. Three hours later the crew frantically radioed that they were under attack, but evidently fell silent before they could identify or describe the attacker.

The transport just made it back to San Diego, flown by its critically injured co-pilot. He died immediately after landing. All other crewmembers were already dead.

Gaping wounds marked the corpses, and the exterior of the aircraft had had huge holes blasted in it. Its interior reeked of hydrogen sulfide (rotten eggs,) and investigators who touched the plane developed a strange skin infection.

Yet in this case full of riddles the most befuddling was that at some point during the fatal flight the pilot and co-pilot had unloaded their .45-caliber automatic sidearms, leaving the unfired cartridges scattered on the cockpit floor. If only the transport had been nearer San Diego or Honolulu when it was assaulted. Some of the crew might have been saved, lessening the tragedy, and providing the answer to (or description of) this enduring, horrible mystery. [129]

A Missouri businessman whose encounter presaged a prolonged association with an invisible entity is so determined to keep his identity secret that he refuses to reveal not only his name, but also the date of his first rendezvous. While driving home from work one night his car broke down on an isolated stretch of road two miles from where he lived. After he began walking he noticed a small, fuzzy light in a field to his left. Although it did not approach him, it kept pace with him, stopping when he stopped. Preoccupied with (and admittedly fearful of) this odd manifestation the businessman did not notice the large UFO behind him until it was almost overhead.

The man stood rooted to the spot, literally paralyzed with terror while simultaneously trying to shield his eyes from an indescribably bright red light. He was able to make out the small light leaving the field and entering the saucer, upon which they departed.

After the shaken witness got home (he had always been a staunch disbeliever in flying saucers) he kept quiet about his experience out of fear of what others might think of his mental faculties. A week later a severe headache was keeping him awake when he heard a voice within his skull. A being calling itself Ashtar telepathically told him he was being contacted by the United Council of Universal Brotherhood, which required his help to avert global destruction.

In ensuing weeks Ashtar correctly foretold newspaper headlines and stock market fluctuations. He told his human contact he would become a godlike messiah who would attract millions of faithful disciples. As a practical-minded businessman he balked at these revelations, and began seeing a psychologist. Not only was he alarmed at Ashtar's becoming an obsessive fixation in his life, but his business was failing from neglect, and his wife had left him.

The psychological counseling did little good, and Ashtar became angered at his contact's recalcitrance. After unsuccessfully trying to threaten the man into submission the unseen being tried bribery, telling the businessman that if he would invest $50,000 in a certain stock he would become fantastically wealthy. The hapless entrepreneur made the investment, and promptly lost $37,000, whereupon Ashtar fell silent and never returned. [130]

It may be significant that the Missourian was by his own admission not deeply religious. Satan may have been searching for such a spiritual vacuum. By offering this ardent capitalist wealth and power (his concept of bliss,) he perhaps was attempting to sow the seeds of a false, theistic movement that would spread and distract others from the message of Christian salvation.

During His earthly ministry Jesus Christ never promised His followers wealth and power in this life, as Ashtar did his human contact. This would indicate Ashtar was not on a mission from the Lord God. Given the overall misfortune to befall his contactee as a result of their intercourse (and assuming the man was not afflicted by some elusive mental condition that went undetected by the psychologist and that appeared and disappeared with peculiar abruptness,) this intrusive entity was either a meddlesome, fallible extraterrestrial on an incredibly pointless mission, or he was a demon. Christ Himself may have sabotaged the $50,000 investment in order to destroy Ashtar's credibility, which is certainly what happened. Realizing this the Ashtar spirit evidently abandoned what it now realized was a failed project, and the harassed businessman was thankfully bereft of this succubus-like being.

Another case that at first glance appears to have been an obvious contact with another world is one in which close inspection uncovers suspicions of dark spirituality. It began in November 1966. In a field outside Owatonna, Minnesota two ladies stood watching an aerial display that had become commonplace to them. They called the blinking, brightly colored lights that cavorted about the skies almost nightly, "little flashers."

One of the lights suddenly dropped to about a yard above the ground on the opposite side of the field from the onlookers and commenced swaying back and forth. One of the women gasped, fell to her knees and went into a trance. "What...is...your...time...cycle?," she asked.

Her shaken companion, Mrs. Ralph Butler, tried to explain the human concept of time as measured in minutes, hours and days.

Then came another question, "What…constitutes…a…night?"

Butler later described how after several more such queries her friend awakened and the little flashers shot upward and out of sight. Sudden, excruciating headaches would strike the two women every time they tried to tell anyone about this incident, which they considered to have been a telepathic exchange between themselves and space aliens.

Butler also had baffling telephone problems, and odd, unidentified voices kept coming through on her CB radio. The following May the Butlers were visited by a peculiar individual calling himself Air Force Major Richard French. He was about five-foot-nine, with a pointed face and dark complexion. His black hair was long, "…too long for an Air Force officer," Butler later remarked. The man spoke perfect English and seemed well educated. He wore civilian clothes—a gray suit, white shirt and black tie. This attire looked brand-new.

He questioned the Butlers about UFOs and CB radios, and then remarked that his stomach was troubling him. Mrs. Butler advised him to eat Jell-O. He replied that if his ailment persisted he would come back for some. As he drove away, Butler wrote down the license plate number of his white Ford Mustang. She later learned it was owned by a Minneapolis car rental agency.

The major returned the next day, and Butler served him some Jell-O. When she set the bowl in front of him he picked it up and tried to drink its contents. She had to show him how to use a spoon to eat something as American as Jell-O.

Later investigation by the Butlers revealed there was indeed an Air Force major named French stationed in their area, but he in no way resembled the man who had visited them. They reached a predictable conclusion about their ersatz major—he was an outworlder who wanted to learn about them and their society, and in order to do so had tried to fool them into thinking he was an ordinary human and had used the authoritative guise of a military officer in order to make them more receptive to his aims. They would be more likely to cooperate with someone from a respected, trusted agency like the U.S. Air Force than they would have been with someone from an unknown or unimpressive background. Of course all this quickly occurred to the Butlers.

This outer space deduction was inevitable. Firstly, the "major's" hair was too long to be a military cut. Secondly, he wore civilian clothes that were brand-new, perhaps just then acquired for the sole purpose of visiting (and disguising himself from) Earthlings. Presumably, whatever he was wearing when he had arrived in his spaceship was inappropriate for his impersonation role, but he was unsurprisingly unable to find a hard-to-obtain authentic Air Force uniform, so instead he was forced to opt for civilian garb. Thirdly, he used a name easily found to be someone else's. Fourthly, the car was almost effortlessly found to be owned by a *civilian* firm. Naturally, he should have been driving a vehicle with some sort of insignia permitting it to be parked on a military base. Lastly, he had to be shown how to use a *spoon.*

Of course "French" was an imposter, but this does not necessarily mean he was an extraterrestrial (as it would seem he was trying to convince his human contacts.) Any group sufficiently advanced to travel through outer space to Earth would surely be capable of doing a much more believable job of dispatching a credible emissary. A considerably more plausible possibility is required to account for this case.

The 1966 UFO/little flashers/Major French affair brought the Butlers more than telephone irregularities, headaches, strange voices on their CB radio, and visits from a bogus Air Force officer. Their home was plagued by poltergeist activity. Objects moved of their own(?) accord, articles of glass spontaneously shattered, and odd sounds echoed through their house. While watching little flashers one night Mrs. Butler felt a hand on her shoulder. When she turned, no one was there.

She later remarked, "Sometimes I've seen some kind of activity, men moving around in the trees behind our house at night, but something keeps me from going near them." It is more than slightly possible that fallen spirits, in an attempt to remain active without appearing too threatening, were masquerading as extraterrestrials. People would be much more likely to pray to the Lord for deliverance from demons than from ETs, so these entities made certain of success by implanting the obvious discrepancies that led to the Butlers' conclusions that French was an imposter, that he was from another planet and hence at least relatively non-threatening. In this situation they would be unlikely to pray for protection. [131] Saucerians have not always been so eager to camouflage themselves, however.

There can be little doubt as to the identity and motives of the darkly mysterious Kachinas, who persistent legends say established the Hopi tribe in their desert home. The Kachinas frankly claimed to be from another world. They went to great lengths to lure a group of natives away from their ancestral homeland into isolation in the arid American Southwest. There they instructed the Hopis in the satanic gospel. It appears the Kachinas intended to establish an entire tribe of devil worshippers, but via some divine intervention the tribe evaded sinking into an occult-centered existence.

Maybe the Kachinas learned a lesson from this abortive venture. Rather than preach an overtly demonic message, perhaps they now work at clandestinely distracting the spiritually vulnerable away from the Gospel of Jesus Christ by godlike displays of technology, telepathy, precognition, etc.

Extraterrestrials would be unlikely to evoke as much fear as obviously satanic powers, and contactees would not be as inclined to turn to God for protection and deliverance. Owatonna, Minnesota had been the site of poltergeist hauntings in earlier years, and the mysterious, elusive airships of 1897 had frequently passed overhead. [132]

Perhaps this secluded town was unwittingly harboring some demonic force that was becoming uneasy over the possibility of being neutralized by the Gospel of Jesus Christ. The Major French encounters may have been staged to mislead townspeople into thinking they were hosting mortal visitors from the stars rather than fallen angels from hell.

Ufonauts' ability to speak our languages may also be relevant here. When German-American Reinhold Schmidt came across a landed, blimplike UFO by a road outside Kearney, Nebraska on November 5, 1957, one of the humanoids who emerged from the machine addressed him in fluent German. [133] A normal-looking individual steps from an abnormal-looking flying machine in the middle of Nebraska, and not only knows German, but knows to speak it to an approaching man who, considering the location, should have preferred English. This is more than a bit suspicious. An actual intergalactic traveler would presumably have used the language of the land he was in, not that of an individual he had never met before. This was no ordinary spaceman.

To ask the obvious, would a mortal from another planet have this fantastic insight? Even considering hypothetical, advanced technology it would still appear unlikely, but it *is* an ability traditionally attributed to demons.

Those who construe the 1948 re-creation of Israel as an indication that this is the final generation before the great tribulation preceding the apocalyptic Second Coming of Christ note that the modern saucer phenomenon sprang upon us at roughly the same time. Maybe somebody was/is trying to distract us from pondering too deeply the possible implications of Israel's re-emergence. Christians may become too preoccupied with studying UFOs to spiritually minister to the lost (i.e. those not saved by the blood of Jesus Christ) in what could be the last days before all Christians are removed from this world by God. Prevention of this sharing of the Gospel in what could be the end times would mean the unsaved would be abandoned and left behind during the coming global holocausts (I Thessalonians 4: 13-18 and Revelation chapters 8 through 11.) The saucers appearing when they did may not have been a coincidence.

Dr. Clifford Wilson, in his book *The Alien Agenda,* flatly states his belief that UFOs are spiritually hostile to the Godhead. He theorizes that an unknown (but great) number of humans may have been abducted, brainwashed and then released by saucerians. These persons would have no conscious memory of their mental rearranging until a worldwide posthypnotic suggestion of some kind galvanizes them into a vast army of zombie-like slave warriors to fight for the ufonaults as they invade Earth. Wilson believes the saucerians are agents of Satan, recruiting unsuspecting humans to fight alongside them against Jehovah at Armageddon in a desperate attempt to disrupt His plans for our world's future as outlined in the Revelation of St. John the Apostle.

In this post-Christian society of ours such a hypothesis initially strikes most persons as inarguably preposterous. The Lord of Darkness may be counting precisely on this. Few things are deadlier than an underestimated enemy, especially if this enemy is also undetected. Satan may *not* be convinced of the inevitability of his eventual consignment to the pit as outlined in Revelation 20: 10. In any case it is unlikely he will go down without a fight. Misery loves company. He will drag as many hapless, lost souls as possible down with him. There are other clues.

Whitley Strieber's interest in Wicca (a form of witchcraft) and his pet cats' going rigid with fear during his ufological encounters lend credence to an occult explanation in his case. An explanation of which he himself appears unaware.

Kelly Segraves, in his book *Sons of God Return,* intriguingly calls to mind the colossal earthquake predicted in Revelation 6: 12-17. He wonders if it could be a devastating side effect of a nuclear war in which demonic saucerians, in their flesh-and-blood guise of mortal extraterrestrials, may be vulnerable. Again we recall ufonauts' repeated warnings against atomic weapons.

When Lorraine Davis, a researcher at John F. Kennedy University in Orinda, California, conducted a survey of 261 UFO witnesses, an unexpected pattern emerged. Although some of the surveyed presumably were Christians, those who had been atheistic or agnostic tended to gravitate toward a sort of universal spirituality following their saucer encounters. [134] Persons who already are committed to a religion are much harder to win over to a new faith (such as Christianity) than those who have no religious convictions at all. By embracing this unfocused but seemingly real and compelling spiritual state, these lost souls play right into Satan's hands. They never realize (at least not until too late) they are taking the wrong path in their quest for eternal salvation.

Although this writer agrees with his collaborator Donovan's surmise that some saucerians may have motives to bolster the Christian faith (additional examples may be found in the Sidney Padrick and Betty Andreasson cases,) he disagrees with Donovan's belief that Christianity is the creation of alien beings. Jesus Christ is the Son of Almighty God, and is Savior of all humanity. He is the sole access to heaven, and the unsaved in the Lorrain Davis study appear to have been distracted from Him specifically because of the flying saucers they encountered. Coincidence? Of course those who suffer this distraction from the route to Holy Redemption would be far from limited to those in the John F. Kennedy University program.

When John Keel conducted his full-scale saucer investigation in the late 1960s he underwent an eerie period of spiritual oppression. It began with odd phone calls from unidentified persons who transmitted strange dispatches from "space people." UFOs followed him. He would select a motel completely at random, only to find that someone had already phoned in a reservation for him and had left incomprehensible messages. On occasion he would awake paralyzed in the middle of the night, and there would be a large dark entity hovering over him.

This harassment spread to his friends and business acquaintances, many of whom were plagued by memory lapses, poltergeists and the smell of rotten eggs. At times he would get calls from contactees who would hand the receiver to someone claiming to be a ufonaut. These conversations sometimes lasted for hours.

During this period these unseen contactees passed along a number of predictions, a frightening percentage of which came true. One is reminded of precognition being a classic symptom of possession.

At one point the saucerians, via their servile contactees, promised a three-day power failure. Keel figured a blackout of that duration would also precipitate a water shortage, so he purchased three quarts of distilled water. He then paid a visit to a contactee who was puzzled by a message he had been given. "Tell John we'll meet with him and help him drink all that water."

On December 15, 1967 a several-week-old prediction of a river disaster came off when the highway bridge connecting Gallipolis, Ohio with Point Pleasant, West Virginia, laden with rush-hour Christmas shoppers, collapsed into the Ohio River. Almost simultaneously with this tragedy, Australia's prime minister vanished without a trace while swimming at his favorite beach. This also had been foretold by the ufonauts. [135] This was not the first instance of saucer-related fortune telling.

A case of what apparently was UFO-connected brainwashing occurred in 1952 when two men were driving through the mountains outside Parana, Brazil. They saw five saucers hovering next to the highway, but did not stop to investigate.

Later, however, one of the witnesses, Aladino Felix, gave in to his curiosity and returned to the scene of the sighting. One of the objects reappeared. Felix was invited aboard by the amiable, human-appearing crew. He conversed freely with the captain, who informed him they were from Venus and just dropping in for a friendly visit. If these beings were benign, however, they had a strange way of showing it. Because of them their new friend's life would take a darkly esoteric turn.

Felix later received a visit from a priest whom he recognized as the saucer captain. As an atheist, Felix was rocked to learn the Catholic Church not only had sent missionaries to Venus, but that converts were journeying to Earth in flying saucers. Through this and many ensuing meetings, the two discussed UFOs and the overall state of the cosmos. Felix became totally immersed in the world of ufology on a very intimate, direct level. He publicized his experiences in his 1959 book *My Contact With Flying Saucers,* using the pseudonym "Dino Kraspedon."

In this work, Felix revealed a respectable knowledge of the occult and the contactee syndrome. It was also the first step in his colorful career as a self-proclaimed UFO prophet. He predicted the devastating flood and earthquake that killed 600 people in Rio de Janeiro in 1965. A year later he warned that the Russians soon would lose a cosmonaut, and on April 24, 1967, Vladimir Komarov became the first human ever to die outside Mother Earth's atmosphere. The following autumn the burgeoning soothsayer of international tragedy went on Brazilian television to forecast the imminent assassinations of Reverend Martin Luther King and Senator Robert Kennedy.

After all this, few were surprised when Felix's predictions of a wave of terrorist activity commenced in 1968. Concentrating on Sao Paolo, newspapers, police stations, the American consulate, Second Army headquarters, and numerous public buildings were bombed while, simultaneously, a mysterious gang robbed armored cars and banks.

Through sheer persistence and determination, the Brazilian police identified and arrested 18 members of the faction. Questioning of the terrorists revealed they had planned to assassinate Brazil's top government officials, paving the way for a complete takeover of the nation. The real surprise was the identity of the group's leader.

The now-infamous Aladino Felix led the gang. After his August 22, 1968 arrest the muddled cosmic necromancer growled:

"I was sent here as an ambassador to the Earth from Venus. My friends from space will come here and free me and avenge my arrest. You can look for tragic consequences for humanity when the flying saucers invade this planet." [136]

No one came to rescue Felix from jail. He remained behind bars, but what if he had not been caught? Would Brazil have fallen under the rule of some unidentified, evidently nonhuman movement? With such a small band it appears extremely unlikely that even one city the size of Sao Paolo could have been taken over, much less the entire, sprawling country. Whoever beguiled Felix and his confederates evidently was using them for purposes other than a military coup. The occult/UFO connection seems a likely possibility.

Venus is a dead planet. Lead would flow like water on its baking surface, and its sulfurous, corrosive atmosphere has been found to be as lifeless as the heat-sterilized exterior. Aladino Felix's saucerians could not have come from Venus.

Being an atheist, Felix would not have thought to pray for discernment and guidance before embarking on what he intended to be the conquest of Brazil. Had he been familiar with Christian concepts of what characterizes the Holy and the profane he would have realized that the precognitive powers bestowed upon him by the "Venusians" are a symptom of demonic possession. In his state of spiritual vulnerability Felix appears to have been used by Satan, who through accurate predictions of monumental events propelled him to a position of high visibility. He had, in the course of announcing his forecasts, proclaimed to an ever-growing number of listeners that the inhabitants of Venus were wonderful and caring. They were so kind and compassionate that they sent one of their priests to inform him of their mission to declare to Brazil (and, it is likely, eventually an even greater area) Venus' gospel of an interplanetary brotherhood. As in the Fatima events, these ufonauts tried to hide behind Catholic imagery, but there is no record of Felix's "priest" ever mentioning the Holy Trinity. It would seem they intended to implant an exotic (and hence fascinating and compelling,) theistic (but non-Christian) movement.

The Lord God would not permit this conspiracy to come to fruition. After the prophet's abortive attempt to take over Brazil (which probably was not anticipated by the ufonauts,) his arrest and exposure, his cause sputtered and died. He dropped back into the obscurity from which he had sprung—a discarded pawn of a failed scheme of Satan's.

Wilson's ideas about Lucifer being behind the flying saucer mystery look to be very compatible with the Aladino Felix case. The saucerians may not have been behind the formation and actions of the terrorist squad (it was hardly in keeping with their flowery doctrine,) but their overzealous, impatient proselyte resorted to force rather than take the slow course of a takeover by a steadily growing body of adherents who would assume power through sheer force of numbers. Even if they were not directly responsible for it, however, the ufonauts do not appear to have attempted to dissuade Felix from his violent, ultimately self-destructive venture.

There can be no doubt that the piously garbed UFO commander lied. He could not have been from scorched Venus, but he likely *was* interested in establishing a pseudo-religious movement. When looked at from the viewpoint provided by Wilson's hypothesis it appears likely this was an early, tentative attempt by demonic forces to pose as benign extraterrestrials. Their sweet-sounding message of a colorful, interplanetary quasi-religion could have been intended to lure the unsaved away from the narrow path to true Christian salvation, but it was foiled by human fallibility, and perhaps also by some unseen, subtle-but-effective act of God.

Christian ufologists Zola Levitt and John Weldon point out that the "Sons of God" mentioned in the sixth chapter of Genesis could have been demonic ufonauts. The Bible never describes them as benevolent, and their taking of human wives hardly seems to be something expected from *Holy* angels. The prevalent wickedness that overspread Earth after their appearance led directly to the Flood, and lends weight to the likelihood that they were *fallen* angels. It also is notable that the group of beings referred to as the "Sons of God" in Job 1:6 included Satan.

Weldon and Levitt frankly state their belief that many UFO contactees are demonically possessed *by ufonauts* and used as mouthpieces to subtly spread a camouflaged demonic gospel in order to keep unsaved humanity unsaved prior to the coming of the Antichrist.

Another who saw the saucers in a paranormal light was Britain's Royal Air Force (RAF) Air Marshall Sir Victor Goddard, who was involved in the RAF's UFO investigations in the 1950s. In a 1969 lecture given in London, Goddard pointed to a lack of evidence that UFOs come from another planet:

"For if the materiality of UFO is paraphysical (and consequently normally invisible) UFO could more plausibly be creations of an invisible world coincident with the space of our physical Earth planet than creations in the paraphysical realms of any other physical planet in the solar system...Given that UFO are paraphysical, capable of reflecting lifelike ghosts, and given also that (according to many observers) they remain visible as they change position at ultra-high speeds from one point to another, it follows that those that remain visible in transition, do not dematerialize for swift back transition, and therefore their mass must be of a diaphanous (very diffuse) nature, and their substance relatively etheric...The observed validity of this supports the paraphysical assertion and makes the likelihood of UFO being Earth-created greater than the likelihood of their creation on another planet." [137]

Sir Victor's phrase "lifelike ghosts" sounds like someone describing what he does not realize are demons. Regardless of precisely what he perceived UFOs to be, it seems certain the Air Marshall's research had led him to conclude the saucers belong in the realm of the paranormal, and the occult is about as paranormal as anything can be.

Kelly Segraves, in his book *Sons of God Return,* details his suspicion that Satan is sending his fallen angels to us in the guise of extraterrestrial astronauts in hopes of diverting us from the worship of the one True God by leading us to believe Jehovah is nothing more than a supertechnological mortal. Segraves points out that if contemporary doomsayers are correct and that we are living in the end times, the Sons of God (fallen angels) are apparently returning in flying disks to convince us God is nothing more than a glorified computer technician. This "god's" fantastically advanced machines would be as incomprehensible to us as color television scenes from the moon would have been to Plato. Although he was a genius, he lived in a much younger, less high-tech world. It is safe to assume that we are no smarter than he was, so what if someone is as far ahead of us as we are ahead of him? To us this technology would seem godlike--perhaps even worthy of veneration.

Segraves believes the ufonauts are launching this campaign in what are likely to be the final days before the rapture of the Christians (when the Lord will remove His true believers from a tribulation-bound world) in order to insure there will be as few believers as possible to remove. There is no telling how many of the unsaved have already been diverted from the straight and narrow path to salvation because of their obsessive fascination with the saucers. In some cases saucerians (such as the Kachina) have expressed an outright, unsettling desire to be worshipped. Only the Messiah truly deserves such veneration, and these beings have done nothing to justify any claim they may make (or imply) of being divine. It is undeniable that the first time He came to Earth the Christ did not arrive in a flying saucer or any other mode of physical transportation. Such would hardly seem necessary for an all-powerful being capable of creating *everything*.

If this occult scenario is even a partial answer to the flying saucer phenomenon, serious ufology by those not strongly committed to (and hence protected by) the Holy Spirit could be an indescribably dangerous venture, especially if the secular ufologist starts getting close to the truth. Who knows what lengths Satan might go to in order to keep his scheme from being exposed?

A young man from Ithaca, New York, involved in an investigation of the UFOs that frequented the vicinity of the radio telescopes outside that city in 1967-1968, may have been the target of an attempted murder by ufonauts. He was in the process of leaving his home to attend a meeting, but got back out of his car. He re-entered his home and performed several pointless, time-consuming tasks such as taking a book from a table and placing it on a shelf, all at the behest of an inexplicable, compelling urge.

After a few minutes he again left the house, and this time drove away. At this point his memory of what happened that night ends. He evidently drove about four miles to a railroad crossing, ignored the warning bells and lights and drove in front of a speeding train. It struck and demolished his car. The young man, incredibly, survived the crash with only minor injuries, but could not recall starting or driving the car. After performing the pointless tasks, the next thing he knew he was in a hospital bed. He could not understand his delay in leaving home. Besides being meaningless it almost got him killed. If he had left home a minute earlier he would have missed the train entirely. Perhaps his investigation was going too well for someone's liking. [138]

This occult angle presents a sobering aspect of the UFO riddle, but maybe it is only one answer among many. As long as we allow ourselves to be limited by blind belief in "absolute" laws of physical science (such as the supposed impossibility of exceeding the speed of light,) we will remain stumped by ufology, which by its seemingly impossible and endlessly complicated nature has kept us bewildered and generally skeptical through the decades. Perhaps we have been trying too hard to decipher it, and maybe somebody somewhere arranged it this way. One wonders what would happen if we stopped *trying* to find out what is happening. All our trying has so far done little but further confuse the matter.

Traces at landing sites range from severe, lasting destruction, to there being no sign whatever of anything having touched down. This would seem to indicate radically divergent propulsion systems, and technologies that have little in com-mon other than being highly superior to ours. There is evidently more than one group up there (or somewhere) that finds us worthy of scrutiny. The highly diverse descriptions of saucer occupants' physical appearances further support this likelihood.

All this would seem to indicate that there is no singular, all-encompassing cause behind the saucer phenomenon. A conclusion to be taken for granted. A band of interstellar explorers landing in, say, Denmark would not be very perspicacious to assume that *all* sentient Earth inhabitants look, sound and act like Danes. It is equally foolish for us to continue to commit ourselves to searching for a single, preferably simple explanation for an issue that is looking more complex all the time.

It is possible that every explanatory hypothesis in this chapter is correct (along with no telling how many others which may not yet have been perceived.) It is illogical to assume that any *one* is the answer, to the same extent that it would be ridiculous to conclude that any single microorganism is responsible for all infectious disease.

Our entire world may be in a situation very similar to that of Western Europe in 1500 A.D. A new age of exploration, discovery and expansion of incalculable proportions might be in its genesis. What effects this will have on humanity, its world and its God are still beyond our knowledge. Only He knows for sure.

Likewise the subject of UFOs. *Something* seems to be in the process of being established. Whether a reality, nonexistence or something totally new, unexpected and therefore indescribable we cannot yet say. To achieve this enlightenment, ufology needs to be categorized into individual classes to be studied meticulously and independently. Extraterrestrial ufology, dimensional ufology, terrestrial ufology, theistic/occult ufology and perhaps others to be discerned later would each be given a lion's share of attention, which seems the most promising route to eventual comprehension.

Unless this overhaul in the methods of investigating this still-embryonic field of science is undertaken we may as well cease delving into it altogether, and simply wait and see. Someone from somewhere else just might step forward and give us the elusive answers.

Appendix I: ET Role in Earth History

by Tim Donovan

OUR ALIEN VISITORS HAVE a great historical Master Plan for Earth. Formulated two thousand years ago, it is now only half a century from spectacular fulfillment. The ETs' purpose is to speed terrestrial development; catapulting Earth into the ranks of the galaxy's superworlds in the shortest time possible. Even strange alien behavior can be understood in the context of this great Master Plan.

Probably the best starting point for explaining the Master Plan is revealing the reasons for the current government saucer cover-up (and the parallel alien inconspicuousness and deception: disclosure would doom Judeo-Christianity and democracy—the heart of present culture.)

Regarding Judeo-Christianity: the saucers represent a great Universal Evolutionary Culmination. They complete Man's knowledge of an anti-Christian Worldview. Evolution means *ascent* from the lowliest and simplest things to the loftiest and most complex—from the simplest matter spewed by the Big Bang to more complex matter forged in stellar interiors, to DNA, primitive life, more sophisticated life, intelligence, civilization and supercivilization.

In such a progressive worldview no form of supremacy exists *initially,* only *ultimately.* No "god," in other words, existed until intelligent life reached the peak of development and became all-powerful. Man is rapidly approaching a great Evolutionary Summit already attained by his alien visitors. Instead of worshipping a nonexistent diety he shall become *almighty himself,* based on ultimate science and technology. That is what our accelerating progress is all about: the eventual attainment of a great summit where Man needn't worship any "god." He *will* be god. Alien saucer races have already reached such a summit. Like them, Man can survive and attain greatness. Obviously, saucer disclosure would imperil religion, to say the least.

As for democracy: dictators have often used outside threats to gain unlimited power, or consolidate it. A saucer scare would give them an unparalleled opportunity. Never has the human race faced a challenge of such dimensions (if obscured for now.) Humanity's great common cause would overshadow individual rights. In its frantic attempts to cope society would undergo the most radical transformation. Extremism would thrive in an atmosphere far exceeding the aftermath of Sputnik--more akin to *War of the Worlds.*

Russian history may provide the best analogy for a post-disclosure world. Peter the Great, and later Stalin ruthlessly modernized Russia to match advanced foreigners quickly. Such leadership and policies are antithetical to democracy. This explains the cover-up or unwillingness to set in motion a vast, sweeping overhaul of the status quo.

Ufologist Stanton Friedman blamed nationalism for the cover-up, since disclosure of aliens would compel a unified world. True enough, but much more is at risk than just the nation-state! Virtually *all* current beliefs and institutions would be imperiled by disclosure. Len Stringfield's sources mentioned alien bodies appearing as if formed out of a mold, and probably cloned. Even government informant "Falcon" (*UFO Cover-Up? Live,* October 1988) believes *some* facts about the aliens should be kept classified. Might it be that theirs is a "Brave New World," and that all civilizations ultimately metamorphose into totalitarianism?

Alien mind control, used to manipulate abductees, suggests an ET supertotalitarianism making Big Brother look tame.

Since 1947 libertarian plutocrats have feverishly cloaked the hair-raising saucer evidence, knowing that disclosure would dynamite their values to smithereens. It is easy for ufologists without access to certain secrets to downplay the consequences of disclosure. *Those in a position to know obviously have reason to be much more pessimistic.* They have resorted to every tactic of concealment, disinformation and intimidation to prevent the truth from being known. What is at stake is nothing less than the survival of our present society.

So Judeo-Christianity and democracy would be utterly disproved and destroyed by disclosure. Fascism (and then some) would probably triumph. Disclosure is therefore impossible as long as Judeo-Christianity/democratic values and institutions are intact. The present system has a vested interest in cover-up and self-preservation. It won't do what is tantamount to suicide.

But if Judeo-Christianity/democracy are wrong, how could they have arisen and flourished for so long? And what was their role in the grand scheme of things? (The ET Master Plan.) The most likely answer:

Christianity, implanted by alien beings (aiding and manipulating Christ,) *is nothing but the suppression or postponement of the Will to Power for the sake of complete, prerequisite technical and scientific progress first* (providing the proper basis for the Will to Power.) How did this work historically?

Ancient Rome represented the great worldly ambition and Will to Power, but was almost totally lacking in the proper technical/scientific foundation for it. Caesar demanded to be worshipped as a god, but was no god. He wasn't backed by much know-how. As long as Rome endured, scientific and technical progress remained stagnant.

It was not until after the fall of Rome (and its would-be successors—Theodoric, Charlemagne, etc.) and the rise of the Christian medieval world that technical (and later scientific) progress got underway. The continuing stream of innovation and progress unique to the Christian West began in the 10th-11th centuries, after the fall of the Roman and Frankish empires.

The Will to Power, in other words, had been eliminated so that all energies could be devoted to building its proper basis first (science, technology.)

By fostering such prerequisite progress (for the ultimate Will to Power) Christianity is steadily digging its own grave. Progress makes Man more successful and powerful in the real world, undermining otherworldly doctrine by degrees (HOW Christianity fosters progress, and the Will to Power hindered it are beyond the scope of this synopsis.) Note that the West wound up with both Christianity, the antithesis of the Will to Power, and the overwhelming scientific and technical basis for the Will to Power. Darwin came from the Christian West, as did this author.

But until the ultimate progress is attained, deeply ingrained Christianity remains strong enough to forestall premature *resurgent* Will to Power. Whereas ancient Rome was almost totally lacking in the technical/scientific basis for the Will to Power, premature resurgent Caesars such as Napoleon and Hitler did not yet have enough. Hitler demanded to be worshipped as a god, but was no god. He had only mid-20th Century technology. Not until the 21st Century shall the Ultimate Master of the world, backed by supertechnology, be a true god worthy of veneration. He will say to his cloned, genetically engineered subjects, "I am your Maker. Worship me."

The Will to Power was still premature in 1945, the year of the Nazi collapse, and may not triumph until 2040 or so. For aforementioned reasons the saucers shall be instrumental in overturning current beliefs and institutions in the end. Arising in the very aftermath of the Reich's fall, the Mideast conflict, the East-West rivalry and saucer phenomenon will one day rejuvenate fascism. Nazism, however, will not revive, but a *new ultimate* rational-Evolutionary Worldview (nonracist.)

When the ultimate basis for the Will to Power is at last attained, the three crises, at their culminating phases, shall produce a Great Reversal of values, overthrowing Christianity and democracy with Caesarism so that Earth's scientific and technical genius can be supplemented by the Will to Power to produce a consummate superworld (it is fallacious to suppose technology alone can produce a superciv-ilization. The space program has stagnated not because technology is lacking, but because current values—religion, hedonism—are hardly conducive to great achievement; only the Will to Power.)

The Mideast conflict shall be first to reach its culminating phase, setting in motion the reversal of western values and institutions. Aid for Israel shall lead to Arab economic retaliation, depression and chaos. Military leaders shall seize power, sweeping away the irresponsible democratic government (with its Zionist lobby.) Fascism shall revive in the aftermath of Judeo-Christian/democratic failings.

World War III shall then make its contribution. The diversion of Russian forces to the China front shall ensure western victory, but democracy will lose. U.S. dictatorship shall be consolidated in wartime (after nuclear deterrence ends.) After WWIII, authoritarianism will be needed to forge a bona fide World Government. Caesarism, not democracy, shall run the ultimate global empire.

The saucers shall make the final and culminating contribution. The alien threat or challenge shall strengthen dictatorship and global unity. Fascists (or Wholeists) shall clone supermen, liquidate the inferior, and colonize the solar system. Earth shall become a consummate superworld on a par with the others.

The aliens originally implanted inverted values to foster prerequisite progress. Foundationless Caesarism was overturned by Christianity so the basis for the Will to Power could arise. When that basis is at last complete the aliens will overthrow the last of the stupidity they were responsible for in the first place (restoring Caesarism with a vengeance,) so Earth can have the ultimate in ideology as well as technology (hence becoming a great, consummate supercivilization.)

Some may have trouble reconciling "inexplicable" alien behavior with this scenario and master plan. Yet it has already been shown that it is still too early to overthrow Christianity and democracy. The ultimate basis for the Will to Power is still years away. So the aliens, like the government, resort largely to secrecy and deception (although only the aliens may know the full Master Plan; the necessity of interim obscurantism. The government probably covers up to preserve current institutions for their own sake. Again, its downfall is the prerequisite to disclosure. Only a new, fascist regime can benefit from disclosure, and hence agree to it, after WWIII.)

The problem for the aliens from is how to get us used to them without wrecking current ideologies too early. The apparent solution is to make humanity semi-conscious of their existence through sporadic, fleeting appearances, and to confuse the picture greatly, to forestall any "premature" conclusions. Occasionally the aliens even bolster religion. Fatima, the Andreasson and Strieber affairs were probably designed to help prevent premature resurgent Will to Power, based on the general perception of the aliens as a supercivilization at the peak of Universal Evolution, with godlike powers. It is still too soon for man to aspire to such greatness. He still lacks the technical foundation, which must be completed first.

Repeated visitations shall familiarize us with saucerians without wrecking existing beliefs prematurely. The aliens still reinforce them occasionally.

Generally the picture remains very confused, even bizarre, compliments of all the trickery a supercivilization can muster.

These may not be popular ideas, but they are the only way to make sense of a complex phenomenon in the context of world history. This is an ultimate wholeistic worldview into which I've integrated virtually everything.

Appendix II: Saucers Deliberately Crashed

by Tim Donovan

THE AVAILABLE RECORD OF downed disks has a few unusual aspects, which do not detract from the credibility of the reports as much as they suggest the crashes were actually planned.

Perhaps the strangest thing about crash accounts is that retrieval by humans was possible. It seems unlikely that several could have fallen into government hands if a superior ET civilization opposed it. Even advanced technology may break down, but that does not explain the failure of a supercivilization to destroy or remove traces before military men recovered them, or afterwards for that matter. Widely scattered debris suggests the Roswell saucer self-destructed. The reported seizure of others intact, however, invites suspicion. And why was nothing done to rescue or free survivors?

Several hours or even days elapsed between the crashes and subsequent retrievals. Surely advanced beings could have disposed of fallen disks if they wished. Military establishments make great efforts to prevent technology from falling into the wrong hands. The aliens, in contrast, seem strangely negligent. They allowed the U.S. government to reap a bounty of advanced gear and bodies.

Another odd feature of crashes is their occurrence very early in the modern saucer era. The term "flying saucer" was barely a week old when one came down near Roswell in 1947. Although some supposedly crashed much later, and one as early as WWII, these were exceptions. Moreover they are not as reliable as Roswell, and may be misinformation. Why haven't crashes occurred in the past decade if they are the result of random accidents? Why the concentration of fallen disks at the beginning of the modern UFO era?

Len Stringfield suggested later crashes were more effectively covered up, or that saucers overcame initial vulnerabilities. Such speculation hardly explains another peculiarity: the apparent geographical concentration of crashes. Saucers generally came down in America's thinly populated areas. The distribution of downed disks is suspiciously odd in that they avoided most foreign countries and U.S. cities, even though saucer sightings were universal. Why would alien craft malfunction only over deserts and hinterland? How could they have been more effectively covered up in other countries? If crashes were the result of random accidents one should not expect them to be bunched up either in space or time. Yet this appears to be the case, lending weight to the hypothesis that the crashes were the result of design, not accident.

Unusual aspects of crash/retrieval tales may lead skeptics to dismiss this whole idea of research, but the Roswell case in particular is too convincing to make that course seem wise. Moreover, all of the odd features can be explained by an interpretation of crashes as a deliberate part of an alien plan. The advanced beings were unerring after all, and ingenious.

What could motivate the aliens to sacrifice several craft and the lives of most of their occupants? They probably sought to contact the government without disturbing our society. Crash landing in the American Southwest enabled the aliens to get in touch with the most influential government on Earth without the public being aware of it, save for a few locals who were long-silenced. The aliens no doubt relied on the Southwest's combination of military bases and sparse population to ensure that contact was limited to the government. There was to be no awareness of their existence.

The probable mission of the alien survivor(s) was to allay fears of an invasion, and to prevent a premature disruption of society. Disclosure of aliens would spark a radical transformation of our culture to better cope. This would be futile because we may not be able to attain parity with aliens for many more years.

Revolutionizing current society prematurely might hinder the very basic research which must culminate before any attempt to match the aliens would be feasible. Note that the Soviet emphasis on revolutionary overviews and causes proved inimical to narrowly focused scientific and technical pursuits. The inevitable failure of the stagnant Soviet system explains why aliens chose to deal with the U.S. government.

Although related saucer waves are probably designed to slowly familiarize us with aliens, publicly known saucer evidence is inadequate to compel a major overhaul of society to reflect the reality of aliens and catch up with them. One day we will be able to do so. For now there is little we can do, since we lack the basic know-how. Why even acknowledge the challenge if we don't have the means to deal with it yet, and which is benign enough to ignore in the meantime? Gaining that expertise, undisturbed by revolution, is the likely purpose of interim secrecy, ensured jointly by aliens and government.

Why didn't the aliens land instead of crash when seeking contact with the government? They probably crashed to minimize the risk of frightening the government initially. Landings might have given the impression an invasion was underway. Crashes were much less threatening, because the alien craft were wrecked and most occupants were dead. There was no need to declare a national emergency. Unlike the space invaders of science fiction, the real, crashed aliens were patently harmless. Alien foresight and self-sacrifice apparently prevented a real *War of the Worlds* scare in 1947. That would have defeated the aliens' purpose. Of course EBE (Extraterrestrial Biological Entity) probably provided formal assurances along with a demand for prolonged secrecy.

How could the government have known initially that the aliens were benign unless it was informed by them? Although secrecy and the preservation of the status quo were in the government's best interest, it would have had nothing to lose by mobilizing society if its survival seemed threatened. UFOs might have been interpreted as harbingers of invasion, necessitating a state of emergency. Obviously it was imperative for the aliens to provide assurances and compel secrecy at the very beginning to prevent major blunders by the government in the face of the new phenomenon.

The aliens must appear sporadically for many years to familiarize us with them. They cannot remain unknown until terrestrial technology peaks, and then suddenly reveal themselves (to induce Earth to quickly catch up and join the intergalactic club.) The shock of "aliens" would be too great if Man was not already semi-conscious of their existence. But even brief, intermittent appearances might have triggered a premature revolution if the government was not reassured and cooperative from the start. The aliens had little to fear from the public once they had secured the cooperation of the government. If a saucer appeared the public could be fooled into thinking it was just Venus or a meteor. The government, with its jets and radar, knew better. It was the one element of society that could not be fooled.

If the aliens have to appear without disrupting society they had to ensure, right away, that the government relax, but keep quiet and deny their existence. Once the U.S. government was set straight the alien plan could not be seriously threatened from any other quarter. After an understanding had been reached there may have been secret landings, while crashes ceased.

Source Notes

UNIT I

1. Shabelle Media Network, Somalia, 3/26/07

2. Trendwatch, 4/27/07

3. *Our Haunted Planet*

4. *Our Haunted Planet*

5. *Flying Saucers: Serious Business*

6. *Flying Saucers: Serious Business*

7. *Flying Saucers: Serious Business*

8. *Flying Saucers: Serious Business*

9. *This Baffling World,* pages 122-126

10. *Dimensions*

11. *Dimensions*

12. *Dimensions*

13. *World of the Odd and the Awesome*

14. *Strange World,* pages 175-181

15. *UFOs: Operation Trojan Horse*

16. *Dimensions,* pages 84-85

17. *UFOs: Operation Trojan Horse*

18. *UFOs: Operation Trojan Horse*

19. *Flying Saucers: Serious Business*

20. *UFOs: Operation Trojan Horse,* pages 13-14

21. *Flying Saucers: Serious Business*

22. *Flying Saucers: Serious Business,* pages 57-58

23. *Flying Saucers: Serious Business*

24. *Flying Saucers: Serious Business,* pages 60-61

25. *Flying Saucers: Serious Business,* page 62

26. Time/Life *Mysteries of the Unknown—The UFO Phenomenon,* pages 53-55

27. *Beyond Earth: Man's Contact With UFOs*

28. Time/Life *Mysteries of the Unknown—Alien Encounters,* pages 84-85

29. Time/Life *Mysteries of the Unknown—Alien Encounters,* pages 84-85

30. Associated Press, 1/15/94

31. *Incident at Exeter,* pages 38-41

32. *Incident at Exeter,* pages 11-15

33. *Incident at Exeter*

34. *Our Haunted Planet*

35. *Incident at Exeter,* page 231

36. *Our Haunted Planet*

37. Time/Life *Mysteries of the Unknown—The UFO Phenomenon*, page 106

38. Time/Life *Mysteries of the Unknown—The UFO Phenomenon*, page 107

39. Time/Life *Mysteries of the Unknown—The UFO Phenomenon*, page 109

40. Time/Life *Mysteries of the Unknown—The UFO Phenomenon*, page 109-110

41. Time/Life *Mysteries of the Unknown—The UFO Phenomenon*, page 111

42. Time/Life *Mysteries of the Unknown—The UFO Phenomenon*, page 115

43. Time/Life *Mysteries of the Unknown—The UFO Phenomenon*

44. *Reader's Digest,* February 1978

Unit II

1. *The Flying Saucer Conspiracy*

2. *The World's Greatest UFO Mysteries*, pages 5-7

3. *Beyond Earth: Man's Contact With UFOs*

4. *Our Haunted Planet*, page 11

5. *Stranger Than Science*

6. *Flying Saucers: Serious Business*

7. *Strange World*, pages 6-7

8. *UFOs: Operation Trojan Horse*, pages 66-67

9. *Strange World*

10. *Flying Saucers: Serious Business*

11. *Strange World*

12. Time/Life *Mysteries of the Unknown—The UFO Phenomenon,* pages 70-73

13. *Strange World*

14. Time/Life *Mysteries of the Unknown—The UFO Phenomenon,* page 73

15. Time/Life *Mysteries of the Unknown—Mysterious Creatures,*

16. *Beyond Earth: Man's Contact With UFOs,* pages 22-34

17. *Our Haunted Planet,* pages 185-187

18. Time/Life *Mysteries of the Unknown—The UFO Phenomenon,* pages 85-86

19. *Beyond Earth: Man's Contact With UFOs,* pages 109-121

20. *The Interrupted Journey*

21. *Dimensions,* pages 23-24

22. Time/Life *Mysteries of the Unknown—The UFO Phenomenon,* page 129

23. *Dimensions*

24. *Dimensions*

25. *Dimensions*

26. *UFOs: Operation Trojan Horse*

27. *Dimensions*

28. *Dimensions*

29. *Dimensions*

30. *Beyond Earth: Man's Contact with UFOs*

31. *The World's Greatest UFO Mysteries,* pages 51-54

32. *Pravda,* 1999-2006

Unit III

1. *Stranger Than Science*

2. *Strange World*

3. *Stranger Than Science*

4. *Stranger Than Science*

5. *Strange World*

6. *Stranger Than Science*

7. *Stranger Than Science*

8. *Stranger Than Science*

9. *Stranger Than Science*

10. *In Search of Extraterrestrials*

11. *In Search of Extraterrestrials*, pages 67-68

12. *Our Haunted Planet*

13. *Sons of God Return*

14. *Charles Berlitz's World of the Odd and the Awesome*, page 147

15. *The Bermuda Triangle*

16. *Flying Saucers: Serious Business*, pages 81-82

17. *Our Haunted Planet*

18. *Not of This World*, pages 74-75

Unit IV

1. *Disneyland of the Gods,* pages 43-46

2. *Chariots of the Gods*

3. *Beyond Earth: Man's Contact With UFOs*

4. *The Spaceships of Ezekiel*

5. *Mysteries From Forgotten Worlds*

6. *Gods and Spacemen in the Ancient East*

7. *Chariots of the Gods*

8. *Is Anyone Out There?*

9. Time/Life *Mysteries of the Unknown—The UFO Phenomenon*

10. *Chariots of the Gods*

11. *We Are Not the First*

12. *The Alien Agenda*

13. *Our Haunted Planet,* page 146

14. *We Are Not the First, Our Haunted Planet*

Unit V

1. *Is Anyone Out There?*

2. Time/Life *Mysteries of the Unknown—The UFO Phenomenon*

3. *Flying Saucers: Serious Business*

Unit VI

1. Time/Life *Mysteries of the Unknown—The UFO Phenomenon*

2. Time/Life *Mysteries of the Unknown—The UFO Phenomenon*

3. *Our Haunted Planet,* page 111

4. *Disneyland of the Gods*

5. Time/Life *Mysteries of the Unknown—The UFO Phenomenon*

6. Time/Life *Mysteries of the Unknown—The UFO Phenomenon*

7. Time/Life *Mysteries of the Unknown—The UFO Phenomenon*

8. Time/Life *Mysteries of the Unknown—The UFO Phenomenon*

9. Time/Life *Mysteries of the Unknown—The UFO Phenomenon,* page 51

10. *Strangest of All*

11. *UFOs: What on Earth is Happening?*

12. *Stranger Than Science*

13. *Charles Berlitz's World of the Odd and the Awesome*

14. *Flying Saucers: Serious Business,* pages 240-241

15. *Flying Saucers: Serious Business,* pages 159-161

16. *UFOs: Operation Trojan Horse*

17. *Our Haunted Planet*

18. *The World's Greatest UFO Mysteries*

19. *UFOs: What on Earth is Happening?*

20. *UFOs: What on Earth is Happening?*

21. *UFOs: Operation Trojan Horse*

22. *Dimensions*

23. *Out There*

24. *Out There*

25. *Incident at Exeter,* page 21

26. *Out There*

27. *Out There*

28. *Out There*

29. *Out There,* page 164

30. *Out There*

31. *UFOs: Operation Trojan Horse,* page 257

32. *UFOs: Operation Trojan Horse,* page 258

33. *UFOs: Operation Trojan Horse,* page 260

34. *UFOs: Operation Trojan Horse,* page 264

35. *UFOs: Operation Trojan Horse*

36. *UFOs: Operation Trojan Horse,* page 266

37. *UFOs: Operation Trojan Horse*

38. *Our Haunted Planet,* page 182

39. *Our Haunted Planet,* page 183

40. *UFOs: Operation Trojan Horse*

41. Time/Life *Mysteries of the Unknown—The UFO Phenomenon*

42. *Our Haunted Planet*

43. Time/Life *Mysteries of the Unknown—The UFO Phenomenon*

44. *Our Haunted Planet*

45. *UFOs: Operation Trojan Horse*

46. *Our Haunted Planet*

47. *Our Haunted Planet*

48. *Beyond Earth: Man's Contact With UFOs,* pages 182-184

49. *Phenomena: A Book of Wonders*

50. *Our Haunted Planet*

51. *Disneyland of the Gods*

52. *UFOs: Operation Trojan Horse*

53. *Beyond Earth: Man's Contact With UFOs,* page 109

54. Time/Life *Mysteries of the Unknown—The UFO Phenomenon,* page123

55. *In Search of Extraterrestrials*

56. *Disneyland of the Gods*

57. *UFOs: Operation Trojan Horse,* page 198

58. *Not of This World*

59. *The Riddle of the Bermuda Triangle,* page110, *Stranger Than Science,* pages 5-6

60. *The Riddle of the Bermuda Triangle,* page 110

61. *The World's Greatest UFO Mysteries*

62. Associated Press, 5/26/94

63. *UFOs: Operation Trojan Horse*, page 146

64. *UFOs: Operation Trojan Horse*

65. *UFOs: Operation Trojan Horse*, page 147

66. *Disneyland of the Gods*

67. *UFOs: What on Earth is Happening?*

68. *Our Haunted Planet*

69. *The World's Greatest UFO Mysteries*

70. Time/Life *Mysteries of the Unknown—Mystic Places*

71. Time/Life *Mysteries of the Unknown—Earth Energies*

72. Time/Life *Mysteries of the Unknown—Mystic Places*, page 108

73. Time/Life *Mysteries of the Unknown—Mystic Places*

74. Time/Life *Mysteries of the Unknown—Mystic Places*

75. *The Bermuda Triangle*-Berlitz

76. *The Bermuda Triangle*-Berlitz

77. *The Bermuda Triangle*-Berlitz

78. *The Bermuda Triangle*-Berlitz

79. *Dimensions*

80. *Dimensions*

81. *Beyond Earth: Man's Contact With UFOs*, page 117

82. *UFOs: Operation Trojan Horse*, page 80

83. *UFOs: Operation Trojan Horse*

84. *UFOs: Operation Trojan Horse*

85. *UFOs: Operation Trojan Horse*

86. *UFOs: Operation Trojan Horse*

87. *UFOs: Operation Trojan Horse*

88. *UFOs: Operation Trojan Horse,* page 128

89. *UFOs: Operation Trojan Horse*

90. *UFOs: Operation Trojan Horse*

91. *UFOs: Operation Trojan Horse*

92. *UFOs: Operation Trojan Horse*

93. *UFOs: Operation Trojan Horse*

94. *UFOs: Operation Trojan Horse*

95. *UFOs: Operation Trojan Horse*

96. *UFOs: Operation Trojan Horse,* page 139

97. *UFOs: Operation Trojan Horse,* pages 140-141

98. *UFOs: Operation Trojan Horse*

99. *Flying Saucers: Serious Business*

100. *The Gulf Breeze Sightings*

101. *UFOs: Operation Trojan Horse*

102. *Flying Saucers: Serious Business,* page 86

103. *Flying Saucers: Serious Business,* pages 87-88

104. *Flying Saucers: Serious Business*

105. *Flying Saucers: Serious Business*

106. *Flying Saucers: Serious Business*

107. *Flying Saucers: Serious Business*

108. *Flying Saucers: Serious Business*

109. *UFOs: Operation Trojan Horse,* pages 176-177

110. *UFOs: Operation Trojan Horse*

111. Time/Life *Mysteries of the Unknown—Mystic Places*

112. Time/Life *Mysteries of the Unknown—Mystic Places*

113. *Secret of the Ages*

114. *Secret of the Ages*

115. *Dimensions*

116. Time/Life *Mysteries of the Unknown—The UFO Phenomenon*

117. *UFOs: Operation Trojan Horse*

118. *UFOs: Operation Trojan Horse*

119. *Alien Contact,* pages 174-213

120. *Disneyland of the Gods*

121. *The Alien Agenda,* page 164

122. *UFOs: What on Earth is Happening?*

123. *Intercept UFO,* page 135

124. *Intercept UFO*

125. *Our Haunted Planet*

126. *Our Haunted Planet*

127. *Our Haunted Planet*

128. *Our Haunted Planet*

129. *Sons of God Return*

130. *UFOs: Operation Trojan Horse,* pages 184-187

131. *UFOs: Operation Trojan Horse*

132. *The Alien Agenda*

133. *Charles Berlitz's World of the Odd and the Awesome*

134. *UFOs: Operation Trojan Horse,* pages 273-278

135. *UFOs: Operation Trojan Horse,* pages 279-281

136. *The Alien Agenda,* pages 154-155

137. *UFOs: Operation Trojan Horse*

Bibliography

ADLER, BILL. *LETTERS to the Air Force on UFOs,* Dell Publishing Co., Inc., 1967.

Adi-Kent, Thomas Jeffery. *The Bermuda Triangle,* Warner Paperback Library, 1973.

Amiin, Mohamed. Shabelle Media Network, Somalia, March 26, 2007.

Associated Press, *Tyler Morning Telegraph,* 1/15/94 and 5/26/94.

Atkins, Thomas. Baxter, John. *The Fire Came By: Riddle of the Great Siberian Explosion,* Warner Books, 1976.

Berlitz, Charles. *Mysteries From Forgotten Worlds,* Dell Publishing Co., 1972.

Berlitz, Charles. *The Bermuda Triangle,* Avon Books, 1974.

Bernard, Dr. Raymond. *The Hollow Earth,* University Books, Inc., 1969.

Bing.com. 8-6-22.

Blum, Howard. *Out There,* Pocket Star Books, 1990.

Blum, Judy. Blum, Ralph. *Beyond Earth: Man's Contact With UFOs,* Bantam Books. 1974.

Blumrich, Joseph. *The Spaceships of Ezekiel,* Bantam Books, 1974.

Blundell, Nigel. Boar, Roger. *The World's Greatest UFO Mysteries,* Octopus Books, Ltd., 1983.

Drake, Dr. Raymond. *Gods and Spacemen in the Ancient East,* Signet Books, 1968.

Edwards, Frank. *Strangest of All,* Signet Books, 1956.

Edwards, Frank. *Stranger Than Science,* Bantam Books, 1959.

Edwards, Frank. *Strange World,* Bantam Books, 1964.

Edwards, Frank. *Flying Saucers: Serious Business,* Citadel Press, 1966.

Explosion! Reader's Digest, February 1978.

Fuller, John. *Incident at Exeter,* G.P. Putnam's Sons, 1966.

Fuller, John. *The Interrupted Journey,* Dell Publishing Co., Inc., 1966.

Good, Timothy. *Above Top-Secret: The Worldwide UFO Cover-up,* William Morrow and Co., 1988.

Good, Timothy. *Alien Contact,* William Morrow and Co., Inc., 1993.

Greene, Stan. smobserved.com, 10/26/16.

Hynek, J. Allen. *The UFO Experience: A Scientist's Inquiry,* Ballantine Books, 1972.

Jacobson, David. *Hartford Courant,* 10/11/89.

Jones, Griffith. *Unsolved Mysteries of Time and Place and Space,* Nutmeg Press, 1979.

Keel, John. *UFOs: Operation Trojan Horse,* G.P. Putnam's Sons, 1970.

Keel, John. *Our Haunted Planet,* Fawcett Books, 1971.

Keel, John. *Disneyland of the Gods,* Amok Press, 1988.

Keyhoe, Donald. *The Flying Saucer Conspiracy,* Henry Holt and Co., 1955.

Kolosimo, Peter. *Not of This World,* Bantam Books, 1971.

Landsberg, Alan. *In Search of Extraterrestrials,* Bantam Books, 1976.

Le Poer Trench, Brinsley. *Secret of the Ages,* Pinnacle Books, 1974.

Michell, John. Rickard, Robert. *Phenomena: A Book of Wonders,* Pantheon Press, 1977.

Peoples' Daily Mail, 6/4/2015.

Pravda, 1999-2006.

Randle, Kevin D, USAF (retired.) *The UFO Casebook,* Warner Books, 1989.

Roberts, Frederick. *Trendwatch,* 4/27/2007.

Segraves, Kelly. *Sons of God Return,* Spire Books, 1975.

Spencer, John Wallace. *Limbo of the Lost,* Bantam Books, 1973.

Stonely, Jack. *Is Anyone Out There?,* Warner Books, 1974.

Stringfield, Leonard. *The UFO Crash/Retrieval Syndrome: Status Report II,* MUFON, 1980.

Strieber, Whitley. *Communion: A True Story,* Avon Books, 1987.

Strieber, Whitley. *Transformation: The Breakthrough,* Beech Books, 1988.

Taylor, John. *Black Holes,* Avon Books, 1973.

Time/Life Books. *Mysteries of the Unknown: Mystic Places,* 1987.

Time/Life Books. *Mysteries of the Unknown: The UFO Phenomenon,* 1987.

Time/Life Books. *Mysteries of the Unknown: Mysterious Creatures,* 1988.

Time/Life Books. *Mysteries of the Unknown: Earth Energies,* 1991.

Time/Life Books. *Mysteries of the Unknown: Alien Encounters,* 1992.

Vallee, Jacques. *Dimensions: A Casebook of Alien Contact,* Contemporary Books, 1988.

Von Daniken, Erich. *Chariots of the Gods?,* Bantam Books, 1968.

Walters, Ed. Walters, Francine. *The Gulf Breeze Sightings,* Avon Books, 1990.

Wilson, Dr. Clifford. *The Alien Agenda,* Signet New Age, 1988.

Winer, Richard. *The Devil's Triangle,* Bantam Books, 1974.

Wolfe, James. *The Riddle of the Bermuda Triangle (Of Time and the Triangle,)* Signet, 1975.

YouTube/LUFOS, 7/16/2018.